Rural Crime
INTEGRATING RESEARCH
AND PREVENTION

Bringing together the most recent research available on rural crime in America, this book provides an overview of the extent and nature of rural crime and an analysis of the important factors contributing to its growth. The philosophy and practice of crime prevention are discussed, and the relationship between crime analysis and rural crime prevention programs is explored. The authors, who include sociologists and criminal justice educators, administrators, and practitioners, have contributed a variety of viewpoints in developing rural crime prevention strategies—both long and short term—in specific areas.

Rural Crime

INTEGRATING RESEARCH
AND PREVENTION

edited by
Timothy J. Carter
G. Howard Phillips
Joseph F. Donnermeyer
Todd N. Wurschmidt

ALLANHELD, OSMUN   PUBLISHERS

ALLANHELD, OSMUN & CO. PUBLISHERS, INC.

Published in the United States of America in 1982
by Allanheld, Osmun & Co. Publishers, Inc.
(A Division of Littlefield, Adams & Company)
81 Adams Drive, Totowa, New Jersey 07512

Library of Congress Cataloging in Publication Data

Carter, Timothy J.
  Rural crime.

  (Studies in crime and deviance in American society)
  Includes index.
  1. Rural crimes—United States—Addresses, essays,
lectures. 2. Crime prevention—United States—Addresses,
essays, lectures. 3. Juvenile delinquency—United States
—Addresses, essays, lectures. 4. Offenses against
property—United States—Addresses, essays, lectures.
I. Donnermeyer, Joseph F. II. Phillips, G. Howard
(Garland Howard), 1926-   . III. Title. IV. Series.
HV6791.C36   364.1′0973   81-65018
ISBN 0-86598-023-3   AACR 2

82 83 84 / 10 9 8 7 6 5 4 3 2 1

Printed in the United States of America

We depart from the traditional
dedication to offer our admiration
and thanks to Professor G. Howard
Phillips, the man who pioneered the
field of rural crime and its
prevention.

THE OTHER EDITORS

Contents

List of Figures

List of Tables

Preface

The impetus for this book stems from the need to document the rapidly emerging rural crime problem and to supplement the limited information available to address this issue from a crime prevention approach. Our work with sheriffs, rural police officers, officials of the court, academicians, community leaders, and interested citizens has revealed only a meager scattering of relevant materials to approach this expanding problem. Most rural crime prevention materials to date consist mostly of worked over ideas designed for urban situations or the best guesses of persons concerned with a particular problem. An increasing number of classes, workshops, and community action programs aimed at developing a fundamental understanding of rural crime prevention has finally pressed us to seek the most appropriate materials we can assemble. To accomplish this we have tried to cover rural crime prevention from the viewpoint both of the researcher and the practitioner. In essence, we go from the theoretical to the applied, recognizing the role of each.

Basically, what we have attempted to accomplish in this book is a "state of the art" commentary on rural crime prevention. We have tried to examine the problem in a general sense (i.e., national data), as well as with some specific case studies. Those of us who have addressed the problems of rural America over time are aware of its diversity. Thus, crime prevention programs must ultimately be locally oriented. We have included several in-depth studies of local crime problems in order to give insight and ideas to persons confronted with a variation of the problem in specific areas of the nation.

As will be apparent in the early chapters, rural crime is property-oriented and perpetrated by youth. Thus, rural juvenile delinquency is examined from several vantage points, but all in a rural context. It is the belief of the authors that a basic understanding of the problem is paramount to developing rational response programs.

Understanding the problem is only the first step toward resolution. Ultimately, rural crime prevention programs tailored to address the problem at the local level are where the rewards culminate.

To deal with this subject matter, we selected authors with solid reputations in crime prevention who could apply knowledge to the problem within specific situational contexts. A police officer discusses rural crime prevention from the perspective of a working policeman; several national crime prevention specialists and administrators share their insights and experiences on this subject; professional researchers discuss theories of crime prevention as well as findings from the application of these theories; and community educators discuss practical approaches to educational efforts.

We hope this book provides the reader with a balanced collection of practical and professional insights into rural crime prevention.

The Editors

Acknowledgments

The editors are indebted to the following persons for lending their knowledge and skills to the completion of this book.

William E. Snizek
Full Professor, Department of Sociology
Virginia Polytechnic Institute and State University

Simon Dinitz
Full Professor, Department of Sociology
The Ohio State University

Ed Sagarin
Full Professor, Department of Sociology
City College of New York and City University of New York

Donna M. Justice
National Rural Crime Prevention Center
The Ohio State University

Jill Loar
Department of Agricultural Economics and Rural Sociology
The Ohio State University

PART ONE
The Dimensions of Rural Crime

Introduction

The readings in Part One, "The Dimensions of Rural Crime," are presented in two sections: 1) the extent and nature of rural crime, and 2) rural juvenile delinquency. In the first section, the reader is given an overview of the extent and nature of rural crime and an analysis of the important factors hypothesized as contributing to the growing problem of rural crime. The focus of the second section is rural juvenile delinquency. Here, differences in urban and rural delinquency patterns are identified. Also, two juvenile delinquent behaviors, that is, involvement in drug use and vandalism, are analyzed in detail.

The Extent and Nature of Rural Crime

Information pertaining to the extent (rates) and nature (offense and offender/victim characteristics) of rural crime is presented in this section. The information is obtained from two sources: official police statistics (*Uniform Crime Reports*) and victimization reports. While neither source provides a totally accurate measure of the true crime rate, together they yield valuable information pertaining to the consequences of crime for both official and private citizens. Additionally, if police and victim crime rates are compared, information on the differences between these rates may be as important as either rate alone. Therefore, official police statistics, victimization reports, and a comparison between the two are necessary for a thorough analysis of the extent and nature of rural crime.

Three out of the four chapters in this section utilize these information gathering strategies. Chapter 2 is based on national official police statistics, while Chapter 3 is a rural victimization survey. Chapter 4 presents information from both official police statistics and victimization report data.

Official police statistics and victimization reports yield two separate measures of crime, each with inherent difficulties associated with their respective source of information (i.e., police or the victim). An understanding of these inherent difficulties is necessary for proper interpretation and application of the findings presented in these chapters.

OFFICIAL POLICE STATISTICS

Official information pertaining to crime includes statistics, as well as police, court, probation, parole, and prison records. However, all such official sources of criminal statistics provide inadequate measures of the true crime rate. Faced with such a measurement problem, researchers often follow the advice of many who maintain that the value of criminal statistics as a measure of criminality decreases as the measurement procedures takes the researcher further away from the actual crime. In practice, this means that police statistics are more accurate measures of crime than court statistics and court statistics are more accurate than prison statistics.

The most widely used police statistics are the *Uniform Crime Reports* (UCR). These reports are gathered annually by participating police departments, sheriffs, and state police throughout the United States. The local police reports are sent to the Federal Bureau of Investigation (FBI) where they are collated and published under one cover. The UCR contains both formal complaints made to the police, and police arrests. Arrest statistics are categorized by age, race, and sex. Because the majority of crimes known to the police are not cleared by an arrest, they are generally preferred to arrest statistics as a measure of crimes committed.

There are several problems associated with the use of police statistics, particularly with respect to crimes known to the police. First, police statistics yield an "official rate" which represents an unknown proportion of the true crime rate. That is, more crimes are actually committed than are reflected in the official crime rate, because not every offense is reported. Second, police statistics are sometimes suspected of being used for political purposes. For example, high official crime rates may be used to bring public attention to the need for increased expenditures, including more operating funds, better equipment, improved working conditions, or increases in police benefits and salaries. High official crime rates also may cause political embarrassment for public criticism of the police. Thus, the police may have good reason to inflate, suppress, or distort the information made available to the public. Third, because laws change over time and vary among police jurisdictions, the accuracy and value of long range comparative analyses is reduced. Finally, census figures are necessary to calculate crime rates, yet the most reliable census information is available only in ten-year intervals. This means that variations in reported crime between such intervals may be partly due to inaccuracies in the estimation procedures used to project population totals for years between the censuses. If the population is underestimated, the crime rate may appear higher than its actual level.

In summary, the above described deficiencies in official police statistics were important in the recent development and use of victimization reports to measure crime.

VICTIMIZATION REPORTS

Victim survey research began during the mid-1960s in the United States. The intent of such research was to uncover crimes which were not included in official data. The presidential commission on Law Enforcement and Administration of Justice offered this explanation for initiation of victimization surveys:

> Since better crime prevention and control programs depends upon full and accurate knowledge about the amounts and kinds of crime, the commission initiated the first national survey ever made of crime victimization. (Hindelang, 1976:21)

The victimization survey method is a data collection procedure which may be used to estimate the extent of crime within a particular geographic area by means of a representative sample of the population from which information about specific criminal incidents within a specified time frame are gathered. The victimization survey is able to record criminal incidents which are not known to the police and also to examine the reasons why some incidents are not reported. The victimization survey is also able to collect information on situational events surrounding the criminal incident as viewed by the victim, as well as to measure the impact of crime on the victim. Victimization surveys are not substitutes for official statistics; rather, they are complementary techniques which provide a more comprehensive view of the nature and extent of the rural crime problem.

Victimization reports, like official statistics, have inherent problems which jeopardize their use as measures of crime. Victimization reports are first and foremost dependent on the knowledge and integrity of the respondent (victim) and the ability to recall relevant incidents and details. Second, crimes in which victims are not clearly identifiable, and those in which victims are not aware of their victimization cannot be measured. Third, cases of victimless crime, including such offenses as drunkenness, prostitution, narcotics and gambling, are not likely to be reported by the victim. Fourth, victims of rape or abuse may be reluctant to divulge such information.

Chapter 1, by Ed Sagarin, Joseph F. Donnermeyer, and Timothy J. Carter, focuses upon the relationship between changes in rural society and the increase in rural crime rates. Subtitled "A Prologue," the chapter represents an "overview to the relatively recent growth of rural crime and its emergence in rural society during the sixties and seventies."

Chapter 2 by Timothy J. Carter presents an overview of the rural crime problem in America, using the *Uniform Crime Reports*. Reported crimes, official crime rates, and the relation between reported crime and police arrests are compared between rural and urban areas. Rural official crime rates are found to have reached a level equivalent to the urban rate of 1966 and to be increasing faster than the rates for America's largest cities since 1970.

In Chapter 3, Joseph F. Donnermeyer reports on the results from a victimization study of a rural county in southwest, Indiana. The chapter reviews the volume, type, and proportion of crime occurring to both small town and open-country residents, and the rate of criminal victimization was compared with national victimization rates and the victimization rates of metropolitan areas. This comparison yielded forcible entry and attempted burglary rates higher than the national averages, and for Standard Metropolitan Statistical Areas (SMSA). Donnermeyer also compared offense rate differentials by location of residence, sex, age, and size of household. Of significance is that Donnermeyer found little difference in the level of victimization by age. In contrast, the National Crime Study found substantial differences in victimization rates by age.

In Chapter 4, G. Howard Phillips and Todd N. Wurschmidt present the findings from the only statewide rural victimization survey available. They report three significant findings. First, vandalism accounted for more than one-third of crimes reported, and theft was the second leading crime. In contrast, a statewide study of crimes reported to Ohio's sheriffs found that theft was the crime most often known, followed by vandalism. Second, the above discrepancies between the findings of the two studies was explained by the fact that only 45 percent of crimes occurring to victims were subsequently reported to local law enforcement agencies. Finally, characteristics of the victims were examined for the crimes of burglary, theft, and vandalism in an attempt to identify patterns of victimization. It was found that households which experienced one or more acts of vandalism were more likely to have higher annual incomes.

Rural Juvenile Delinquency

In this section of Part One, comparative information on the extent and nature of rural juvenile delinquency is presented as are detailed information on juvenile vandalism and drug use. All of the studies presented in this section use a self-reported method of data collection. In contrast to methods used to collect data for official statistics, the self-report method goes directly to juveniles themselves, by questionnaire or interview, to discover the actual incidents of youth involvement in crime and why they become involved in such activity.

SELF-REPORT STUDIES

The strengths and weaknesses of self-report studies are similar to those of the victimization survey previously discussed. Briefly, there are four major advantages for the use of self-report studies. First, self-report studies provide information on the extent of undetected illegalities. Second, they provide information on the types of law violations with which delinquents are most involved. Information on the extent and type of undetected law violations may be quite different from the extent and type of detected law violations. Thus, the third advantage of self-report studies is that they provide information on the "dark figure" of crime. Most self-report studies provide information on the offenses which often are not known to the police. Finally, self-report data enhance the comparison of theortically relevant factors of crime for delinquency causation. Comparisons between delinquents and nondelinquents and comparisons of the illegal activities between urban vs. rural, male vs. female, white vs. nonwhite, lower class vs. middle class are a major component of self-report studies.

Again, self-report studies, like other measures of crime and delinquency, have problems associated with their use. Like the victimization survey, self-report measures are dependent upon the knowledge and integrity of the respondents and their ability to recall relevant incidents and details. Some respondents may be motivated to embellish their involvement in illegal activities while others may not admit to their actual involvement. This becomes a serious problem if the motivation to exaggerate or deny law violations is associated with a particular segment of the population (systematic error). In addition to these problems associated with research on human subjects, self-report studies are not systematic. They are not conducted on an annual basis and investigators seldom use standard lists of criminal or delinquent acts. This impedes a trend analysis and the comparison between studies.

In Chapter 5, Kathleen Natalino examines the comparative frequency of self-report involvement in delinquency among rural and urban adolescents. These data are then used to test two prominent theories of delinquency, control theory and peer subculture theory, among rural delinquents. Natalino reports that rural youth were significantly less involved in personal injury offenses and drug use than their urban counterparts, but there was no significant difference between rural and urban youth for serious property offenses. Theoretically, control theory and peer subculture theory are found to be applicable to an explanation of rural delinquent involvement. These findings are then applied to suggestions for reducing circumstances conducive to rural delinquency.

Martin G. Miller, Eric O. Hoiberg, and Rodney F. Ganey, in Chapter 6, compare self-reported delinquency rates between urban, rural non-farm, and rural farm youths from a statewide sample of 3,947 Iowa middle and secondary school students. Special attention is given to the rural farm population. The authors found the highest delinquency rates to be among urban youths and the lowest delinquency rates among rural farm youth. However, the structural and attitudinal correlates of delinquency appeared to be similar for all groups. These authors conclude by applying the findings to approaches designed toward the prevention of juvenile delinquency.

In Chapter 7, Ted L. Napier and Mary Christine Pratt examine the extent and nature of drug use among rural high school students. These researchers found that urban patterns of drug use have been diffused to rural areas. Within the southwest Ohio rural county investigated, students reported a level of drug use that exceeded the drug use of students found in previous, urban-based, studies. The analysis of social correlates of drug use leads these authors to suggest that "existing theories and standard predictive variables will probably prove less crucial than the development of new theoretical approaches and identification and utilization of more relevant variables." These authors concluded their study with a call for innovative prevention programs applicable to rural social problems.

The final study in Part One, Chapter 8, by Joseph F. Donnermeyer and G. Howard Phillips, investigates the extent and patterns of vandalism committed by sophomore and junior students from five rural high schools in Ohio and Indiana. The results revealed that slightly more than one-half of these students had committed at least one act of vandalism. Vandalism was not perceived as "unacceptable" behavior by these rural students. Motivational factors were found to be the "root cause" of vandalistic behavior. Based on the results of this study, the authors suggest that long-run prevention strategies aimed at attitudinal and behavioral changes to the potential offender may prove to be the most effective approaches.

Reference

Hindelang, J.J. 1976. *Criminal Victimization in Eight American Cities*. Boston: Ballinger Publishing Co.

1

Crime in the Countryside— A Prologue

EDWARD SAGARIN, JOSEPH F. DONNERMEYER, and TIMOTHY J. CARTER

This chapter is an attempt to provide an overview to the relatively recent growth of rural crime and its emergence in rural society during the sixties and seventies. It does not attempt to provide a comprehensive theoretical model. Instead, this chapter represents part description and part exploration of the changes and trends which have modified the face of rural America, and which perhaps have contributed to the increase in rural crime.

Rural Crime in Industrial America

That the United States is an industrial rather than an agricultural country is self-evident. Few countries of the world have such a large part of their population in urban areas (75 percent). Few have such a high proportion of their employed in industry and in service fields largely dependent upon or serving nonagricultural related industries. Finally, the United States has one of the lowest percentages of the Gross Domestic Product devoted to agricultural products (United Nations 1979:724-37).

Yet, despite the obvious industrial characteristics of the United States, there is another group of statements that can be made that emphasize the rural nature of this so-called "industrialized" nation. The total acreage of the United States utilized for farming (1,049,000,000 acres) is one of the largest among all nations (U.S. Department of Commerce 1979:439). This country also is the most productive agricultural nation in the world. The United States accounts for over 60 percent of all the wheat produced in the world, about one-half of all corn, 30 percent of all cotton, and 11 percent of all eggs from hens (United Nations 1979).

While most industrial countries have some agriculture, and most largely agricultural countries have some industry, seldom does one country have such a large concentration of both, as in the United States. No wonder, then, that mechanization of American agriculture has gone far beyond what it has in Western Europe and elsewhere in the modern world. For instance, nearly two out of every five tractors used in agriculture may be found in the United States. Likewise, American farmers own 42 percent of all harvesters (United Nations 1979:100-105).

Yet, rural America means more than agriculture. Of the 56 million rural persons in the United States, about 8 million reside on farms. Thus, rural nonfarm residents outnumber their farm counterparts by 6 to 1.

The rural population of the United States alone would make it the 14th most populous country in the world today. Its size is greater than such economically and militarily powerful countries as Great Britain, West Germany, and France.

Crime in the countryside is a challenge to a major industry—the industry of farming. However, crime challenges not just the world of wheat fields and meadows, of forests and grazing animals, but the uniqueness of a way of life that persists among millions of Americans.

The Increasing Crime Rate

During the sixties and seventies, urban and rural Americans experienced sizeable increases in crime. Although thousands of journalistic reports and hundreds of scientific articles have been devoted to the problem of "crime in the city," similar accounts of "crime in the countryside" have been rare. However, recent editions of several magazines and trade journals have highlighted the growth and nature of rural crime. Authorities in Arkansas, Kansas, Texas, and California reported dramatic increases in the theft of farm machinery, some valued at as much as $100,000. Often thieves will load heavy farm equipment onto flatbed trucks, to be shipped to countries in Central and South America (U.S. News and World Report 1980; Swanson and Territo 1980). Theft of irrigation equipment from farms in western states runs into millions of dollars (Footlick et al. 1977). Theft of hogs in one Indiana county was valued at $200,000 (Russell 1976), and in South Dakota losses due to seed and chemical thefts were estimated to be at least several hundred thousand dollars (McGrane 1980). In a recent study of farm roadside markets and "pick-your-own" operations, three-quarters were found to have experienced at least one type of property crime, such as vandalism, shoplifting, employee theft, burglary, and larceny/theft (Phillips and Donnermeyer 1980).

It would be erroneous to conclude, however, that crime experienced by farmers involves only "big money" items. The most frequent crime occurring to farmers is vandalism (Bean and Lawrence 1978; Donnermeyer and Cox 1981). A single incident of vandalism is often minor when compared to the theft of a tractor. In addition, most cases of farm-related larceny are of tools, guns, batteries, and other items of much less value than a single combine. However, total dollar losses from these so-called "petty" crimes may exceed losses from all heavy equipment thefts.

It would be equally erroneous to conclude that rural crime is synonymous with "agri-crime." Rural nonfarm residents, on a per capita basis, experience as much crime as the farm population (Donnermeyer and Cox 1981). Much like their counterparts in farming, the most frequent types of crimes experienced by the rural nonfarm population are relatively minor incidents of vandalism and larceny.

Two basic points must be made about the growth of rural crime. First, factors which account for the growth in rural crime may be different from factors contributing to the growth in urban crime. On the rural scene, opportunities have increased for several reasons: increasing inventory of farm equipment and other operational inputs; advent of the interstate highway system and other improvements in transportation; and growth of the rural population due to relocation of industry, the "Boom Town" phenomenon associated with energy development, construction of suburbs and "strip housing," and migration of retired households into small town and open-country environments.

Second, an interesting feature of crime during the sixties and seventies is the increased participation of suburban (Richards 1979) and rural youth (Feldhusen et al. 1965; Phillips 1976b) in unlawful behavior. For instance, a Gallup Poll "youth survey" of participation in shoplifting activities revealed that 29 percent of those from metropolitan areas, 27 percent from suburban areas, and 22 percent from rural areas had been involved in shoplifting. The motivation behind shoplifting was primarily "for kicks," as opposed to economic reasons. This was true whether the adolescent shoplifter was from the city or the country.

Rural youth have probably never been as law-abiding as their image painted them to be. Today, however, a greater proportion is indulging in vandalism, in malicious mischief, and in other lesser offenses for which adults become impatient, and sometimes in more serious offenses that are so often the precursors of criminal careers.

One Society: Many Faces

How can one account for the rise in rural crime? As yet, the facts are only now beginning to be amassed, and the research has only begun to be conducted. One must be content with description of the situation along with some speculation, inspired in part by the study of change in rural American society during this century, and in part by the more general study that has been made of urban crime.

How does social change relate to the growth of crime within society? The outline of such a paradigm is suggested in a recent article by Cohen and Felson (1979) on social change and the rise in crime. The authors delineate three elements whose "convergence in space and time" is necessary for "direct-contact predatory violations" (i.e., violent crime) to occur. These three elements include: (1) suitable targets; (2) the absence of guardians (i.e., police or citizens) capable of preventing the violations; and (3) motivated offenders. The authors argue that the absence of any one of these three elements would be "sufficient" to prevent crime from occurring (Cohen and Felson 1979:588-91).

This basic paradigm may be found, albeit in a less formalized manner, in thousands of flyers, brochures, and manuals on crime prevention distributed each year by law enforcement agencies. This literature stresses that protection of person or property (suitable target) against the would-be criminal (motivated offender) requires reduction of opportunity (guardianship).

The major point is that rural America has experienced an increase in all three elements: suitable targets, opportunities, and motivated offenders. The discussion below is organized according to this paradigm, and the crime prevention literature of law enforcement officials. However, the second element of "opportunity" will be used in place of "guardianship" in order to redirect the discussion toward property crime, the predominant type occurring in rural areas.

SUITABLE TARGETS

There have been several changes in rural society which contribute to the increase in suitable targets. First, rural people have experienced the same rise in affluence during the sixties and seventies as Americans in general. Rural households own the same quantities of televisions, stereos, microwave ovens and other home appliances. These items are "fenceable," and therefore serve as attractive targets.

In part, the increased affluence of rural society is due to the growth of suburbs in open-country areas, and the more general movement of the population back to rural locations (i.e., population turnaround). As well, in an increasing proportion of rural households, both spouses are working (U.S. Bureau of Census 1979).

Beyond the general trend of affluence is the more specific aspect of the decrease in small, economically marginal farms and the increase in large acreage, highly mechanized and capital intensive agricultural enterprises. American farmers rely heavily on expensive tractors, combines, and other farm implements. Pesticides, herbicides, and other farm inputs are equally expensive. As the earlier discussion indicated, farm equipment and supplies have become suitable targets for thieves.

OPPORTUNITY

Opportunity refers to those factors which facilitate the commission of a crime. During the sixties and seventies, there has developed in rural areas a structure of opportunity for crime to occur, especially property crime. There are six factors which may be identified as affecting the formation of this opportunity structure.

The first aspect may be defined as a precondition and relates to the low population density of rural areas. Low population density is perhaps the most distinctive characteristic of rurality. Remoteness and distance between homes, however, increase the likelihood that crimes can be committed unobserved.

A second factor relates to the improvement in transportation systems and, in particular, the construction of interstate highways. Despite the relative isolation afforded by low population density, most rural areas today are easily accessible. The impact of improved transportation has increased opportunity in two ways. It has, first of all, provided logistical means for offenders to operate over extensive geographic area. The emergence of this phenomenon was observed nearly 50 years ago by Smith (1933:3-4):

The new means of transportation have often brought the teeming life of city streets to the open countryside. Depredations upon farm buildings and standing crops are now of frequent occurrence. Roadhouses cater to the passing motorist with one or more forms of commercialized vice, and the city gangster establishes his retreat far outside the regularly patrolled areas. Various types of crime and disorder naturally increases under these circumstances.

Second, improved transportation has spurred the development of recreational and leisure facilities in rural locations. The density of traffic in many rural areas has increased to such an extent that local residents are no longer able to differentiate between neighbors and strangers. In part, this has lessened the cohesiveness of many rural communities.

A third factor related to increased opportunity is the growth of suburbs and strip housing in rural areas. Generally, suburban areas experience a higher per capita rate of burglary and larceny than inner-city locations. As more residential developments of this type are located in rural areas, property crime rates will more than likely increase.

A fourth aspect of opportunity is related to the increased vacancy of rural homes during day-time and early evening hours. Four changes have taken place in rural society which contribute to this trend. The first change is that of rural school consolidation. Most rural young people must travel long distances to school. Second, in an increasing proportion of rural households, both spouses work away from the home (U.S. Bureau of Census 1978:9). Third, workplaces for 85 percent of the rural labor force are factories or offices in distant cities or other rural locations far from home. Fourth, just as improved transportation has allowed greater access to rural areas, rural people have increasingly oriented their lifestyles away from the local community. This is especially evident in retail shopping patterns of rural households. Many now travel great distances for retail purchases, such as groceries, clothes, and furniture. These items used to be purchased at nearby trade centers. This trend is also evident in the leisure time and recreational pursuits of rural people, who increasingly manifest a nonlocal orientation.

As a result of these changes in mobility patterns, rural residents are more vulnerable to crime. For example, Smith and Donnermeyer (1979) found that nearly 50 percent of the personal larcenies (without contact) experienced by rural residents of Benton County, Indiana occurred in an adjacent metropolitan county. Many of these thefts occurred at shopping malls and other retail outlets, or at their workplaces in the metropolitan area.

A fifth aspect of opportunity concerns minimal law enforcement resources available for patrol, investigative, and other police functions.

Although crime has increased in rural areas, law enforcement resources have not kept pace. For example, in a typical rural midwestern county there are only one or two officers available for patrol duties in a jurisdictional area that covers several hundred square miles.

The sixth and final aspect of opportunity structure is attitudinal in nature. Although rural crime has markedly increased, public perception and awareness of the problem has not. This is reflected in the fact that rural residents have not adopted home and farm security measures to the same degree as their urban cousins. For instance, Phillips (1976a:14) found that 40 percent of rural Ohioans seldom or never locked their doors when leaving home and sixty percent did not lock their fuel storage tanks. Similar results were obtained in separate rural crime studies among the farm and non-farm populations in West Virginia (Bean and Lawrence 1978:5–6), and Missouri (Galliher et al. 1980).

MOTIVATED OFFENDERS

The profile of the rural offender is not well known. However, the few sociological studies which have been published indicate that most are single males less than 25 years old, from a nearby community. They are "amateurs" or non-career criminals who get involved in petty acts of vandalism and larceny, and occasionally more serious offenses (Polk 1969, 1980; Phillips 1976b). These observations are similar to some of the earlier writings on rural crime by Clinard (1942, 1944) who found rural offenders did not manifest the characteristics generally associated with the criminal social type, such as: (A) an early start in criminal behavior; (B) progressive knowledge of criminal techniques and crime in general; (C) the use of crime as the sole means of support; and (D) the development of a self-concept of being criminal.

Although there is evidence that farm machinery theft and residential burglary are performed by the "professional" criminal, the vast majority of rural offenders are of a different type. It can be argued that much of the increase in rural crime during the sixties and seventies may be attributed to the entrance of nonprofessionals into illegal and deviant behavior.

How does one explain the increased involvement of rural youth? There appear to be two separate, but interrelated, dimensions to such an explanation. The first dimension suggests that increased participation is due to lifestyle changes.

Radio, television, automobiles, industrialization, nuclear families, the ease and actuality of geographic mobility: these are among the forces that have tended to efface the distinction between rural life and urban life. Although there remain many differences between rural and urban life, there has been a gradual and steady erosion of these differences over the decades.

A primary force underlying this trend is the influence of mass media. Their importance in the development of adolescent role models, both those in conformity with the dominant adult culture and those deviant to this culture, has long been recognized by criminologists. Glaser (1956), for instance, building upon Sutherland's differential association theory, developed a theory of "differential identification" to account for the acquisition of role models through the more impersonal communication channels of radio, television, movies, and music.

However, the diffusion of new role models from urban centers into the countryside would not in itself result in behavioral change toward deviant lifestyles without positive reinforcement from reference groups significant to rural youth (Richards 1979; Wurschmidt 1980). The second dimension to understanding the increased participation of young people relates to the fundamental shift in the importance of institutions primarily responsible for socialization. The basic nature of change has been the shifting of influence from the family to the youth peer group.

The increased influence of peers may be understood by examining the impact of television as a form of technological change on the rural family. The rapid diffusion of television as a major form of leisure time behavior has changed the interactional patterns of the family. This occurred at the same time the nuclear family structure was becoming the predominant familial arrangement in the United States (Glenn 1979). By 1970, the average television viewing time per day for both adults, adolescents, and children was approximately five hours (Glenn 1979). This has generally been at the sacrifice of "time shared" in interaction between parents and children (Glenn 1979).

With the decline of influence of the family, there has been an increase in the importance of the peer group. As Richards (1979:484) pointed out, vandalistic behavior among middle-class adolescents may be understood as an "age-status conflict" in which partial "exclusion from the adult status system is thought to lead adolescents to construct alternatives within the peer group." The so-called alternatives generated within the peer setting are often "pseudo-autonomous behavior that is likely to be defined as delinquent," according to the standards of the adult status system (Richards 1979:484).

In rural society, many other changes have occurred which contribute to this process. For example, there has been an increase in the number of single parent households, and of households in which both parents work. Second, occupational opportunities in rural areas have changed, resulting in a decreased availability of agricultural and unskilled jobs for rural youth. For a vast majority of youth living in rural areas today, the experience of "growing up on the farm" is no more salient than it is for urban youth.

Summary

Rural society in the United States will change whether or not there is a problem with crime, but the presence of crime only promises to take from rural society the very characteristics that in this century have made rural life distinctive from urban life. Perhaps the major contribution of crime prevention to rural society is a reduction in the negative aspects of this inevitable change.

References

Bean, T.L. and L.D. Lawrence. 1975. *Crime on Farms in Hampshire County, West Virginia—Pilot Study.* R.M. No. 69. Morgantown: Center for Extension and Continuing Education, West Virginia University.

Clinard, Marshall. 1942. "The Process of Urbanization and Criminal Behavior: A Study of Culture Conflict." *American Journal of Sociology* 48:202-13.

———. 1944. "Rural Criminal Offenders." *American Journal of Sociology* 50:38-45.

Cohen, Lawrence E. and Marcus Felson. 1979. "Social Change and Crime Rate Trends." *American Sociological Review* 44(August):588-607.

Donnermeyer, Joseph F. and Robin Cox. 1981. "Criminal Victimization and Attitudes Toward Crime and Crime Prevention Among Farm Operators: A Comparative Analysis." Paper presented at the annual meeting of the North Central Sociological Association, Cleveland, Ohio. April.

Feldhusen, John F., John R. Thurston, and Elvira Ager. 1965. "Delinquency Proneness of Urban and Rural Youth." *The Journal of Research in Crime and Delinquency.* 2(January):32-44.

Footlick, Jerrold F., Paul Brinkly-Rogers, and Chris Harper. 1977. Crime on the Farm. *Newsweek* (October 3):101.

Glaser, Daniel. 1956. "Criminality Theories and Behavioral Images." *American Journal of Sociology* 61:433-44.

Glenn, H. Stephen. 1979. "Education for Alternative Behavior." Keynote Address, 1st Annual Southeast Drug Conference, Atlanta, Georgia.

McGrane, Martin. 1980. "Big Money in Farm Crime." *Rural Electrification* 38(June):14-16.

Phillips, G. Howard. 1976a. *Rural Crimes and Rural Offenders.* EB 613. Columbus, Ohio: Department of Agricultural Economics and Rural Sociology, Ohio Cooperative Extension Service, The Ohio State University.

———. 1976b. *Vandals and Vandalism in Rural Ohio.* Research Circular 222. Wooster, Ohio: Ohio Agricultural Research and Development Center.

Phillips, G. Howard and Joseph F. Donnermeyer. 1980. "Extent of Crime Against Farm Retailers and Suggested Remedies." In M.E. Cravens and Susan Sullivan, eds. *Proceedings of the 20th Annual Ohio Roadside Marketing Conference*. ESO 731. Columbus, Ohio: Department of Agricultural Economics and Rural Sociology, The Ohio State University.

Polk, Kenneth. 1969. "Delinquency and Community Action in Nonmetropolitan Areas." In Ronald R. Cressey and David A. Ward, eds. *Delinquency, Crime and Social Process*. New York: Harper and Row, Publishers.

———. 1980. "Not So Peaceful in the Country." *Rural Electrification* 38 (June):16-17, 50.

Richards, Pamela. 1979. "Middle-Class Vandalism and Age-Status Conflict." *Social Problems* 26 (April):482-497.

Russell, John. 1976. "Stamp Out Hog Rustling." *Hog*, September.

Smith, Brent L. and Joseph F. Donnermeyer. 1979. "Victimization in Rural and Urban Areas: A Comparative Analysis." Presented at the annual meeting of the Rural Sociological Society, Burlington, Vermont. August.

Smith, Bruce. 1933. *Rural Crime Control*. New York: Institute of Public Administration.

Swanson, Charles R. Jr. and Leonard Territo. 1980. "Agricultural Crime: Its Extent, Prevention and Control." *FBI Law Enforcement Bulletin* 49 (May):8-12.

United Nations, Department of International Economics and Social Affairs. 1978. *Statistical Yearbook*. New York: United Nations.

U.S. Department of Commerce, Bureau of the Census. 1978. *Farm Population of the United States: 1977*. Current Population Reports, Series P-27, No. 51. Washington, D.C.: U.S. Government Printing Office.

———. 1979. *Statistical Abstract of the United States 1977*. Washington, D.C.: U.S. Government Printing Office.

U.S. Department of Justice, Law Enforcement Assistance Administration. 1979. *Criminal Victimization in the United States, 1977*. Washington, D.C.: U.S. Government Printing Office.

U.S. News and World Report. 1980. "Lawbreakers Turn to Greener Pastures." (May 26):67-69.

Wurschmidt, Todd N. 1980. *Property Crime Victimization and the Practice of Home Security Behaviors Among Ohio Rural Residents: An Examination of the Response-Consequence Contingent*. M.S. Thesis, The Ohio State University.

2

The Extent and Nature of Rural Crime in America

TIMOTHY J. CARTER

Introduction

Over time, the city has had the reputation of being the "breeding ground" for crime. The rural community, by contrast, is viewed as one of the last remaining bastions of law and order. The informal social relationships among neighbors in rural areas are thought to generate a recognition for the rights and property of others, and for conformity to the law. As a result, the image of rural life is one relatively free from the human traumas of crime, or at least, free from any "serious" crime problem. This view is perpetuated by criminologists who, in the past, have almost exclusively directed their investigations toward urban populations, for both theoretical and practical considerations. Theoretically, the heterogeneous populations of American urban communities provide a fertile setting for testing a variety of theories about criminal behavior. Practically, urban crime affects that segment of the population most able collectively to register their concern and thereby to insist on some form of ameliorative response from government.

Given the current absence of any systematic analysis of the extent and nature of rural crime on a national level, the purpose of this chapter is to present an overview of the rural crime problem, using the Federal Bureau of Investigation's *Uniform Crime Reports,* which has provided one of the few continuous sources of crime data in the United States since 1930. In addition, the social impact of crime on rural community life is discussed.

Extent and Nature of Rural Crime

The Uniform Crime Reports' (UCR) "The Index of Crime" has been developed by the FBI to indicate annual changes in serious crimes in the United States. Data for the index are assembled from reports submitted by nearly 15,000 law enforcement agencies from throughout the country. The Index of Crime is composed of seven major offenses, including the violent crimes of murder, rape, robbery, and aggravated assault, and the property crimes of burglary, larceny-theft, and motor vehicle theft.[1] The Index of Crime represents the total number of offenses reported to law enforcement per each 100,000 population.

The Index of Crime is published for three areas of the United States: metropolitan areas, other cities, and rural areas. This analysis will focus principally on the Index of Crime for rural areas. The FBI defines a rural area as "that portion of a county outside the Standard Metropolitan Statistical Area excluding areas covered by city police agencies" (U.S. Department of Justice 1978:306). Urban includes the remaining two classifications, Standard Metropolitan Statistical Area (SMSA) and other cities.

Figure 2.1 shows the trend in the UCR Index of Crime for rural areas of the country since 1959. From 1959 to 1979, the Index of Crime increased nearly 450 percent for rural areas. Perhaps an even more telling feature of the seriousness of the present rural crime problem is revealed by the fact that the index rate in 1979 exceeded the 1966 index rate for metropolitan areas of the U.S. In the middle 1960s the crime rate had become so alarming, especially in the nation's largest cities, that President Johnson, in an address to Congress, declared "war on crime." The President stated that "we must arrest and reverse the trend toward lawlessness, . . . crime has become a malignant enemy in America's midst" (Quinney 1977:6). Responding to the President's declaration, Congress enacted The National Institute of Law Enforcement and Criminal Justice and the Law Enforcement Assistance Administration

Figure 2.1
THE U.S. RURAL CRIME INDEX
(UNIFORM CRIME REPORTS, 1959-1978)

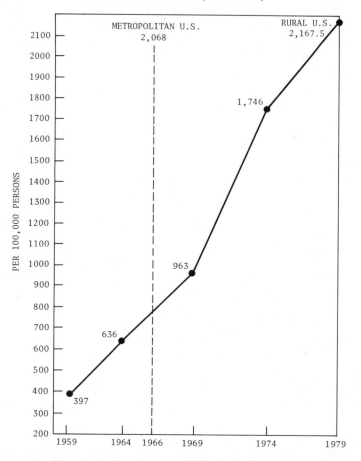

under the "Omnibus Crime Control and Safe Streets Act of 1968" (U.S. Dept. of Justice 1974:111).

The seriousness of the rural crime problem noted above may also be illustrated by comparing the percentage increase in reported crimes between rural and urban areas. Table 2.1 presents the percentage change in crime index rates for rural and urban (SMSA and other cities) areas over a 20 year period. Percentage increases are tabulated for five year interims, (except the period 1976-79) and for the total 20 year period (1960-79).

Table 2.1 reveals that there has been a consistently higher percentage

Table 2.1.   Percent Change in FBI Total Crime Index For
             Urban and Rural Areas, 1960-1979

Area	1960-1964	1964-1968	1968-1972[a]	1972-1976	1976-1979	1960-1979
Urban	+31.8%	+66.4%	+25.5%	+26.1%	+4.9%	+368.1%
Rural	+50.4%	+38.2%	+31.3%	+39.1%	+5.9%	+412.5%

[a] Beginning with the year 1973, the crime rate based on the index crimes
includes a figure for total larceny. For the period 1960-1972, the crime
rate included only larceny $50 and over. The 1973 Uniform Crime Report
provided revised figures for 1972 which included total larcenies. The
percent changes included in the 1972-1976 column reflect the revised
definition of larceny for 1972. The percent changes included in the
1968-1972 column reflect the unrevised definition of larceny for 1972.

increase in the rural crime rate over the urban crime rate beginning with
the 1968-72 period. The trend of larger percentage increases in reported
index crimes for rural areas continues in the most recent interim for
which data are available, 1976-79.

For the period 1976-79, the percentage increases are considerably
lower for both areas than the two previous time frames. This results
from the fact that, for urban areas, the crime index rate peaked in 1975
(5,890.1 per 100,000 persons) and declined slightly in 1976 (5,840 per
100,000 persons). The rate then dropped in 1977 to 5,587.0 per 100,000
persons. However, both in 1978 and 1979, it resumed an upward trend.
Rural areas followed a similar pattern, but lagged a year behind. The
rural crime rate did not peak until 1976 (2,047.5 per 100,000 persons),
and then declined slightly in both 1977 (2,012.5 per 100,000 persons)
and 1978 (1,997.9 per 100,000 persons). However, the rural crime rate
rose again in 1979 to a level that was 5.9 percent higher than the crime
level in 1976.

The fact that the reported rural index crime rate now approximates
the reported metropolitan index crime rate of the mid-1960s and that
the reported rural index crime rate has been increasing faster than that
of the metropolitan areas over the past decade, clearly indicate rural
crime to be an emerging problem. But what is the nature of this emerging
problem? Two sets of statistics will be examined in order to answer this
question. First, crime reported to rural and urban law enforcement will
be subdivided into violent offenses and property offenses and their relative proportions to the total crime index will be examined from 1960 to
1979. Second, reported rural and urban violent and property crime rates
are compared for nine U.S. census regions from 1974 to 1979.

Table 2.2.   The Proportion of Reported Violent and Property
Offenses for Urban and Rural Areas, 1960-1979.

Area	Year				
Urban	1960	1965	1970	1975	1979
Violent Crime Rate	162.4	234.2	501.2	539.8	598.3
Percent of Total Index	12.4	12.9	14.0	9.2	9.8
Property Crime Rate	1,146.1	1,574.5	3,087.6	5,350.4	5,529.2
Percent of Total Index	87.6	87.1	86.0	90.8	90.2
Rural					
Violent Crime Rate	67.3	81.1	120.0	167.3	187.4
Percent of Total Index	15.9	13.1	12.9	8.4	8.6
Property Crime Rate	355.8	535.7	807.4	1,829.9	1,980.1
Percent of Total Index	84.1	86.9	87.1	91.6	91.4

Table 2.2 shows the proportion of violent and property crime for urban and rural areas, from 1960 to 1979. For both areas, property crimes are the predominant type reported by citizens to law enforcement. The proportion of violent crime reported in rural areas slightly exceeds the proportion of violent crime reported in urban areas for 1960 and 1965. This pattern is reversed in 1970, 1975 and 1979.

The decrease in the proportion of violent crime between 1970 and 1975 for both urban and rural areas was due in part to the change in the definition of larceny in 1973 from "$50 and over" to "total larceny." From 1960 to 1970, the proportion of reported violent crime in urban areas had increased from 12.4 percent to 14.0 percent. In rural areas, the proportion of violent crime had decreased from 15.9 percent to 12.9 percent. In 1975, the proportion of violent crime in urban areas dropped to 9.2 percent. In rural areas, reported violent crime fell to 8.4 percent of all reported crimes. In 1979, the proportion of violent crime in urban areas rose to 9.8 percent of the total, and in rural areas increased slightly to 8.6 percent of all offenses reported.

To this point analysis has focused on the comparison between urban and rural reported index crime rates over time for the nation as a whole. National statistics may inflate or supress and thereby distort the extent and nature of crime in a particular area. To explore further the extent and nature of rural crime, analysis now turns to comparative examination of reported crime rates for the nine Census Regions of the United States: New England, Middle Atlantic, East North Central, West North Central, South Atlantic, East South Central, West South Central, Mountain and Pacific.[2]

Table 2.3 contains both violent and property crime rates for all regions, the percentage change for each region from 1974 to 1979, and the proportion of reported violent and property of the total crime index. These data are presented for rural and urban places within all regions.

In 1974 the highest rural and urban rate of reported violent crime occurred in the South Atlantic Region of the United States (277.3 and 713.1 per 100,000 persons, respectively), followed by the Pacific region (224.5 and 571.1 per 100,000 persons, respectively). The region reporting the lowest violent crime rate in 1974 was the West North Central for rural places (60.2 per 100,000 persons), and New England for urban places (304.1 per 100,000 persons). By 1979, the highest rate of reported violent crime shifted to the Pacific Region for both rural (357.9 per 100,000 persons) and urban (752.3 per 100,000 persons) places. The lowest reported violent crime rate was in the West North Central (63.5 and 412.0 per 100,000 persons, respectively).

The largest percentage increase in reported rural violent crime between 1974 and 1979 appeared in New England (102.6 percent). For urban places the largest percentage increase in reported violent crime occurred in the West South Central Region (63.3 percent) and the New England Region (44.3 percent). While no other region, rural or urban, approximated the slightly more than doubling in reported violent crime that occurred in New England, rural places in other regions also experienced substantial increases in reported violent crime, including: Pacific (59.4 percent), Mountain (53.0 percent), Middle Atlantic (49.0 percent) and East North Central (43.1 percent). Decreases in reported crimes of violence occurred in urban places within the East North Central Region (−5.3 percent); rural places within the East South Central Region (−7.4 percent); and in both rural (−7.7 percent) and urban (−6.3 percent) places within the South Atlantic Region.

In 1974, and again in 1979, the highest rural and urban property crime rates appeared in the far western regions of the United States. For rural places the reported property crime rate in both 1974 and 1979 was highest in the Pacific Region (3,489.3 and 3,822.5 per 100,000 persons, respectively) followed by the Mountain Region (2,488.0 and 2,516.9 per 100,000 persons, respectively). For urban places the highest property crime rate in 1974 and 1979 was reported in the Mountain Region (6,661.6 and 7,187.5 per 100,000 persons, respectively) followed by the Pacific Region (6,340.6 and 6,747.2 per 100,000 persons, respectively). The lowest reported property crime rate for both rural and urban places, and in both 1974 and 1979, occurred in the East South Central Region. In 1974, the East South Central region reported a property crime rate of 701.4 per 100,000 persons in rural places and 3,658.3 per 100,000 persons for urban places. In 1979 the respective property crime rates were 1,055.1

Table 2.3. Reported Violent and Property Crime Rates, Percentage Change and Proportions for Urban and Rural Areas by U.S. Census Region, 1974-79.

Region	1974 Rate Per/100,000 persons[b]		1979 Rate Per/100,000 persons		Percent Change '74-'79	
	Violent Crime[a]	Property Crime	Violent Crime	Property Crime	Violent Crime	Property Crime
NEW ENGLAND						
Urban	304.1	4,640.5	438.9	5,398.3	44.3	16.3
Percent of Total Index	6.2	93.8	7.7	92.3	1.5	-1.5
Rural	77.2	1,597.3	156.4	2,513.5	102.6	57.4
Percent of Total Index	4.6	95.4	5.9	94.1	1.3	-1.3
MIDDLE ATLANTIC						
Urban	597.2	3,828.5	679.2	4,751.0	13.7	24.1
Percent of Total Index	13.5	86.5	12.5	87.5	-1.0	1.0
Rural	97.8	1,953.4	145.7	2,442.2	49.0	25.0
Percent of Total Index	4.8	95.2	5.6	94.4	.8	-.8
EAST NORTH CENTRAL						
Urban	525.3	4,843.2	497.4	5,142.8	-5.3	6.2
Percent of Total Index	9.8	90.2	8.8	91.2	-1.0	1.0
Rural	91.6	2,091.5	131.1	2,212.6	43.1	5.8
Percent of Total Index	4.8	95.2	5.6	94.4	.8	-.8
NORTH CENTRAL						
Urban	353.5	4,747.8	412.0	5,245.8	16.5	10.5
Percent of Total Index	6.9	93.1	7.3	92.7	.4	-.4
Rural	60.2	1,140.5	63.5	1,391.3	5.5	22.0
Percent of Total Index	5.0	95.0	4.4	95.6	-.6	.6

SOUTH ATLANTIC						
Urban	713.1	5,216.3	668.3	5,884.8	-6.3	12.8
Percent of Total Index	12.0	88.0	10.2	89.8	-1.8	1.8
Rural	277.3	1,529.6	255.9	2,053.7	-7.7	34.3
Percent of Total Index	15.4	84.6	11.1	88.9	-4.3	4.3
EAST SOUTH CENTRAL						
Urban	407.3	3,658.3	440.9	4,339.6	8.2	18.6
Percent of Total Index	10.0	90.0	9.2	90.8	-.8	.8
Rural	108.6	701.4	167.3	1,055.1	-7.4	50.4
Percent of Total Index	20.5	79.5	13.7	86.3	-6.8	6.8
WEST SOUTH CENTRAL						
Urban	350.5	4,611.0	575.2	5,626.2	63.3	22.0
Percent of Total Index	7.1	92.9	9.3	90.7	2.2	-2.2
Rural	153.7	1,111.4	109.8	1,512.1	24.1	36.1
Percent of Total Index	12.1	87.9	11.2	88.8	-.9	.9
MOUNTAIN						
Urban	463.3	6,661.6	572.9	7,187.5	23.7	7.9
Percent of Total Index	6.5	93.5	7.4	92.6	.9	-.9
Rural	172.6	2,488.0	264.0	2,516.9	53.0	1.2
Percent of Total Index	6.5	93.5	9.5	90.5	3.0	-3.0
PACIFIC						
Urban	571.1	6,340.6	752.3	6,747.2	31.7	6.4
Percent of Total Index	8.3	91.7	8.1	89.9	-.2	.2
Rural	224.5	3,489.3	357.9	3,822.5	59.4	9.6
Percent of Total Index	6.1	93.9	8.6	91.4	2.5	-2.5

a. Violent crimes include: murder and non-negligent manslaughter, aggravated assault, forcible rape and robbery. Property crimes include: burglary, larceny and auto theft.
b. All rates are standardized per/100,000.

per 100,000 persons for rural places and 4,339.6 per 100,000 persons for urban places.

All nine regions in both rural and urban places demonstrated an increase in property crime from 1974 to 1979. Overall, the largest increases in reported property crime rates occurred in rural places. The largest increase in rural places appeared in New England (57.4 percent), followed by the East South Central (50.4 percent), West South Central (36.1 percent), and South Atlantic Regions (34.3 percent). Thus, for rural places, New England experienced the largest increase both for reported violent and property crimes between 1974 and 1979. For urban places, the largest increase in reported property crime occurred in Middle Atlantic Region (24.1 percent), followed closely by the West South Central Region (22.0 percent).

In addition to violent and property reported crime rates and the percentage change in these rates from 1974 to 1979, Table 2.3 presents the proportion of reported violent and property crime to the total crime index for 1974 and 1979, and the proportionate change over this time period.

As Table 2.2 had indicated, for both rural and urban areas, property crimes are the predominate type reported to law enforcement. However, differences do exist between regions. In 1974, the highest proportion of reported violent crime for rural areas occurred in the East South Central (20.5 percent) and South Atlantic (15.4 percent) Regions. The lowest proportion of reported violent crime for rural places in 1974 appeared in New England (4.6 percent), followed closely by the Middle Atlantic and East North Central Regions, each with a proportion of 4.8 percent of reported violent crime to the total crime index.

In 1979, the highest proportion of reported rural violent crime remained in the East South Central Region, but the proportion had decreased to 13.7 percent. The lowest proportion of rural violent crime had shifted to the West North Central Region (4.4 percent).

For rural places the largest increase in the proportion of violent to the total reported crime index from 1974 to 1979 occurred in the Mountain (3.0 percent) and Pacific (2.5 percent) Regions. The most dramatic decrease occurred in the rural East South Central (−6.8 percent) and South Atlantic (−4.3 percent) Region where the proportions of reported violent crime had been the highest in 1974. Two other regions experienced slight decreases in the proportion of reported violent crime for rural places: the West South Central (−.9 percent) and West North Central (−.6 percent) Regions.

In 1974, the Middle Atlantic Region yielded the highest proportion of reported violent crime for urban places (13.5 percent), while New England yielded the lowest for urban places (6.2 percent). In 1979, the Middle Atlantic Region remained the highest in proportion of reported urban violent crime (12.5 percent), however, the lowest proportion of reported urban violent crime had shifted to the West North Central (7.3 percent), followed closely by the Mountain (7.4 percent) and New England (7.7 percent) Regions. For urban places, the West South Central Region experienced the largest increase in the proportion of reported violent crime to the total crime index from 1974 to 1979 (2.2 percent). The largest decrease for the proportion of violent crime occurred in the South Atlantic Region (−1.8 percent). The Middle Atlantic, East North Central, East South Central and Pacific Regions also showed slight decreases in the proportion of reported violent crime to the total crime index for urban places.

Although the reported violent and property crime rate for urban places has and continues to be substantially higher than the respective rates reported in rural places, in three regions the proportion of reported rural violent crime actually exceeded that proportion reported in urban places within those same regions. In 1974 and again in 1979, the proportion of reported violent crime to the total crime index was higher in the rural East South Central, South Atlantic and West South Central Regions than for urban places in those regions. In 1974, the proportion of reported violent crime to the total crime index in the East South Central Region slightly more than doubled that proportion for urban places (20.5 percent vs. 10.0 percent). By 1979, the proportionate difference in the East South Central Region had decreased, but the proportion of violent crime reported in rural places (13.7 percent) remained higher than that for urban places (9.2 percent).

These findings simply document the seriousness of the emerging crime problem in rural America. An overview of law enforcement statistics cannot answer the critical question of why crime has emerged as a major problem in rural areas, nor can these data verify the many reasons that have been suggested. Rather these data represent the need for an in-depth crime analysis in order to identify research questions and practical approaches to crime prevention. However, scholars and practitioners alike must be aware of, and, if possible, help leaders lessen the negative social impact crime has on the rural community.

The Social Impact of Crime

There has been be a growing awareness about crime as a problem among rural residents. A series of national public opinion polls by the Gallup organization illustrates this increased concern. In 1972, respondents to a national opinion survey were asked: "Is there more crime in your area now than a year ago or less?" Forty percent of the respondents residing in cities of 500,000 persons or more said that crime had increased during the past year, compared to only 27 percent of the respondents from rural areas and towns of less than 2,500 persons. In 1977, this question was repeated in another national opinion survey. The percent of respondents from the large cities who perceived an increase in crime had declined slightly to 38 percent. In contrast, the percentage of rural respondents who perceived an increase in crime had climbed to over 46 percent. As has been revealed by the trend analysis of *Uniform Crime Report* data, these perceptions are accurate. However, the influence that this awareness has on shaping the attitudes of rural citizens about crime is critical to the overall impact that crime will have on the rural social structure. It is at this critical point that social scientists can make their greatest contribution to reducing crime and maintaining rural social relationships.

There are two schools of thought about the impact of crime on the solidarity of communities and neighborhoods. One theory is that a growing awareness of crime encourages an attitude of distrust and heightened fear. The social repercussions of such an attitude could result in a breakdown in the rural community's network of close interpersonal relations. As Conklin (1975:9) has noted about crime in urban areas: "Crime generates suspicion, and distrust and this diminishes social interaction. As a community is atomized, solidarity weakens and informal social controls dissipate. The result is a high crime rate, since restraints on criminal behavior are released." Some social scientists suggest that fear of crime leads to the adoption of target-hardening (i.e., lights, locks, and alarms) devices but does not reduce, and may even contribute to increased fear and distrust among neighbors (Quinney 1977). If true, this could critically affect the quality of life of particular subsectors of the rural population. For instance, given the proportion of the rural elderly who live alone or who are socially isolated (Donnermeyer et al. 1980), and given the higher levels of fear of crime among senior citizens (Conklin 1975), a crime prevention program could serve to enhance this fear and to increase further the social isolation of rural older persons.

A second school of thought is that crime, because it represents a violation of deep-set normative standards within a community, serves to strengthen the "collective consciousness" among law-abiding citizens. Coser (1956) has noted that a threat (i.e., crime as a threat to order and tranquility) will unite persons around a common cause of action. In this instance, community solidarity is enhanced.

One of the critical issues in the development of educational programs on crime prevention is the potential for the creation of fear and distrust. Community-based approaches to crime prevention, such as Neighborhood Watch and the CB (Citizens Band Radios) Patrol, stress the responsibility of the individual as a member of the larger community. Viewed as a community problem requiring a community response, crime may function to strengthen social relationships.

Summary

The analysis of *Uniform Crime Report* data can be summarized in ten major findings:

1. Rural communities presently face a major crime problem. The rural crime index rate of 1979 exceeded the metropolitan crime index rate of 1966.
2. Rural crime is an emerging problem. The rural crime index rate has been increasing faster than the urban crime index rate since the late 1960s.
3. Rural and urban crime are predominantly against property. Since 1970 a slightly higher proportion of crime in rural areas is against property than in urban areas.
4. The highest reported rates of violent crime for both urban and rural places has shifted from the South Atlantic (1974) to the Pacific Region (1979).
5. The highest reported rates of property crime for rural places in both 1974 and 1979 occurred in the Pacific Region. For urban places the highest reported property crime rate in both 1974 and 1979 appeared in the Mountain Region.
6. The largest increase in reported rural violent crime occurred in New England. For urban places the largest increase in reported violence appeared in the West South Central Region.
7. In all regions, both urban and rural, reported property crime increased. For rural places the largest increase was in New England. For urban places the largest increase was in the Middle Atlantic Region.
8. In both 1974 and 1979 the highest proportion of reported violent crime to the total crime index for rural places appeared in the East South Central Region. For urban places this proportion was highest in the Middle Atlantic Region.
9. For rural places the largest increase in the proportion of reported violent crime occurred in the Mountain Region. The largest increase in the proportion of urban reported violence appeared in the West South Central Region.
10. Reported urban violent and property crime has been and continues to be substantially higher than the respective rates for rural areas. However, in both 1974 and 1979, the proportion of reported violent crime was higher in the rural East South Central, South Atlantic and West South Central Regions than for urban places in those regions.

Thirty years ago, in the "big" city, crime and fear of crime were factors in the "flight to the suburbs." Fifteen years ago, the "flight from the suburbs" and the "back to the country" movement began. In part, this resulted from the rapid increase in crime and drug-related problems, which served to shatter the "idyllic" image of suburban living. Crime has now come to the hinterlands, and there are no more "crime free" places to move. Rural crime prevention is a must if the negative social impacts are to be contained at a tolerable level.

Notes

1. Arson has been added as an eight index crime, beginning in 1980.
2. States included with each Census Region include: (1) New England—Connecticut, Maine, Massachusetts, New Hampshire, Rhode Island, and Vermont; (2) Middle Atlantic—New Jersey, New York, and Pennsylvania; (3) East North Central—Illinois, Indiana, Michigan, Ohio, and Wisconsin; (4) West North Central —Iowa, Kansas, Minnesota, Missouri, Nebraska, North Dakota, and South Dakota; (5) South Atlantic—Delaware, Florida, Georgia, Maryland, North Carolina, South Carolina, Virginia, and West Virginia; (6) East South Central—Alabama, Kentucky, Mississippi, and Tennessee; (7) West South Central—Arkansas, Louisiana, Oklahoma, and Texas; (8) Mountain—Arizona, Colorado, Idaho, Montana, Nevada, New Mexico, Utah, and Wyoming; and (9) Pacific—Alaska, California, Hawaii, Oregon, and Washington.

References

Bean, T.L. and L.D. Lawrence. 1978. *Crime on Farms in Hampshire County, West Virginia—Pilot Study*. R.M. No. 69. Morgantown, West Virginia: Center for Extension and Continuing Education, West Virginia University.

Conklin, John E. 1975. *The Impact of Crime*. New York: MacMillan Publishing Co., Inc.

Coser, Lewis. 1956. *The Functions of Social Conflict*. New York: The Free Press.

Donnermeyer, Joseph F., Gerald Wibert, and Bill Beach. 1980. "Developing Programs for the Rural Elderly: A Community Development Approach." Paper presented at the annual meeting of the Community Development Society, Arcata, California. August.

Lentz, William P. 1956. "Rural-urban Differentials and Juvenile Delinquency." *Journal of Criminal Law, Criminology and Police Science* 47(October):331-39.

Polk, Kenneth. 1967. "Juvenile Delinquency in Non-metropolitan Areas." In the *President's Task Force on Law Enforcement and Administration of Justice: Juvenile Delinquence and Youth Crime*. Washington, D.C.: U.S. Government Printing Office.

Quinney, Richard. 1977. *Class State and Crime*. New York: David McKay Company, Inc.

Smith, B.L. and J.F. Donnermeyer. 1979. "Criminal Victimization among Rural Residents: A Case Study of Benton County, Indiana." Presented at the annual meeting of the Rural Sociological Society, Burlington, Vermont. August.

U.S. Department of Justice, Federal Bureau of Investigation. 1959-80. *Uniform Crime Reports*. Washington, D.C.: U.S. Government Printing Office.

U.S. Department of Justice, Law Enforcement Assistance Administration. 1978. *Myths and Realities about Crime*. Washington, D.C.: U.S. Government Printing Office.

3

Patterns of Criminal Victimization in a Rural Setting: The Case of Pike County, Indiana

JOSEPH F. DONNERMEYER

Introduction

Crime in the rural United States is rising rapidly.[1] The exact magnitude of the increase is readily available through such official statistics as the Federal Bureau of Investigation's *Uniform Crime Reports,* or through other police and court figures. However, perhaps the most important evidence that crime today is defined as a "serious" problem in America's hinterlands may be found in the growing concern expressed by leaders of rural and farm organizations and by public officials from rural areas.

A spokesman for the American Farm Bureau has indicated that U.S. farmers suffer losses of over one billion dollars annually from theft, vandalism, and other crimes (Cheatham 1979). Farm thefts exceed $6 million in Kentucky (Dogin 1980), while farmers in California suffer losses due to theft of over $30 million per year (Footlick et al. 1979). Rural electric cooperatives in Virginia spend more than one million dollars each year to repair and replace vandalized and stolen property. Georgia power cooperatives lost nearly $250,000 in copper wire, tools, and equipment in the first half of 1980 (Anderberg 1980).

The topic of rural crime has recently been highlighted in the *FBI Law Enforcement Bulletin* (May 1980), and *U.S. News and World Report* (May 26 1980). The trade magazine, *Rural Electrification* (June 1980) devoted an entire issue to rural crime.

The level of crime in rural areas is now beginning to receive nationwide attention. A "Rural Working Paper" was presented at the 1980 meeting of the National Governor's Association (Rideout 1980). Recently, a National Extension Workshop on Rural Crime Prevention was held under the auspices of the National Rural Crime Prevention Center at The Ohio State University. At the workshop, representatives from 16 State Cooperative Extension Services met to examine various crime prevention strategies for rural homes and farms.

As concern about the issue grows, there will be an increasing need for research concerning the extent and pattern of rural crime. The purpose of this chapter is to review the findings from a criminal victimization research study conducted in Pike County, a rural county in southwest Indiana. It will examine the extent of crime occurring by the type of victimization and will compare the incidence of crime in the study area with national victimization data available through the National Crime Study (U.S. Department of Justice 1979). A second purpose of the chapter is to examine area, sex, age, and household size differentials in victimization rates. The chapter will conclude with suggestions for future research into the extent and pattern of rural crime.

Research Method

Pike County (pop. 12,300) was selected as the research site for two reasons (Department of Health, Education, and Welfare 1978:41). First, it is primarily a rural county, with a mixed economic base of agriculture and coal mining. Petersburg, the county seat, had a population at the time of the study of nearly 2,800 persons. It is located approximately 42 miles north of Evansville, Indiana. Second, one of the subgoals of the study was to examine the comparative rate of victimization between younger and older age groupings. According to Department of Health, Education, and Welfare (HEW 1978:41) estimates, the proportion of the population 60 years of age and over in Pike County was 21.8 percent in 1976. This is considerably higher than the state average of the population 60 and over, which was estimated at 14.3 percent in 1976.

A simple random sample of households from the county telephone directory was utilized. Each residential listing in the telephone book was enumerated and a sample of 400 telephone numbers was randomly selected. Only one listing per the same address was counted, unless the address indicated an apartment dwelling.

The survey instrument was administered by telephone. A total of 366 interviews was completed with one adult member (20 years or older) of the household. Of those households contacted, a total of 66 refused to be interviewed. The completion rate was 84.7 percent for those households which were contacted. In addition, 62 households originally selected for inclusion in the study could not be contacted for a variety of reasons.[2]

The victimization section of the survey instrument was modeled after the National Crime Study (National Research Council 1976) in order to insure comparability of the Pike County crime data with national crime rate statistics. The victimization questions were divided into two parts: a series of items on household level crimes (burglary, household larceny, motor vehicle theft, and vandalism), and crimes against the person (personal larceny, assault and robbery). Unlike the National Crime Study, the Pike County victimization study included the crime of vandalism because previous research by Phillips (1975) and Smith (1979) have indicated it to be one of the most frequently experienced by rural residents. The crime of rape was omitted from the Pike County study due to the sensitivity of the subject and the mode by which the data was collected.

The household victimization questions could be answered by any adult member of the household. However, questions pertaining to crimes against the person were directed specifically to the respondent, who then was not asked if such crimes had occurred to other members of the household. This is dissimilar to the National Crime Study method which addresses the personal victimization items occurring to each household member (over 12) during person-to-person interview sessions. The telephone format employed in the Pike County Study restricted administration of the total survey instrument, including the personal crime items, to only one adult member of the household (over 20).

Household victimization rates are expressed in this chapter as the number of specific criminal incidents per 1,000 households. Victimization rates for crimes against persons are presented as the number of specific incidents per 1,000 persons.

Similar to the National Crime Study (National Research Council 1976), a specific time period (12 months) was used, and all crime statistics refer to annual rates. The time period for the Pike County study was the 1978 calendar year. The telephone interviews were conducted during the first several months of 1979. In order to verify positive responses to the crime questions, a series of follow-up items were utilized. These included details regarding the day and month during which the criminal incident occurred and additional information on the nature of the incident, such as the type of property stolen or damaged, the location of the incident, and whether or not the incident was reported to a law enforcement agency. If an incident described by the respondent did not occur during the 1978 calendar year, it was not counted in the calculation of the crime rates.

Distribution of Offenses

A total of 126 criminal incidents were reported by the respondents (Table 3.1). Of 366 completed interviews, 85 (23.2 percent) respondents experienced one or more criminal incidents during the 1978 calendar year. Fifty-nine reported only one offense, while 26 described two or more separate criminal offenses which occurred during this period.

Vandalism (destruction or attempted destruction of property) was the most frequently reported crime, representing about 28 percent of all incidents. Household larceny (theft or attempted theft of property from the yard with entry into the house or other buildings) was the second most frequently mentioned criminal incident, comprising about one out

Table 3.1. Number and Percent of Criminal Incidents, by Type of Incident

Crime Type	Number	Percent
Household		
Forcible Entry Burglary	11	8.7
Attempted Forcible Entry	9	7.1
Unlawful Entry Without Forced	8	6.3
Household Larceny	31	24.6
Vandalism	35	27.8
Motor Vehicle Theft	4	3.2
Personal		
Personal Larceny Without Contact	22	17.5
Personal Larceny With Contact	2	1.6
Robbery	0	0.0
Assault (Simple and Aggravated)	4	3.2
Total	126	100.0

of every four crimes. Personal larceny with contact (purse-snatching or pick-pocketing) and personal larceny without contact (theft of personal property while at work, school, shopping or other places away from the place of residence) together accounted for nearly 20 percent of all crimes reported. Household and personal larceny added together represent the largest share of the crimes (more than 40 percent of the total incidents).

The results from Table 1 indicate that property-related crimes make up the vast majority of those suffered by the residents of Pike County. These results appear consistent with other rural victimization research (Dinitz 1973; Phillips 1975; Kelley and Burdge 1979; and Smith 1979), which suggests that property offenses account for 90 percent or more of all criminal incidents likely to be experienced by persons residing in most rural areas of the United States.

Table 3.2 compares the rate of criminal victimization for Pike County with the most recently published results of the National Crime Study for the United States, for Standard Metropolitan Statistical Areas (SMSAs), and for non-SMSA areas. The results indicate that for some types of victimizations, the Pike County crime rates were equivalent or equal to the national rates and to those for SMSA areas. The forcible entry burglary and attempted forcible rates were very near to the SMSA levels and exceeded both the U.S. average and the rate for non-SMSA areas. In contrast, the rate of unlawful entry without force was lower in Pike County than in the other three comparative units.

The rate of household larceny in Pike County (85.2 per 1,000 households) was nearly identical to the non-SMSA average (85.9 per 1,000 households). On the other hand, the motor vehicle theft rate in Pike County (11.0 per 1,000 households) was twice as high as the non-SMSA rate (5.4 per 1,000 households), but considerably lower than both the U.S. average (17.0 per 1,000 households) and the SMSA rate (21.0 per 1,000 households).

The vandalism rate in Pike County, an offense which is not included in the National Crime Study, was 96.1 per 1,000 households. Vandalism ranks as the most extensive criminal offense occurring to Pike Countians, affecting nearly one-tenth of all households on an annual basis. This finding, plus the earlier cited research by both Phillips (1975) and Smith (1979), indicates the need to explore further the impact of vandalism to the rural population. In addition, this finding suggests that future victimization research under the auspices of the National Crime Study needs to include the crime of vandalism.

A direct comparison between Pike County and SMSA and non-SMSA areas is impossible because the personal offense rates found in Table 3.2 are based upon different age groupings. However, a discussion of the

Table 3.2.   Comparative Victimization Rates for Pike County, Indiana (1978) and
National Crime Study, by Metropolitan and Non-Metropolitan Areas (1977).

Crime Type	Pike County (1978)	National Crime Study[a] U.S. Average (1977)	SMSA Areas (1977)	Non-SMSA Areas (1977)
Household (Per 1,000 Households)				
Forcible Entry Burglary	30.3	30.1	35.4	18.6
Attempted Forcible Entry	24.8	19.7	23.0	12.4
Unlawful Entry Without Force	22.0	38.8	39.4	37.3
Household Larceny	85.2	114.0	127.0	85.9
Motor Vehicle Theft	11.0	17.0	21.0	5.4
Vandalism	96.1	NA[b]	NA	NA
Personal (Per 1,000 Persons)	Persons ≥ 20 years	Persons ≥ 20 years	Persons[c] ≥ 12 years	Persons[c] ≥ 12 years
Personal Larceny Without contact	60.4	83.2	106.3	69.7
Personal Larceny With Contact	5.5	2.7	3.3	1.2
Robbery	0.0	5.3	7.8	2.6
Assault (Simple and Aggravated)	11.0	21.5	30.4	18.9

a. U.S. Department of Justice, Law Enforcement Assistance Administration, and the
National Criminal Justice Information Statistics Service. Criminal Victimization
in the United States, 1977: A National Crime Survey Report. Washington, D.C.:
U.S. Government Printing Service, December 1979.

b. Not available

c. The rate for personal crimes from the Pike County study is limited to persons
20 years and older. The personal crime rates from the National Crime study were
recalculated to include only persons 20 years and older for the United States
average. However, for metropolitan and non-metropolitan areas, the personal crime
rates were for persons 12 years and older. The reports available from the
National Crime Study did not provide age-specific victimization rates for personal
crimes by community size.

relative differentials between Pike County and the U.S. average is possible, because the national personal offense rates are reported in an age-
specific format in the official publications of the National Crime Study.

The personal larceny without contact (i.e., theft of personal property
or cash from any place other than the victim's place of residence without
a direct contact between victim and offender) rate in Pike County was
60.4 offenses per 1,000 persons. This is about three-fourths the per capita
volume of crime on a national basis. The difference in the personal
larceny without contact offense rates may be due in part to the differences
between the types of jobs held by and the commuting patterns of rural
and urban residents. Many personal larcenies take place at the victim's
place of work (i.e., the factory or the office). A greater proportion of the
labor force in a rural environment works at home, such as farmers and
farm laborers. This reduces the opportunity for this type of offense to

occur. In addition, a theft on the farm would be reported as a household larceny.

The personal larceny with contact rate (i.e., purse-snatching and pick-pocketing) in Pike County was twice as high as the national average. However, the relatively smaller sample size of the Pike County study precludes a definite conclusion that this offense occurs more often in rural areas. There were no robberies (i.e., theft by force) reported by residents to the Pike County study. The national average for robbery was 5.3 incidents per 1,000 persons. The total assault rate (simple and aggravated) in Pike County was about one-half the rate of the United States. Interestingly, half of the assaults reported by respondents occurred outside of Pike County, in large metropolitan areas.

The Pattern of Crime in Pike County

The preceding section of this chapter establishes that the predominant types of crime occurring in Pike County were property offenses. This section of the chapter extends analysis of property offenses by examining their relative occurrence according to location of residence, sex, age and household size. Table 3.3 displays the proportion of households to which one or more incidents of vandalism, burglary, and household larceny occurred, and the proportion of persons to which one or more incidents of personal larceny occurred, according to the location of residence. Residence was divided into three types: county seat (residence in Petersburg, the county's largest town), small towns (residence in all other incorporated and unincorporated places less than 2,500 persons), and open-country (all other respondents, including both farm and non-farm residences).

The results in Table 3.3 indicate statistically significant differences for two of the four property offenses. First, vandalism was far more likely to occur among those households located in the small towns (14.9 percent) than in either the county seat (5.5 percent) or in the open-country (7.0 percent). An oft-repeated comment of respondents from the several small towns in the study was the problem of unsupervised groups or so-called "marauding" gangs of youth during the evening hours. Coupled with this type of comment was often the complaint that there was no visible signs of law enforcement, which the respondents perceived as necessary to deter these youth from "getting into trouble." This style of commentary was consistently volunteered by the small town respondents, regardless of whether or not their household had been the victim of vandalism. Although it was not within the scope of the Pike County

Table 3.3.   Proportion of Pike County Households and Persons
             To Which One or More Property Crime Victimizations
             Occurred, By Place of Residence

Location	Vandalism (Percent)	Burglary, All Types (Percent)	Household Larceny (Percent)	Personal Larceny, All Types (Percent)
County Seat (N=110)	5.5	0.9	6.3	4.5
Small Towns (N=141)	14.9	10.8	10.8	4.1
Open Country (N=171)	7.0	9.9	8.2	5.8

$$x^2 \leq .05, \text{ C=S.} \quad x^2 \leq .05, \text{ C=S.} \quad x^2 > .05, \text{ C=N.S.} \quad x^2 > .05, \text{ C=N.S.}$$

crime study to examine age or other characteristics of probable offenders, these comments do suggest that less opportunity for young persons to gather at the county seat (due perhaps to the more visible presence of the police) or at open-country locations may be an important contributor to the relatively high probability of vandalism to small town households in Pike County.

Burglary and attempted burglary were far more likely to be experienced by households located in either the small towns (10.8 percent) or in the open-country (9.9 percent) than in the county seat (0.9 percent). Nearly all of the burglaries and attempted burglaries were to houses, rather than to barns, garages, or other buildings.

Two explanations are suggested for the higher incidence of burglary to households located outside the county seat. Among open-country households, the fact that nearly one-tenth experienced one or more burglaries within a 12 month period may be due to the increased opportunity afforded by greater distances between houses. Open-country homes are more likely to be physically isolated, so that they are less visible to neighbors. This allows the potential burglar to attempt an illegal entry with less chance of being seen.

Among the small town households, however, neighbors would be physically nearer, and this explanation appears less plausible. The absence of full-time law enforcement in the small towns may present a more viable alternate explanation for the higher level of burglary. However, it should be emphasized that both these explanations represent hypotheses and are not meant to exclude the consideration of other rationales.

Table 3.4.   Proportion of Pike County Households and Persons
             To Which One or More Property Crimes Occurred,
             By Number of Persons in Household

Number of Persons In Household	Vandalism (Percent)	Burglary, All Types (Percent)	Household Larceny (Percent)	Personal Larceny (Percent)
One Person (N=75)	9.3	4.0	12.0	2.6
Two Persons (N=146)	6.8	6.2	4.8	4.1
Three or More Persons (N=137)	8.0	9.5	6.6	7.3

$x^2 > .05$, C=N.S. $x^2 > .05$, C=N.S. $x^2 > .05$, C=N.S. $x^2 > .05$, C=N.S.

For both household and personal larceny, there were no major differences between county seat residents, small town residents, and open-country residents. Again, there was a slightly greater chance that households located in the small towns were more likely to experience one or more incidents of household larceny (10.8 percent) than either open-country households (8.2 percent) or county seat households (6.3 percent). There was also little or no difference by location in terms of the proportion of respondents experiencing at least one incident of personal larceny.

SIZE OF HOUSEHOLD

Contained within Table 3.4 is displayed the proportion of households and persons to whom one or more property offenses occurred, broken down by household size. As the data in Table 3.4 indicates, there were no statistically significant differences for any of the four offense categories. With respect to vandalism, there was only a slight tendency for single member households to have experienced one or more incidents. In contrast, a burglary or attempted burglary was more likely to be reported by households with three or more members. This pattern is similar to the findings of the National Crime Study (U.S. Department of Justice 1979:36): the burglary rate increases with household size.

The National Crime Study (U.S. Department of Justice 1979:38) also found that the rate of household larceny is higher for larger households. However, in Pike County, the trend was in the opposite direction. Twelve

Table 3.5.   Proportion of Pike County Households To Which
One or More Household Level Property Crimes
Occurred, By Age of Household Members

Age of Household Members	Vandalism (Percent)	Burglary All Types (Percent)	Household Larceny (Percent)
Some Members $\leq$ 60 (N=241)	7.1	7.9	8.3
All Members > 60 (N=117)	9.4	4.3	6.8

$x^2 >$ .05, C=N.S. $x^2 >$ .05, C=N.S. $x^2 >$ .05, C=N.S.

percent of the single member households experienced one or more incidents of larceny, in contrast to 6.6 percent for households of three or more persons. Finally, the proportion of respondents to whom one or more personal larcenies occurred were more likely to be from households with three or more persons.

AGE OF HOUSEHOLD MEMBERS

Households were dichotomized according to the ages of all household members. The two categories were those in which all members were 60 years or older, and those in which at least one member was less than 60 years old. The proportion of both types to which vandalism, burglary, and household larceny occurred is found in Table 3.5. There were no statistically significant differences between older and younger households on the probability of victimization for each of the three offense categories. Older households were slightly more likely to have experienced an incident of vandalism, but less likely either to be burglarized or to have a larceny occur.

This finding is significant because it suggests that the pattern of victimization in rural areas may be different from urban areas. In urban places, the probability of victimization decreases with age. The nature of the impact of crime on the urban elderly has more to do with their greater levels of fear about the probability of victimization, although vulnerability to certain crimes, such as fraud, and purse-snatching, are also problems.

The results in Table 3.5 indicate that there exists a small differential

Table 3.6.   Percentage Distribution of Household-Related
             Victimizations to Older Households in Pike
             County, By Place of Residence and Household Size

Location of Household (All Members > 60)	None (Percent)	One or More (Percent)	Total (Percent)
County Seat (N=36)	83.3	16.7	100.0
Small Town (N=28)	71.4	28.6	100.0
Open-Country (N=46)	82.6	17.4	10.0

$$x^2 > .05, \ C=N.S.$$

Size of Household (All Members > 60)	None (Percent)	One or More (Percent)	Total (Percent)
1 (N=59)	79.7	20.3	100.0
2 (N=56)	83.9	16.1	100.0

$$x^2 > .05, \ C=N.S.$$

between older and younger persons in rural areas with respect to the direct experience of victimization, than in urban areas.

This is not to be interpreted as meaning that older persons in rural areas do not have special problems associated with the impact of crime. Quite to the contrary, the increased physical vulnerability and generally lower incomes of older persons mean that the effects of direct victimization may be differentially higher among the rural elderly than among the urban elderly, when compared to younger age groupings in the same respective environments.

LOCATION AND HOUSEHOLD SIZE OF
OLDER VICTIMIZED HOUSEHOLDS

Who among the elderly are more likely to be victimized in Pike County? In order to further examine criminal victimization among older households, household-related offenses by location of residence and household size was completed. Table 3.6 shows the results of this analysis. First, looking at the location of residence, it may be seen that the proportion of older households from small towns to whom at least one victimization occurred was 28.6 percent. This is higher than the proportion of older households from either the county seat (16.7 percent) or from the open-country (17.4 percent) who were victimized. However, the difference is not large enough to be statistically significant. The pattern of victimization to older households found in Table 3.6 is similar to that of the total sample. Households located in the small towns were more likely to have been victimized than in any other part of Pike County.

In the bottom half of Table 6 is shown the proportion of older households which have been victimized by the size of the household. There was a slightly higher likelihood for single member older households to have experienced a victimization than older households with two or more members. However, the difference is not of statistical significance.

The results in Table 3.6 are preliminary in nature and suggest the need for more in-depth research on the effects of crime on the rural elderly. Vulnerability to crime, and the fear of crime may be different among the rural elderly than among the urban elderly. Realization of these differences will be crucial to the design of crime prevention and victim compensation programs targeted for the rural elderly.

AGE, SEX, AND PERSONAL LARCENY VICTIMIZATION

The sex and age distribution of persons who reported one or more personal larceny offenses is reported in Table 3.7. As the results there indicate, there were no significant percentage differences by either the sex or age of victims to personal larceny offenses. According to the sex of the victim, a slightly higher percentage were female (5.3 percent) than male (4.5 percent). By the age of the victims, the proportion who experienced one or more personal larceny offenses was 6.8 percent for those between 20-39 years old, 4.8 percent for those between 40-59 years old, and 2.5 percent for those 60 years of age and over.

The pattern of victimization for personal larceny in Pike County by the sex of the victim is slightly different than the pattern found in the National Crime Study (U.S. Department of Justice 1979:26). On a national basis, males were reportedly more likely to experience a personal larceny. However, the differential percentage of larceny incidents between younger and older persons in Pike County is very similar to the national pattern.

Generally, vulnerability to personal larceny may be understood in large part on the basis of mobility patterns related to employment and shopping habits. Persons who are employed away from the home, such

Table 3.7.   Percentage Distribution of Personal Larceny
Victimizations in Pike County, By Sex and Age

| A. Sex | Personal Larceny, All Types | | |
	None (Percent)	One or More (Percent)	Total
Male (N=177)	95.5	4.5	100.0
Female (N=189)	94.7	5.3	100.0

$x^2 > .05$, C=N.S.

B. Age	None (Percent)	One or More (Percent)	Total
20-39 (N=117)	92.2	6.8	100.0
40-59 (N=104)	95.2	4.8	100.0
60 (N=120)	97.5	2.5	100.0

$x^2 > .05$, C=N.S.

as in a factory or office, and persons who shop frequently at large retail centers are generally more likely to have a personal larceny occur than persons whose everyday activities are centered around the home. For this reason, the national pattern has found more males than females, and younger rather than older persons, to have higher personal larceny rates. The occurrence of personal larceny by sex and age in the Pike County Study indicates a similar pattern.

Summary and Conclusions

This chapter has reviewed and discussed the results of a criminal victimization study conducted in Pike County, Indiana, a rural community in the southwest part of the state. The study focused upon a series of criminal offenses which may have occurred to the study sample during 1978. In brief, highlights of findings from the study included:

1. Nearly one-quarter of the households experienced at least one criminal incident.
2. The predominant type of crimes which occurred were property-related offenses. Larceny, including both the theft of household-related property and of personal property, was the most frequently occurring offense. Van-

dalism was the second most frequently reported incident. Burglary (all types) ranked third in frequency.

3. The rates of forcible entry and attempted forcible entry burglary in Pike County were slightly higher than the national averages and nearly equal to the rates for SMSA areas.
4. The rates of household and personal larceny were lower than the national averages.
5. The proportion of households located in the small towns of Pike County experiencing property crime victimizations, in particular, vandalism and burglary (all types), were higher than at other locations in the county.
6. There were only slight differences in the proportions between older and younger households experiencing vandalism, burglary, and household larceny. The pattern of victimization on a national basis for burglary and household larceny is different. Nationally, the younger the household head, the higher is the rate of burglary and household larceny.
7. Older households from the small towns were more likely to experience a household-related victimization, although the difference between this group and older households from either the county seat or the open-country was not statistically significant.
8. There were only slight differences in the proportion of persons experiencing personal larceny victimization by either sex or age. This pattern is dissimilar from the national pattern, which has found males and younger persons to have higher rates of personal larceny.

There are two significant conclusions to be drawn from the Pike County rural crime study. First, the per capita volume of crime in this almost exclusively rural community is not overall much lower than the national average. This runs counter to the traditional image of the low level of rural crime. Second, crime in Pike County displays a different pattern than what the national statistics indicate. For instance, in Pike County there were only minor differences in the proportion of older versus younger households experiencing household-related offenses, and between older and younger persons experiencing personal larceny offenses.

The first major conclusion (using Pike County as case in point) suggests that crime in many rural communities today is at a level as high as the typical American urban community. In urban America, crime has long been defined as a significant "social problem."

It is now time for many rural communities to address their crime problem, and the alternatives range from increasing and improving law enforcement personnel and facilities, to strengthening criminal penalties as a method of deterrence, to implementing crime prevention programs, such as home security and personal protection measures. However, the second major conclusion suggests that before any type of action occurs, it is imperative that rural communities determine the nature of their local crime problem.

Victimization studies of specific locales, such as the Pike County crime study, are especially valuable in the design of crime prevention programs which seek to reduce the vulnerability of potential victims. This is because victimization research focuses on the "victim," rather than the "offender:"

This chapter has demonstrated that rural crime is not a problem to be ignored. It is real and exists at a level in some rural communities that rivals the level of many urban communities. As response strategies are proposed to reduce crime levels in rural areas, accurate knowledge of the extent and pattern of the problem will be needed. Victimization research, as illustrated by the Pike County crime study, assists in the development of this knowledge.

Notes

1. The author would like to acknowledge the invaluable contribution of Linda Blackwell, Resource Developer, Area 13A Agency on Aging. Her assistance in conducting many of the interviews and in recruiting, training, and monitoring the other interviewers was essential to the successful completion of the project.
2. Sixty-two households could not be reached by telephone for the following reasons: (A) phone out of order or disconnected (13); (B) respondent had moved out of the county (10); and (C) after at least five attempts at calling, either the phone was busy and/or there was no answer (39).

References

Anderberg, Ken. 1980. "There's Gold in Copper." *Rural Electrification* (June):18-19.

Cheatham, Kenneth. 1979. "Crime and U.S. Agriculture." Speech presented at the Crime in Rural Virginia Conference, Virginia Polytechnic Institute, Blacksburg, Virginia.

Dinitz, Simon. 1973. "Progress, Crime and the Folk Ethic: Portrait of a Small Town." *Criminology* 11 (May):3-21.

Dogin, Henry S. 1980. "Rural Areas at Disadvantage in Crime Prevention." *Rural Electrification* 38 (June):25.

Footlick, Jerrold K. 1977. "Crime on the Farm." *Newsweek.* October 3.

Kelley, R.M. and Rabel J. Burdge. 1979. "Rural-Urban Crime Victimization Ratios: Comparisons from a Statewide Study in Illinois." Paper presented at the annual meeting of the Rural Sociological Society, Burlington, Vermont. August.

National Research Council. 1976. *Surveying Crime.* Washington, D.C.: National Academy of Sciences.

Phillips, G. Howard. 1975. *Crime in Rural Ohio.* ESO 363. Columbus, Ohio: Department of Agricultural Economics and Rural Sociology, The Ohio State University.

Rideout, Richard. 1980. "Rural Crime Working Paper." Paper presented at the National Governor's Association Committee on Criminal Justice and Public Protection, Subcommittee on Criminal Justice, Baltimore, Maryland.

Rural Electrification. 1980. "Rural Crime." June issue.

Smith, Brent L. 1979. *Criminal Victimization in Rural Areas: An Analysis of Victimization Patterns and Reporting Trends.* Ph.D. dissertation, Purdue University.

U.S. Department of Health, Education, and Welfare, Administration on Aging. 1976. *The Elderly Population: Estimates By County, 1976.* Washington, D.C.: National Clearinghouse on Aging.

U.S. Department of Justice, Federal Bureau of Investigation. 1980. *FBI Law Enforcement Bulletin.* May issue.

U.S. Department of Justice, Law Enforcement Assistance Administration. 1979. *Criminal Victimization in the United States: 1977.* Washington, D.C.: U.S. Government Printing Office.

U.S. News and World Report. 1980. "Lawbreakers Turn to Greener Pastures." May 26.

4

The Ohio Rural Victimization Study

G. HOWARD PHILLIPS
and TODD N. WURSCHMIDT

This descriptive report is an attempt to merge two yet barely probed areas of inquiry, rural crime and rural victimization.[1] It is the result of an attempt to illuminate the "dark figures" of crime (i.e., crimes not revealed by official data) by examination of the nature and extent of crimes committed against rural residents as reported by the victims of those crimes. The authors believe that the Ohio study reported herein is the first major statewide victimization study to involve exclusively open country rural residents.[2]

The Problem

Rural crime is increasingly becoming a "manifest" problem for our rural communities. Traditionally believed to be a "social ill" confined within city boundaries, crime in the country was perceived as quite manageable by rural police and judicial resources. The operation of effective formal social controls, coupled with the existence of time-honored informal ones (e.g., the rural family), generally perpetuated a now erroneous view of rural America as a sanctuary of security. The view of rural crime as a problem not worthy of concerted attention is aptly reflected by the paucity of literature available heretofore. A meager total of six related articles, for example, have been published in *Rural Sociology* since its inception in 1937.

For a multiplicity of reasons, the level and pervasiveness of rural crime has increased dramatically in Ohio (Figure 4.1). Although the level of officially documented incidents of crime remains higher for U.S. cities, the escalation in the rate of nonurban crime now surpasses that of our largest cities. The crime rate for rural America for the 15 year period 1963-1977 increased 351 percent; for America's SMSAs, 287 percent (Phillips et al. 1979:2).

The seriousness of the existing rural crime problem is accurately demonstrated by Phillips' et al. (1979:2) observation that "the 'high' U.S. and SMSA crime rates of the middle sixties were a major impetus for the 1968 legislative enactment creating the Law Enforcement Assistance Administration." Today, the level of rural crime equals or exceeds the SMSA levels for the middle sixties. Statements, precipitated principally by the level of the urban crime problem in the mid sixties describing crime as ". . . the ultimate human degradation" (Clark 1970:8), and one which could if left unchecked ". . . destroy the fiber of the nation" (Stewart et al. 1971:29) regrettably seem applicable to the present rural crime problem.

In order to gain further insight into the rural crime problem, several research questions are examined in this chapter. What are the types of crimes occurring to rural residents as reported by victims? Are crimes known to law enforcement authorities different from those reported by rural residents? If so, why? How does property crime compare to violent crime? What is the nature of property crime? Are the socioeconomic characteristics of victims vs. nonvictims significantly different? Can types of victims be identified according to socioeconomic criteria? These and other questions are addressed and examined following a discussion of the study's research tool, unit of analysis and methodology.

Victim Survey Research

Victim survey research was designed to unearth that proportion of crimes which never found their way into the tabulations of official records (i.e., were never reported or not judged by law enforcement personnel to be labeled as crime) (Hindelang 1976). For instance, it is estimated that less than half of crime experienced by citizens is reported to law enforcement (U.S. Department of Justice 1977).

Additionally, the intent was to elaborate on the circumstance of crime,

Figure 4.1:   The U.S. and Ohio rural crime index. [3,4]
Source: U.S. Department of Justice, Federal Bureau of Investigation.
Uniform Crime Reports.   1970–1979.

Per 100,000 Persons

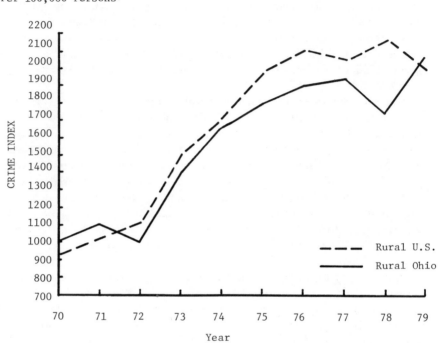

that is, to convey for purposes of criminological theory, research and policy, situational variables surrounding its occurrence. The limitations of the most widely used and reputable document of official crime statistics, the *Uniform Crime Reports,* are readily admitted in the UCR's staff's introductory comment, "Population size is the only correlate of crime utilized in this publication" (FBI, 1977:V).

In the words of Glaser, ". . . victim survey research should not be viewed as a replacement for police reports on the volume of crime, but as a continually necessary supplement to police figures. If both police and victim survey crime rates are tabulated, information on the difference between these rates may be just as valuable as either rate alone" (1970:139-140). The valuable contribution of victim research is indeed ". . . more lucidity for the murky concept of crime" (Glaser 1970:138).

The Victim

In addition to the criminal, crime spawns a second category of partici-pant; namely, the victim. Although acknowledging the validity of the postulate, "In some way everyone involved in a crime is a victim" (Barkas 1978:6), for purposes of understanding the type of individuals likely to be encountered during interview phases of victim survey research, "vic-tim" is here defined according to more limited criteria. The victim is the individual or institution injured and/or whose property is taken or dam-aged, and who following the incident remains consciously aware of his circumstance.

Such a definition departs in degree from Drapkin and Viano's (1974:1) in that the victim need not suffer "severely" nor be the recipient of "cruel or oppressive treatment," although such occurrences are possible. The individual whose car antenna is broken or whose fuel storage tank is emptied is likely to share such incidents with the survey interviewer, and subsequently be classified as the victim of vandalism or larceny-theft, even though it can be argued, he has not suffered "severely." Addition-ally, Glaser's use of the qualifier "deliberately injured individual" re-sults in his conceptualizing two distinct categories of victims, those resulting from "predatory crimes" and those from "negligence crimes" (Glaser 1970:137). In doing so, his schema focuses on the deliberate intentions, or lack thereof, of the offender. We find it more appropriate to base our schema on the predicament of the victim. Accordingly, the individual whose lawn or corn field is damaged as a result of losing control of a vehicle, although not the victim of deliberate action, remains quite cognizant and rather irate that his property has been damaged. Such damage is likely to be narrated to the interviewer.

It might also be noted that the inherent approach employed in victim survey research is likely to exclude certain categories of victims. Those crime situations in which the victim is not clearly identifiable or remains unaware of his straits (e.g., the victim of fraud or shoplifting) are excluded (Glaser 1970:137). Additionally, the victim of "victimless crime," that is where the victim and offender can be one and the same (e.g., crimes involving drunkenness, narcotics, prostitution, and gam-bling) are likely to remain unreported (Dada 1979:3-4). Further, we realize that victims of particular types of offenses (e.g., rape and spouse abuse) will likely hesitate to share such incidents during an interview.

And thus, as with most methods of data collection, judgmental eval-uation finds the utility of the victim survey technique outweighing its limitations.

Methodology

Nine counties were selected on a stratified nonrandom basis to represent the state of Ohio. The state was first divided in a manner reflecting the three major economic regions of the state: Appalachia region; Cornbelt region; and Industrial Northeast region. Second, three counties per region were selected. According to region, they were: Appalachia region: Athens, Hocking, and Perry; Cornbelt region: Clark, Fayette, and Madison; and Industrial Northeast region: Ashland, Medina, and Wayne. Adjacent counties were chosen so that patterns extending across county lines could be examined. The counties were selected on the basis of criteria such as type of agriculture, topographical features, population density, distance from metropolitan areas, and proximity to interstate highways.

In order to test the representativeness of the rural population within the selected counties vis-a-vis the 1970 Ohio rural population, a comparison of population age profiles was performed. No statistically significant differences were revealed (Phillips 1975). The rural population of the nine selected counties, it was concluded, was representative of the rural population of Ohio.

The following steps were employed to select the study's sample. First, ten townships were randomly drawn from all townships in each of the nine counties. From a local map, an intersection of two roads was then randomly picked in each township. This became the starting point for a continuous type sample. Interviewers were instructed as to the direction to proceed and the households to be selected. Thus, ten families per township were selected. Because of road arrangements and size of farms, additional interviews were required. Three additional townships were selected in Clark, two in Wayne, and one in Medina.

A total of 889 questionnaires were completed via a drop-off pick-up method. Assistance was rendered in less than ten situations where individuals were unable to complete the questionnaire independently. Residents were instructed to report only those incidents which had occurred during the one-year period, August 1973-July 1974. Incidents occurring to any member of the household were noted.

Findings

OFFENSES

One of the first questions prompting this research was: What were the leading crimes occurring to rural residents in Ohio as reported by victims? Data in Figure 4.2 reveal vandalism (38 percent) as the leading

Figure 4.2:   Percent of offenses by major categories of crime occurring to Ohio rural residents as reported by victims.

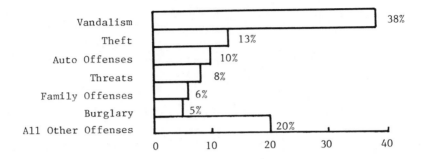

crime, with theft (13 percent) a distant second. It should be noted that serious crimes such as rape and robbery were reported at such low frequencies relative to all other crimes that they were included along with a large variety of miscellaneous crimes in the category "all other offenses."

The acts of vandalism involved a host of infractions including marring, destroying or defacing of cars, windows, lawns, shrubs, mailboxes along with destruction of a multitude of other kinds of property. The vandalizing acts reported in this study did not involve public property in rural areas such as churches, schools, business places, and cemeteries. The addition of these frequently vandalized public places would have markedly increased the percent of all crimes that are destructive in nature.

Theft constituted the second largest category of crime in rural Ohio (Figure 4.2). If the different types of theft had been added together, that is, larceny, burglary, fraud, consumer fraud, robbery and auto theft, they would have exceeded vandalism in scope. Gasoline was the item most often stolen in rural areas. Twenty percent of all thefts involved this product. Many rural residents, farmers in particular, maintained gasoline storage facilities which were reported as most frequently not locked (67 percent).

Slightly more than half (53 percent) of larceny-theft incidents occurred to rural residents while at home. The other 47 percent happened away from home. For example, one-quarter of the crimes which occurred away from home occurred at school. Two-thirds of the victims of larceny-theft were rural nonfarm residents, with the remainder holding full or part-time farming occupations.

In order to ascertain if a significant difference existed between crimes known to police against those reported by residents participating in this

Figure 4.3:   Percent of offenses by major categories of crime known to
Ohio sheriffs for the period June 1974 through May 1975

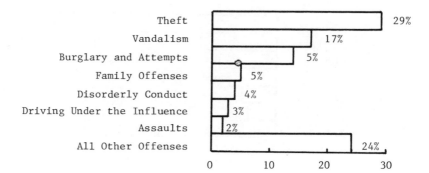

study, victimization data were compared to data collected via an Ohio
Sheriffs' Offenders Study (see note 2). Data in Figure 4.3 reveal theft
(29 percent) as the leading crime known to rural Sheriff's, with vandalism (17 percent) and burglary (14 percent) second and third, respectively.

Comparison of the data shown in Figures 4.2 and 4.3 reveals a notable
discrepancy between crimes known to police and those self-reported by
victims. It is additionally worthy of note that in both studies the overwhelming types of crimes were property crimes as opposed to personal
crimes. Property crimes represented over 90 percent of the rural crime
total.

Such differences were anticipated as a result of preparatory review of
urban victimization studies. Therefore, respondents were asked to indicate whether they had reported to a law enforcement agency the crime(s)
which had occurred to them or members of their household. Data in
Figure 4.4, broken down by major crime-categories, reveal a range of
percentages for those types of crimes reported to law enforcement agencies. Sixty-three percent of burglaries were reported, whereas only 15
percent of cases of fraud were reported. Overall, only 45 percent of the
crimes narrated during the interview process were reported to law enforcement authorities. The scope of the rural crime problem was at least
twice as extensive as was known to police agencies.

Probing still further, respondents were asked why crimes were not
reported. The data on this issue were compared to findings collected
from an attitudinal study of Ohio's Farm Bureau Council members
(Phillips 1974:28). Respondents from both studies indicated similar
reasons why crimes were not reported. The primary and foremost justi-

Figure 4.4: Percent of crimes reported to a law enforcement agency by category

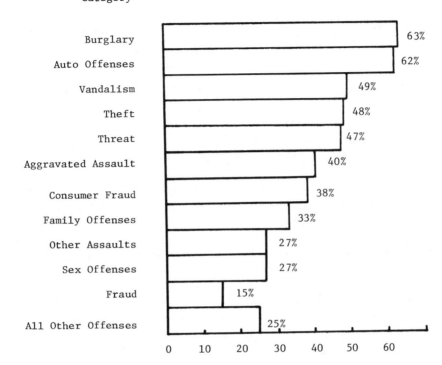

fication related was reflected in the statement, "It was no use." Included within this category were descriptive phrases like "difficult to enforce," "lack of enforcement," "slow follow-up," "too much leniency in the courts," "red tape," "lack of legal evidence," and "would do no good." The second most frequent response suggested unwillingness to get involved. These responses implied a number of things: unwillingness to get someone they knew in trouble; the value of lost items did not justify the time required for follow-up; and mere negligence in following through. A third category noted "fear of reprisal." This was generally fear of reprisal against property more than fear of physical harm.

SOCIOECONOMIC CHARACTERISTICS

Another dimension of the study involved examination by household of socioeconomic characteristics of sample participants to determine if there were notable differences between victims and nonvictims or if identifiably

Table 4.1.   Percent of Households Containing Rural Ohioans
             Who Were Victims of Burglary, Theft, or Vandalism
             by Occupation of the Head of the Household

Occupation	Burglary Victims (Percent)	Theft Victims (Percent)	Vandalism Victims (Percent)
Farmer	1.4 (141)	7.1 (140)	18.1 (138)
Other	4.5 (638)	7.4 (631)	13.9 (634)
Total	4.0 (779)	7.4 (771)	14.6 (772)
	$x^2 > .05$, C=N.S.	$x^2 > .05$, C=N.S.	$x^2 > .05$, C=N.S.

distinct categories of victims existed. The dependent varibles used as
indicators included the property crimes of burglary, theft, and vandalism.

The three property crime offenses were examined in terms of the
primary occupation of the head of the household. These data were viewed
from the perspective of farmers as compared to nonfarm rural residents.
It was hypothesized that farm residents were more likely to spend more
time at home than rural nonfarm residents because of the proximity of
their work and because of the confining nature of certain types of farming. Information shown in Table 4.1 suggested farmers were not burglarized or subject to thievery or vandalism any less than nonfarmers
living in rural areas. However, there was a tendency for nonfarmers to
be burglarized more often than their farmer neighbors, and to be vandalized less often.

Family size was then investigated as potentially a discriminating variable in victimization. It was hypothesized that households with four or
more members would be victimized less often than households with three
or less members. The rationale of this hypothesis was based upon the
notion that households with more members would probably have someone at home for greater periods of time. Additionally, when away from
home, members would more likely be accompanied by others. Data
presented in Table 4.2 did not support this hypothesis. Size of the
household was not related at a statistically significant level to the number of burglaries, thefts, or vandalistic acts.

It was further hypothesized that where the major occupation of the
spouse was a housewife, crime rates would be lower due to, for example,
the increased time in occupancy of the home. The data revealed no
significant differences in the incidents of burglary, theft, or vandalism,

Table 4.2.   Percent of Households Containing Rural Ohioans
             Who Were Victims of Burglary, Theft, or Vandalism
             by Number of Persons in the Household

Number of Persons in Households	Burglary Victims (Percent)	Theft Victims (Percent)	Vandalism Victims (Percent)
3 or Less	2.9 (411)	7.1 (410)	13.8 (405)
4 or More	4.8 (419)	7.8 (412)	15.3 (418)
Total	3.9 (830)	7.4 (822)	14.6 (823)

$$x^2 > .05, \text{ C=N.S.} \qquad x^2 > .05, \text{ C=N.S.} \qquad x^2 > .05, \text{ C=N.S.}$$

no matter whether the spouses' occupations were housewife or some
other.

The age of the head of the household was broken down into those 64
and under and those 65 and over. The rationale was that most people
over 65 would be retired and thus likely to be spending more time at
home than those persons who were younger and employed. It must be
remembered that in the crimes being examined herein, that is, all property crimes, offenders generally go to extremes to avoid being observed
while committing these acts. With those crimes where physical and
mental agility of the victim are deterring factors, the elderly are more
vulnerable. It was expected therefore that with the crimes of burglary,
thievery, and vandalism, visibility would be a more important deterring
factor than one's physical or mental state. As seen in Table 4.3, those
65 and over tended to be victimized slightly less than their younger

Table 4.3.   Percent of Households Containing Rural Ohioans
             Who Were Victims of Burglary, Theft, or Vandalism
             by Age Group

Age Group	Burglary Victims (Percent)	Theft Victims (Percent)	Vandalism Victims (Percent)
64 and Under	4.2 (734)	7.4 (725)	15.4 (727)
65 and Over	2.4 (124)	6.4 (124)	9.8 (122)
Total	4.0 (858)	7.3 (849)	14.6 (849)

$$x^2 > .05, \text{ C=N.S.} \qquad x^2 > .05, \text{ C=N.S.} \qquad x^2 > .05, \text{ C=N.S.}$$

Table 4.4.   Percent of Households Containing Rural Ohioans
Who Were Victims of Burglary, Theft, or
Vandalism by Income

Income	Burglary Victims (Percent)	Theft Victims (Percent)	Vandalism Victims (Percent)
Less than $6,000	2.6 (157)	9.6 (157)	12.2 (156)
$6,000-12,000	3.6 (333)	6.3 (333)	12.7 (331)
More than $12,000	4.9 (209)	9.6 (198)	22.5 (200)
Total	3.8 (693)	8.0 (687)	15.4 (687)

$x^2 > .05$, C=N.S. $x^2 > .05$, C=N.S. $x^2 \leq .05$, C=S.

neighbors, but not at a statistically significant level. On a preliminary basis, this finding is markedly different from a recent national study (U.S. Department of Justice 1979:34) examining property crime victimization by age. Findings from the national study found those 65 and above experienced much less property victimization than persons under 65.

Income was viewed from the position that higher income persons were likely to display their income differential through more costly homes, more expensive equipment, more decorative surroundings, that is, reveal in numerous ways their income advantage. Therefore, it was hypothesized that higher income individuals would be burglarized, victimized by thieves, and/or vandalized at a greater frequency than medium- and lower-income persons. Extending the argument, it was hypothesized that

Table 4.5.   Percent of Households Containing Rural Ohioans
Who Were Victims of Burglary, Theft, or Vandalism
by Religious Affiliation

Religious Membership	Burglary Victims (Percent)	Theft Victims (Percent)	Vandalism Victims (Percent)
Member	4.1 (655)	7.3 (649)	16.5 (649)
Non-Member	4.0 (151)	8.0 (149)	9.3 (151)
Total	4.1 (806)	7.4 (798)	15.1 (800)

$x^2 > .05$, C=N.S. $x^2 > .05$, C=N.S. $x^2 \leq .05$, C=S.

medium-income people would be victimized more than lower-income people.

Data are presented in Table 4.4. There were no statistically significant differences among income groups relative to the incidence of burglary. However, there was a definite tendency for those with lower incomes to be burglarized less frequently than the higher-income group. Thefts were not statistically related to income levels. The lower- and upper-income groups were the same; the middle-income group slightly lower. A significant difference was revealed, however, for the crime of vandalism. The higher-income group reported almost twice as much vandalism as the middle- and lower-income groups.

Religious affiliation was examined in terms of behavior which may be related to one's chance of becoming a victim. Religious behavior is usually patterned around the ritualism of a particular church organization. In this regard, it was hypothesized that church members as a group would differ from nonchurch members in that church members would follow a pattern which would make them more vulnerable to property related crimes. Findings related to the examination are presented in Table 4.5.

Nonmembers did not differ significantly from church members on burglary and theft. However, church members were more often victims of vandalism than nonchurch members. There were also notable differences in numbers of property crimes committed against members of various church organizations. However, these data should be viewed with a degree of caution as the numbers of members reporting for some church organizations were small.

It was hypothesized that how well one knew his neighbors would be a factor in explaining differences in rates of crime. Potential criminals are easier to detect in a neighborhood where most people know one another. More than 80 percent of rural residents interviewed said they know their neighbors moderately well to well. Data in Table 4.6 revealed that differences in the degree of acquaintance did not result in significant differences in rates of burglary, theft or vandalism.

Summary and Conclusions

Several tentative conclusions are readily apparent from the findings. Property crimes constituted the major category of crime occurring to rural Ohioans during the 1974 study period. Vandalism was the crime most often affecting ruralites, with larceny-theft second. This was in contrast to crimes known to the sheriffs from the same study counties. Larceny-theft was the crime most often known to the rural sheriffs. It

Table 4.6.   Percent of Households Containing Rural Ohioans
             Who Were Victims of Burglary, Theft, or Vandalism
             by Degree of Acquaintance with Neighbors

Degree of Acquaintance	Burglary Victims (Percent)	Theft Victims (Percent)	Vandalism Victims (Percent)
Well or Moderately Well	3.6 (688)	7.2 (680)	15.0 (681)
Some or Not Very Well	5.2 (155)	7.1 (154)	14.3 (154)
Total	3.9 (843)	7.2 (834)	14.9 (835)

$x^2 > .05$, C=N.S. $x^2 > .05$, C=N.S. $x^2 > .05$, C=N.S.

would appear the difference in the two findings could be accounted for by the difference in crime which occurred to rural people vs. those which were subsequently reported to police authorities. Only 45 percent of the crimes to which rural persons were victims were later reported. This finding is consistent with that from an urban study conducted in a county lying adjacent to two of the study counties. A report on the Dayton (Ohio)—San Jose victimization problem noted, "Half of the crimes committed in both Dayton and San Jose in 1970 were not reported to the police" (U.S. Department of Justice, Law Enforcement Assistance Administration 1974:24).

Vandalism was the leading crime in rural Ohio accounting for more than a third of all crimes. Vandalistic incidents were too often passed off as "pranks" or rationalized as normal occurrences, represented by comments like, "boys-will-be-boys." This data suggests that vandalism may be far more serious than previously estimated. Vandalism may now exceed all forms of thievery in terms of economic costs. A 1977 study conducted by the American Management Association estimated that vandalism cost U.S. businessmen $2.5 billion annually. Vandalism was equal to burglary in cost and exceeded the cost of shoplifting, insurance fraud, check fraud, and credit-card fraud (*U.S. News and World Report* 1979:59).

Selected characteristics of victims and nonvictims were examined to determine if noticeable differences existed between the two groups or within the victim category. Independent variables included occupation of the head of household; the number of persons in the household; age; income; religious affiliation; and acquaintance with neighbors. These were tested against the dependent variables of burglary, theft, and vandalism. The three crimes were viewed as general indicators of rural property crimes.

All the independent variables centered about the notion of visibility. Those circumstances which perhaps contributed to increased occupancy in or around the residence on a day-to-day basis were hypothesized as decreasing the chances of that house being victimized. Additionally, the nature of particular lifestyles were viewed as decreasing the opportunity for property victimization both in and away from home. Simply stated: few crimes, especially those involving the acquisition or destruction of property, are perpetrated within full view of the intended victim. Additionally, whatever the underlying motivation for committing the offense, a high motivational level to complete the act undetected and/or without capture is operative in all but the most isolated of cases.

Only two independent variables proved significant. First, residents in the highest-income group were almost twice as often victims of vandalism than middle- and lower-income groups. Second, church members, from every denominational group, owned property which was more often vandalized than that owned by nonchurch members. The potential relationship between the two findings has not been tested. It is, however, noteworthy that among the selected variables only the crime of vandalism showed any marked difference. Preliminary conclusions would suggest that the crimes of burglary and theft appeared to occur randomly throughout the rural sample. Vandalism appeared to occur more selectively.

Two additional tentative conclusions appear worthy of comment. First, the elderly were not disproportionately more frequent victims of property crimes. Secondly, the high rate of admitted acquaintance with neighbors in rural areas may have eradicated differences in victimization that appear to be significant in urban areas (Newman 1972:37). Only eight percent of respondents said they did not know their neighbors "very well."

Investigations endeavoring to describe and explain the growing problem of rural crime and rural victimization are only now beginning. This study was undertaken in an effort to uncover descriptive information on the nature and extent of Ohio's rural crime problem. In addition, in an effort to discern susceptibility of certain population groups to victimization, several general socioeconomic characteristics of members of participating households were tested against reported incidents of property victimization. Such general relationships must now be followed by more refined tests of association as we move toward explanatory phases of rural crime research. Hopefully, the preliminary findings from the Ohio rural victimization study will provide some grist for generating hypotheses for much-needed future research.

Notes

1. Victimization, as defined in this report, refers to the study of victims of crimes from the viewpoint of the victims.
2. In order that data collected via an Ohio Sheriffs' offenders study be comparable with data collected during this victimization study, the rural sample was restricted to open-country rural residents (i.e., persons residing outside of incorporated places). Ohio Sheriffs' have operational jurisdiction over such areas. The Ohio Sheriffs' offenders study was conducted during an overlapping time period and in the same counties selected for this victimization study (Phillips 1975).
3. The crime rate index for the *Uniform Crime Reports* is based on offenses of murder, forcible rape, robbery, aggravated assault, burglary, larceny-theft, and auto theft per 100,000 inhabitants.
4. The most current available *Uniform Crime Reports* data is utilized in this report, even though the present study was conducted in 1974. No apparent dissonance should surface as the rural crime problem has continued to climb unabated.
5. A farm bureau council is a group of approximately six to seven families who gather together once a month to discuss, contribute to, change, critique, etc., farm bureau policy and program areas. Farm bureau councils tend to have a high concentration of active or retired farmers and spouses. Members of 391 councils (46 percent) said they were aware of unreported crimes.

References

Barkas, J.L. 1978. *Victims*. New York: Charles Scribner's Sons.

Clark, R. 1970. *Crime in America*. New York: Pocket Books.

Dada, H. 1979. *A Study of Selected Socio-Economic Variables Associated with Criminal Victimization in Rural Ohio*. M.S. Thesis, The Ohio State University.

Drapkin, I. and E. Viano, eds. 1974. *Victimology*. Massachusetts: Lexington Books.

Glaser, D. 1970. "Victim Survey Research: Theoretical Implications." In Anthony L. Guenther, ed. *Criminal Behavior and Social Systems: Contributions of American Sociology*. Chicago, Illinois: Rand McNally & Company.

Hindelang, M.J. 1976. *Criminal Victimization in Eight American Cities*. Boston: Ballinger Publishing Co.

Newman, O. 1972. *Defensible Space*. New York: MacMillan Co.

Phillips, G. Howard; Timothy J. Carter; and Joseph F. Donnermeyer. 1979. *Rural Crime in the United States: A Victimization Survey*. Research Proposal. Columbus, Ohio: The National Rural Crime Prevention Center, The Ohio State University.

Phillips, G.H. 1974. *Rural Crime as Perceived by Members of Farm Bureau Councils*. Report 1. Wooster, Ohio: Department of Agricultural Economics and Rural

Sociology, Ohio Agricultural Research and Development Center and The Ohio State University.

―――. 1975. "Crime in Rural Ohio." ESO 363. Columbus, Ohio: Department of Agricultural Economics and Rural Sociology, The Ohio State University.

Stewart, L. and W. Clarke. 1971. *Priorities for the 70's Crime*. New York: The John Day Company.

U.S. Census Bureau. 1970. *U.S. Census Population*. PC(1)-C37 Ohio. Washington, D.C.: U.S. Government Printing Office.

U.S. Department of Justice, Federal Bureau of Investigation. 1979. *Uniform Crime Reports*. Washington, D.C.: U.S Department of Justice.

U.S. Department of Justice, Law Enforcement Assistance Administration. 1974. *Crimes and Victims*. Washington, D.C.: U.S. Government Printing Office.

―――. 1979. *Criminal Victimization in the United States: 1977*. Washington, D.C.: U.S Government Printing Office.

U.S. News and World Report. 1979. "In Hot Pursuit of Business Criminals." July 23.

5

Family, Peers and Delinquency: A Rural Replication of Urban Findings

KATHLEEN WEINBERGER NATALINO

Introduction

Juvenile delinquency traditionally has been viewed as primarily the domain of the urban male youth.[1] While existing theoretical and empirical analyses of urban delinquency are in great abundance, less attention has been given to the systematic study of delinquent behavior as it occurs among rural adolescents. Writings about rural delinquency have usually concluded that rural offenses are less frequent, less serious and of a less sophisticated nature than urban delinquent acts (Clinard 1942, 1944; Lentz 1956). The prevailing view has furthermore held that rural youth are not subjected to the same peer pressures as are urban adolescents. Hence the rural offender has been characterized as chiefly a "lone offender," not likely to be part of a delinquent gang. Some of these traditional assumptions can be found in an early article about rural crime and delinquency:

As long as there exists a predominant measure of personal relationship and informal social control in the farm and village areas, it will be impossible for a separate criminal culture to exist. Without the presence of criminal social types, the volume of crime committed by rural residents will continue to be small as compared with that of more urban areas. (Clinard 1942:202).

A number of factors thought to be responsible for the lower rates of delinquency in rural areas include the inhibiting influence of close personal ties, informal mechanisms of social control, and lack of a delinquent subculture and delinquent role models.[2]

However, serious doubts recently have arisen with regard to the conception of rural delinquency as relatively minor, unsophisticated, and infrequent. Most of the early studies claiming a significant urban-rural difference in the incidence and nature of delinquency were based on official statistics (Clinard 1942, 1944; Lentz 1956). Since the advent of research using self-report measures of delinquent behavior, several studies have found little or no significant urban-rural differences (Dentler and Monroe 1961), and one comparative study even revealed higher rates of delinquent behavior in rural areas (Hindelang 1973).[3]

The conflicting evidence from official data and self-report data may be partially explained by a difference in formal agencies of social control in rural and urban areas. It is quite possible that law enforcement personnel in rural areas, being better acquainted with all residents in the area, are more likely to let youthful offenders off with a stern warning to them or their parents, rather than resorting to formal arrest and charges. In fact, some research indicates that rural offenders are less likely to be institutionalized than are urban offenders; rural cases are more often closed at intake without further formal court action (Polk 1965:228). It has also been suggested that rural residents have a fairly high tolerance for some lawbreaking and are more likely than urban residents to approve lenient treatment for offenders (Esselstyn 1953; Lowe and Peek 1974). The confounding effect of different methods of social control thus raises the possibility that urban-rural differences in delinquent behavior may not be as great as official statistics indicate.

Perhaps the most cogent evidence that the traditional view of rural delinqency may need some revision comes from a recent study which found that 93 percent of all acts of vandalism admitted by rural adolescents were committed in the company of peers (Phillips and Bartlett 1976). This certainly suggests that a youthful troublemaking subculture may exist among rural as well as urban youth. While studies of rural delinquency in the past have generally claimed that theories used to explain urban delinquency are not applicable to the rural case, a better understanding of the problem of rural delinquency might be gained by putting existing theories to the test with rural as well as urban adolescents.

The remainder of this chapter is addressed to a dual purpose: (1) to compare the involvement of rural and urban adolescents in a broad range of both minor and serious delinquent activities, and (2) to test two theories of delinquency, control theory and peer subculture theory, in order to to determine their relevance for explaining rural delinquent behavior.

Theoretical Orientation

Control theory holds that nondelinquent youth are insulated from delinquency by strong ties to the conventional social order; delinquency occurs when these bonds are weakened or broken (Hirschi 1969). It is a logical choice for testing with rural adolescents since it fits the image of rural youth who are less delinquent because of strong primary group ties in the rural setting. According to control theory, an important part of the bond to the conventional order lies in attachment to conventional others, such as parents.[4] "The essence of internalization of norms, conscience, or superego thus lies in the attachment of the individual to others" (Hirschi 1969:18). Hirschi (1969:85) further observes, "the fact that delinquents are less likely than nondelinquents to be closely tied to their parents is one of the best documented findings of delinquency research."

There is some evidence that both rural and urban delinquents are more likely to come from homes that are broken by death, divorce or separation than are non-delinquents (Rodman and Grams 1970; Phillips and Bartlett 1976). However, there is also evidence that the quality of family interaction may be more important than the family structure per se (Dentler and Monroe 1961). Degree of parental control, nature of discipline, degree of parental affection, and attachment to parents have all been shown to be related to delinquency in both urban and/or rural settings (Glueck and Glueck 1950; McCord and McCord 1958; Dentler and Monroe 1961; Hirschi 1969; Hindelang 1973).

Four variables were used to test the applicability of control theory in explaining rural delinquent behavior. These variables include: (1) family structure; (2) home satisfaction; (3) degree of parental control attempted; and (4) adolescent reponse (i.e., degree of willing conformity) to parental controls.

According to *peer subculture theory*, adolescents engage in delinquent behavior to earn approval and status within the delinquent peer group (Cohen 1965; Cloward and Ohlin 1960; Miller 1958). While these authors focus chiefly upon the tightly knit urban gang, other writers suggest that delinquent peer influence can operate in the absence of highly cohesive gangs (Matza 1964). In this less structured conception, a "subculture of delinquency" is merely "a setting in which the commission of delinquency is common knowledge among a group of juveniles" (Matza 1964:33). Involvement in such a loosely defined peer subculture has two dimensions: (1) a cultural or normative aspect, consisting of shared values, norms, and symbols; and (2) a social or behavioral aspect, referring to activities and association with peers who act out delinquent norms and values (Lerman 1967).

In order to examine these two dimensions of peer subculture theory, three variables are tested. They include: (1) perceptions of peer norms; (2) number of evenings spent with peers; and (3) degree of involvement with peers who engage in delinquent activities.

One would also expect that the degree of adolescent involvement in a peer subculture might be substantially influenced by such control theory variables as the adolescent's home situation. The chapter therefore includes an examination of interrelationships among control and peer subculture variables as they jointly influence adolescent involvement in delinquency.

Data and Method

The observations, discussion, and conclusions in this chapter are based upon an analysis of self-report questionnaire data about adolescents' attitudes and behavior. The data were obtained anonymously from 514 white students in four rural consolidated high schools and 660 white students in three urban high schools.[5] All high schools were located in northwestern Ohio.

DELINQUENCY MEASURES

Involvement in delinquent behavior was measured by scales composed of 36 victimless, property, and personal offense items. These items range from very serious (e.g., "Used a weapon to attack or beat up on somebody") to relatively trivial (e.g., "Made loud noises or did things just to bother and disturb people"). Respondents were asked whether they had committed the acts "Never; Once or Twice; Several Times; or Very Often."

Because the items used to measure delinquency encompass different types of offenses of varying degrees of seriousness, the statistical technique of factor analysis was used to determine whether there were different patterns of offense behavior characteristic of the rural and urban male and female adolescents in the sample. Results of this procedure revealed eight types of offense patterns.[6] (1) *Drug* offenses include using, selling or driving under the influence of hard drugs (LSD, "speed," barbiturates, or heroin), or marijuana. (2) *Hedonist* behavior consists of using or driving under the influence of alcohol, using fake identification to obtain alcohol, sex with the opposite sex, and skipping school. (3) *Personal injury* offenses are comprised of gang fighting, carrying a weapon, assault with or without a weapon, and extorting money by threats or force. (4) *Serious property* offenses include stealing more than $50, stealing a car, motorcycle or car parts, serious vandalism, breaking and entering, and robbery. (5) *Hellraising* behavior consists of minor vandalism, gambling, and being a public nuisance. (6) Offenses against *family* include disobeying, defying parents to their faces, and running away from home. (7) *Minor theft* involves taking less than $2 or taking from $2 to $50 in value. (8) *Car* offenses are comprised of taking cars without permission and joyriding.[7] All 36 offenses are included in the measure of total delinquency.

CONTROL MEASURES

Family structure was measured by a single question about whom the adolescent lived with. A dichotomous variable was constructed in which the adolescent was classified as residing (1) with both parents, and (2) with a single parent, stepparent or other relatives. *Home satisfaction* was a single item measure about the degree to which the adolescent was satisfied with family life. A scale indicating the *degree of parental control* imposed was derived from a series of questions about the extent to which parents imposed curfews, gave advice about appropriate behavior or companions, and wanted to be informed about the adolescent's whereabouts and companions. The scale measuring adolescent conformity was derived by asking how often the respondent generally complied with parental rules and guidelines for behavior.

PEER SUBCULTURE MEASURES

Scales measuring *perceptions of peer norms* were formulated from a series of questions asking what the respondent's girlfriend (or boyfriend), same-sex peer group and opposite-sex peer group would think about getting involved in an assortment of delinquent activities. *Evenings spent with peers* was measured by a single question which asked the adolescent to indicate how many evenings per week were spent out with friends.

Table 5.1. Percent Who Answered 'Never' To All Items in Nine Delinquency Scales

	"Percent Never"				Significant Differences	
	Males		Females		U–R[a]	M–F[b]
	Rural (1)	Urban (2)	Rural (3)	Urban (4)	(5)	(6)
Serious Property	60%	58%	88%	84%	n.s.	M***
Drugs	55	32	65	39	U***	n.s.
Taking Cars	49	59	64	70	n.s.	M***
Personal Injury	42	29	75	64	U***	M***
Minor Theft	30	29	44	42	n.s.	M***
Hedonist	7	4	7	8	U*	M***
Hellraising	6	6	19	12	n.s.	M***
Family	2	4	3	2	U**	F*
Total Delinquency	1	1	1	1	U***	M***
(N Cases)	(250)	(290)	(264)	(370)		

a. Column 5 indicates the significance of the urban-rural difference. Letters (U or R) indicate which group is higher in delinquency.

b. Column 6 indicates the significance of the male-female difference. Letters (M or F) indicate which group is higher in delinquency.

*** Significant at .001 level
** Significant at .01 level
* Significant at .05 level

Degree of involvement with peers was measured by determining the extent to which friends got involved in actions that could be termed delinquent.

Rural-Urban Differences in Delinquent Behavior

It should be noted that most rural and urban adolescents do not habitually engage in most forms of delinquency. Table 5.1 displays the percent of rural and urban males and females who answered "Never" to all items in the eight delinquency scales. Even though only 1 percent of all subgroups reported no overall involvement in delinquency, this was largely a function of their participation in only a few minor offenses.

Table 5.2.   Percent Who Answered "Very Often" to the Most
Frequently Admitted Offenses

| | Percent "Very Often" | | | |
| | Males | | Females | |
	Rural	Urban	Rural	Urban
Drink Alcohol	34.0%	31.4%	26.1%	27.0%
Gamble	19.6	29.0	5.3	9.7
Smoke Pot	13.2	33.1	12.1	29.7
Sex With Opposite Sex	12.0	21.0	21.6	14.1
Disobey Parents	11.2	20.3	16.3	24.3
Skip School	9.2	18.6	8.0	23.5
Drive Hi/Alcohol	6.8	7.9	4.2	4.6
Carry Weapon	6.4	6.9	0.8	2.7
Drive Hi/Pot	5.6	12.8	3.4	7.3
Noisy Public Disturbance	4.4	11.7	3.0	5.9
Steal Less Than $2	4.4	3.8	1.9	2.7
Take Car Without Permission	3.2	3.8	1.5	2.4
Defy Parents to Face	2.4	1.7	2.7	4.9
Use Fake I.D. to Drink	2.4	4.8	1.5	3.8
(N Cases)	(200)	(290)	(264)	(370)

The only offense types for which most adolescents admitted to at least one offense in the scale were hedonist, hellraising, and family offenses, all of which are relatively minor in nature. Over half of all groups also admitted to some minor theft. However, it appears that those youth who were heavily involved in the more serious delinquent behaviors constitute a relatively small minority of urban and rural youth. While urban youth have higher admitted involvement in all types of delinquent behavior, this difference was only statistically significant in the case of drugs, personal injury, family, and, to a lesser extent, hedonist offenses (as shown in column 5 of Table 5.1). The most dramatic difference by far was the much higher urban involvement in drugs.

For all types of offenses except drugs and family offenses, males admitted significantly more delinquent involvement than did the females (as shown in column 6 of Table 5.1). In fact, the sex differences in extent of delinquent involvement were far more striking than the urban-rural differences. Urban males were found to be the most delinquent group, while rural females admitted the least delinquent involvement.

The use of scales unfortunately masks the fact that many adolescents admitted to only one or two items in particular scales. Another perspective can be gained by examining Table 5.2, which lists the individual offense items most frequently admitted by rural youth, together with the percent of all respondents who claimed to be involved in these activities "Very Often."

It can be seen that drinking was the most frequent problem behavior among rural adolescents, with more than a third of the males and a quarter of the females claiming to be frequent drinkers. Frequent marijuana use was somewhat less common among rural adolescents, but nevertheless ranked high on the list of rural problem behaviors.

Another interesting finding from Table 5.2 was the fact that more rural females than urban females admitted having sex with the opposite sex "Very Often." This seems contrary to popular beliefs. However, the percent who answered "Never" to that question was also higher for rural females (49.2 percent) than it was for urban females (45.4 percent).

The data in Table 5.2 indicate that the majority of the offenses committed frequently by more than 2 percent of the rural adolescents can be characterized as "victimless" offenses. Serious transgressions against property and persons, while naturally of great concern to a community when they occur, did not appear to be habitual behaviors for more than a very small percentage of rural (and urban) youth. We shall now turn our attention toward the search for causal factors related to rural delinquency.

Control Theory:
Home, Delinquency and Rural Youth

The data indicate that broken homes were much more prevalent among urban adolescents than they were among rural youth. Table 5.3 shows that in the rural area, 84.6 percent of the high school students in this survey reported living with both parents, while only 67.9 percent of the urban respondents indicated that both parents were living in the home.

For the rural youth, satisfaction with home life appeared to drop off sharply when adolescents came from a broken home (as can be seen in Table 5.4, upper portion). Of considerable interest was the fact that for the urban adolescents there appeared to be very little difference in home satisfaction for those who lived with both parents and those who live

Table 5.3.   Family Structure of Rural and Urban Respondents

	Both Parents (Percent)	Mother or Father (Percent)	Parent and Stepparent (Percent)	Other (Percent)	Total (N Cases) (Percent)
Rural	84.6	7.2	6.6	1.6	(514)
Urban	67.9	16.7	9.2	6.2	(660)

with only one parent (Table 5.4, lower portion). It is not surprising that living with stepparents or in other less conventional arrangements is less than satisfying, since the adolescent probably experiences some strain in adjusting to new personalities in the home situation. However, the difference between rural and urban youth regarding satisfaction in living with either mother or father alone may reflect a difference in the way urban and rural communities view a broken home. Since almost a third of the urban adolescents in this study came from broken homes, it seems reasonable to expect that their situations were viewed as more commonplace and were therefore less stigmatized in the urban school and community. This suggests that rural schools and communities might well devote more effort toward sympathetic understanding of the special problems of rural adolescents from broken homes and attempt to reduce the social stigma which may be incumbent upon that position in the rural area.

The importance of the emotional climate of the home is illustrated by data in the top portion of Table 5.5. When involvement in delinquency is dichotomized into Low and High groups,[8] it is apparent that degree of home satisfaction was intimately related to level of delinquent involvement for rural males. Nearly three-fourths of all rural males who expressed dissatisfaction with their home situations were also found to have above average rates of delinquent behavior. The effect was less pronounced (and not statistically significant) for rural females, but it must be remembered that rural females as a whole were found to be markedly less delinquent than all other groups in the survey. The data clearly support control theory's claim that the emotional climate of the home is an important factor in predicting the extent to which adolescents become involved in delinquent behavior.

According to control theory, the adolescent who is content at home is more likely to conform to parental wishes and guidelines for behavior. What is thought to be crucial is not the amount of overt control attempted by parents, but rather the extent to which the adolescent willingly conforms and lives up to parental expectations. Most adolescents

Table 5.4.   Crosstabulation of Home Satisfaction By Rural
             Family Structure

| Home Satisfaction | Rural Adolescents Living With: | | | |
	Both Parents (Percent)	Mother or Father only (Percent)	Parent and Stepparent (Percent)	Others (Percent)
Satisfied	67.1	40.5	32.4	37.5
Neutral	12.1	16.2	14.7	12.5
Dissatisfied	20.9	43.2	52.9	50.0
Total	100.1	99.9	100.0	100.0
(N Cases)	(431)	(37)	(34)	(8)

$$x^2 = 30.2, \ P \leq .001, \ 2 \ d.f.^b$$

| Home Satisfaction | Urban Adolescents Living With: | | | |
	Both Parents (Percent)	Mother or Father only (Percent)	Parent and Stepparent (Percent)	Others (Percent)
Satisfied	57.6	56.4	36.1	29.3
Neutral	12.5	12.7	18.0	14.6
Dissatisfied	29.9	30.9	45.9	56.1
Total	100.0	100.0	100.0	100.0
(N Cases)	(441)	(110)	(61)	(41)

$$x^2 = 8.9, \ P \leq .02, \ 2 \ d.f.^b$$

a. Totals do not sum to 100% due to rounding off percents.

b. In computing Chi Square, categories "Mother or Father Only," "Parent and Stepparent," and "Others" were collapsed into a single category for comparison with the "Both Parents" category.

perceive that their parents expect lawabiding behavior whether or not it is expressed in stated rules and regulations. The data in the middle and lower portions of Table 5.5 clearly support this contention that willing conformity was more important than overt control in accounting for degree of delinquent involvement. Overt parental control (as measured by amount of rules and advice given by parents) was only minimally related to the delinquent involvement of rural males, and actually had a slight reverse effect among rural females (see the middle portion of Table 5.5). On the other hand, the data demonstrate a striking (inverse) correspondence between degree of willing conformity to parental wishes

Table 5.5. Crosstabulation of Rural Juvenile Delinquent Behavior,
           By Sex, For Control Measures of Home Satisfaction,
           Parental Control, and Conformity to Parental Expectations

Control Measures	Low Delinquency (Percent)	High Delinquency (Percent)
(A) Degree of Satisfaction With Home		
(1) Rural Males		
Satisfied (N=54)	50.9	49.1
Neutral (N33)	45.5	54.5
Dissatisfied (N=159)	25.9	74.1
X^2 = 14.1, P .001, 1 d.f.[a]		
(2) Rural Females		
Satisfied (N74)	69.0	31.0
Neutral (N31)	64.5	35.5
Dissatisfied (N=158)	58.1	41.9
X^2 = 2.3, N.S., 1 d.f.[a]		
(B) Amount of Parental Control Imposed		
(1) Rural Males		
High Control (N=97)	50.5	49.5
Low Control (N=153)	40.5	69.5
X^2 = 2.3, N.S., 1 d.f.		
(2) Rural Females		
High Control (N=156)	64.1	35.9
Low Control (N=107)	67.3	32.7
X^2 = 0.3, N.S., 1 d.f.		
(C) Conformity to Parental Expectations		
(1) Rural Males		
High Conformity (N=135)	62.2	37.8
Low Conformity (N=114)	23.7	76.3
X^2 = 37.2, P $\leq$ .001, 1 d.f.		
(2) Rural Females		
High Conformity (N=176)	79.5	20.5
Low Conformity (N=87)	36.8	63.2
X^2 = 47.1, P $\leq$ .001, 1 d.f.		

a. In Part A of this table, Chi Square was computed with 1 degree of
    freedom by comparing 2 categories: "Satisfied or Neutral" vs.
    "Dissatisfied."

Table 5.6. Crosstabulation of Rural Conformity By Home Satisfaction

| | Degree of Home Satisfaction | | | | | |
| | Rural Males | | | Rural Females | | |
Conformity	Satisfied (Percent)	Neutral (Percent)	Dissatisfied (Percent)	Satisfied (Percent)	Neutral (Percent)	Dissatisfied (Percent)
High Conform	63.5	51.5	27.8	73.9	64.5	52.7
Low Conform	36.5	48.5	72.2	26.1	35.5	47.3
Total (N Cases)	100.0 (159)	100.0 (33)	100.0 (54)	100.0 (157)	100.0 (31)	100.0 (74)
	$x^2 = 19.2$ P $\leq$ .001, 1 d.f.			$x^2 = 9.2$ P $\leq$ .01, d.f.		

Chi Square was computed with 1 degree of freedom by comparing 2 categories: "Satisfied or Neutral" vs. "Dissatisfied."

and degree of delinquent involvement (Table 5.5, bottom portion). Rural adolescents who obeyed their parents were much less likely to have high delinquency scores.

Since it is degree of willing adolescent conformity rather than extent of direct parental control that counts most as a deterrent to delinquency, the importance of the emotional climate of the home is further substantiated by the data in Table 5.6, which indicate that willing conformity was related to degree of home satisfaction. Rural adolescents who were satisfied with home relationships were significantly more likely to conform to parental expectations than those dissatisfied at home.

It has been suggested that involvement in a peer subculture has both normative and behavioral dimensions. Turning first to the normative aspect, we address the extent to which adolescents perceive peer reference groups as extending approval for delinquent exploits. Figure 5.1 depicts perceived peer reference group support for delinquent activity. Three types of significant reference groups were identified: the respondent's girlfriend or boyfriend, the group of opposite-sex friends, and the group of same-sex friends that the respondent associated with. Level of approval perceived from each of these reference groups was computed by summing response scores for nine questions, (scored from 1-Strongly Disapprove to 4-Strongly Approve). Scale scores for each of the reference groups can therefore range from 9 (lowest approval) to 35 (highest approval).

Both rural and urban adolescents in this study indicated that their

Figure 5.1:

Mean Scores of Four Subgroups for Peer Approval
from Three Peer Reference Groups

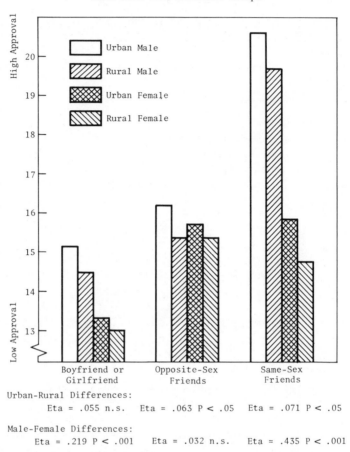

Urban-Rural Differences:
    Eta = .055 n.s.   Eta = .063 P < .05   Eta = .071 P < .05

Male-Female Differences:
    Eta = .219 P < .001   Eta = .032 n.s.   Eta = .435 P < .001

friends generally would disapprove of serious transgressions; most perceived peer approval only for a limited amount of minor hedonistic and
hellraising behavior. Overall, there was surprisingly little urban-rural
difference in perceived peer approval for delinquent activity, significant
only at the .05 level for approval from opposite-sex friends and same-
sex friends. However, there was a distinct sex difference, as shown in
Figure 5.1. While both sexes indicated least support for delinquent acts
from the girlfriend or boyfriend, the males indicated significantly more
support for delinquent acts from their male peers than the two female

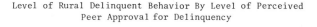

Figure 5.2:

Level of Rural Delinquent Behavior By Level of Perceived
Peer Approval for Delinquency

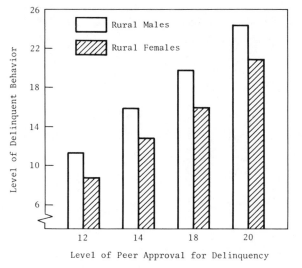

Level of Peer Approval for Delinquency

Zero-Order Correlation between Delinquent Behavior
and Peer Approval for Delinquency:

Rural Males: r = .497 P < .001
Rural Females: r = .409 P < .001

groups perceived from their same-sex friends. This striking male-female difference in approval for delinquent acts from same-sex peers can be seen in Figure 5.1. In general, Figure 5.1 shows that urban-rural differences were not as great as male-female differences regarding peer approval for delinquent behavior.

This relationship between peer approval and delinquency can be seen in Figure 5.2. The delinquency scale scores were computed by summing responses to 36 delinquency questions (scored from 0 = Never to 3 = Very Often). The delinquency scale thus has outer limits of 0 (lowest possible) to 108 (highest possible). The results from Figure 5.2 reveal that regardless of the source of approval, those adolescents who reported their friends as most approving of delinquency also reported higher rates of their own involvement in delinquent acts. While rural females had consistently lower rates of delinquency than rural males at every level of peer approval, it can nevertheless be seen that as the level of peer support for delinquency rose, so also did the level of involvement in

Table 5.7.   Crosstabulation of Rural Juvenile Delinquent Behavior By
Nights Out With Peers and By Having Delinquent Friends

Peer Subculture Measures	Low Delinquency (Percent)	High Delinquency (Percent)
(A) Number of Nights Per Week Spent Out With Friends		
0-2 nights (N=233)	66.5	33.5
3-4 nights (N=162)	46.9	53.1
5-7 nights (N=103)	38.8	61.2
$x^2 = 27.5$, $P \leq .001$, d.f.		
(B) With Friends Who Do Things That Get Them in Trouble With The Police or Sheriff		
No, seldom (N=299)	68.6	31.4
Yes, but not often (N=151)	41.7	58.3
Yes, pretty often (N=41)	8.9	91.1
$x^2 = 53.7$, $P \leq .001$, 1 d.f.[a]		

a.   Chi Square for Part B of this table was computed with 1 degree
of freedom by collapsing "Yes, pretty often" and "Yes, but not
often" into a single category "Yes."

delinquent behavior for rural females, and rural males. Contrary to past assumptions about rural delinquency, the evidence here indicates that rural youth were also influenced by delinquent peer norms when they perceived them among their friends.

On the behavioral level, there is even more striking evidence that rural adolescents who engage in delinquent acts do so in the company of delinquent peer groups. The overwhelming majority of all rural and urban adolescents indicated that they regularly went around with the same groups of friends. The crucial issues appear to be what kind of friends (i.e., delinquent or conforming), and number of nights per week spent in the company of these friends. From the data in Table 5.7, upper portion, it can be seen that the number of nights spent out with peers was significantly related to extent of delinquent involvement among rural youth. Those who said they spent 5-7 nights a week out with friends were almost twice as likely to have above average rates of delinquent behavior as were those who said they went out no more than a couple of nights a week.

The critical importance of the kind of friends adolescents associate

Table 5.8.   Crosstabulation of Home Satisfaction
By How Many Friends Rural Parents Know

Rural Home Satisfaction	"How many of your friends do your parents (or guardians) know?"		
	All or Most (Percent)	Some (Percent)	Few or None (Percent)
Satisfied	66.9	40.7	39.1
Neutral	12.4	13.6	8.7
Dissatisfied	20.7	45.8	52.2
Total	100.0	100.1[a]	100.0
(N Cases)	(426)	(59)	(23)

$$X^2 = 27.7, \; P \leq .001, \; 2 \; d.f.[b]$$

a. Total does not sum to 100.0 percent due to rounding
    of percents.

b. Chi Square was computed with 2 degrees of freedom by
    collapsing "Some" and "Few or None" into a single
    category.

with is pointed up by the data in the lower portion of Table 5.7. More than 90 percent of those rural adolescents who said that their friends very often did things that could get them in trouble, also indicated that they themselves had above average involvement in delinquent activities.[9] It thus appears that similar to findings from urban studies, being part of a delinquent peer group is an important correlate of rural delinquency.

Joint Effects: Home, Peers and Delinquency

The adolescent's relationships with family and peers are intermingled in a number of ways. From the evidence of the present research it appears that rural parents were more likely to be acquainted with their children's friends than were the parents of urban adolescents. In fact, only 5 percent of all rural respondents said that their parents knew few or none of their friends. However, the extent to which rural parents knew youthful friends turned out to be not significantly related to adolescent involvement in delinquent behavior. However, a relationship was detected between adolescent home satisfaction and parents knowing their adolescent's friends, as shown in Table 5.8. Homes in which parents knew most friends also tend to be characterized by more adolescent satisfaction

Table 5.9. Crosstabulation of Having Delinquent Friends
            By Rural Home Satisfaction

| | Degree of Home Satisfaction | | | | | |
| | Rural Males | | | Females | | |
Are Friends Delinquent?	Satisfied (Percent)	Neutral (Percent)	Dissatisfied (Percent)	Satisfied (Percent)	Neutral (Percent)	Dissatisfied (Percent)
No, seldom	60.3	45.5	42.3	70.9	67.9	58.3
Yes, but not often	34.0	30.3	34.6	25.2	21.4	33.3
Yes, pretty often	5.8	24.2	23.1	4.0	10.7	8.3
Totals (N Cases)	100.1 (156)	100.0 (33)	100.0 (52)	100.1 (151)	100.0 (28)	99.9 (72)
	$x^2 = 4.01$, $P \leq .05$, 1 d.f.[b]			$x^2 = 3.39$, N.S. 1 d.f.[b]		

a. Totals do not sum to 100.0 percent due to rounding of percents.

b. Chi Square was computed with 1 degree of freedom by collapsing the two "yes"
    categories into a single category and combining "Satisfied or Neutral."

with life. It may be that knowing who adolescents associate with is an indicator of parental concern and interest in the well-being of their sons and daughters.

Adolescent home satisfaction was somewhat related to the type of friends adolescents socialized with outside of the home, particularly among the rural males. According to the data in Table 5.9 rural males who were happy were significantly less likely to identify their friends as delinquent. For rural females the relationship was in the same direction, but not statistically significant.

Finally, the strongest evidence of the joint effects of home and peers comes from the dramatic inverse relationship between going out with delinquent friends and conformity to parental guidelines. It has already been shown that willing conformity to parental expectations is what counts most as a deterrent to involvement in delinquent behavior (see Table 5.5). The data in Table 5.10 offer compelling evidence that rural adolescents who had delinquent friends were much less likely to have conformed to parental expectations for behavior than were those who did not have delinquent friends. Relationships with peers thus reflect upon parent-child relationships in the home.

Summary and Discussion

This chapter has examined the comparative incidents and nature of self-reported delinquent behaviors of rural and urban adolescents. The find-

Table 5.10.   Crosstabulation of Rural Conformity By Having
Delinquent Friends

| | "Do friends do things that could get them in trouble?" | | | | | |
| | Rural Males | | | Rural Females | | |
Conformity	No (Percent)	Not Often (Percent)	Yes Often (Percent)	No (Percent)	Not Often (Percent)	Yes Often (Percent)
High Conform	66.2	51.8	10	73.1	61.8	33.3
Low Conform	33.8	48.2	90	26.9	36.8	66.7
Totals (N Cases)	100.0 (130)	100.0 (83)	100.0 (30)	100.0 (167)	100.0 (68)	100.0 (15)
	$x^2 = 15.9$, P $\leq$ .001, d.f.[a]			$x^2 = 6.8$, P $\leq$ .01, 1 d.f.[a]		

a. Chi Square was computed with 1 degree of freedom by combining "Not Often" and "Yes Often" into a single category.

ings of the research indicate that while there was very little rural-urban difference in offenses of a minor nature, rural adolescents were still significantly less involved than urban adolescents in regard to drugs and personal injury offenses. The finding of no significant rural-urban difference in serious property offenses tends to confirm the traditional image of rural transgressions being primarily against property rather than against persons. While the rural community may understandably feel most concerned about sporadic incidents of vandalism (since the community is in the position of "victim" in those cases), the research suggests that more attention might well be devoted to the rather extensive problem of teenage drinking among rural youth. Adolescent drinking may be a less visible problem than vandalism. Nevertheless, it is somewhat disconcerting to note that about a third of all rural high school students in this research claimed to drink regularly. Marijuana use was also commonplace among rural youth, although still to a much lesser extent than on the urban scene.

The search for social correlates of rural delinquency revealed connections among home, peers and delinquency. Although broken homes were less common among rural youth than they are for urban adolescents, the pains of a broken home were more keenly felt by rural youth than they were in the urban case. The degree of adolescent contentment with family life was important because lack of home satisfaction resulted in more time spent with peers who were involved in delinquent activities, especially among rural males.

This research indicates that it was not sheer volume of parental rules and curfews, but rather the adolescent's willing conformity to parental expectations (whether expressly stated or merely implied) that counted most as a deterrent to delinquency. Hirschi (1969) apparently was correct when he suggested that adolescents who respect and like their parents will also obey their rules. In fact, overly strict parental controls in a home with an unhappy emotional climate can actually be counterproductive.

The research confirms that, to at least a limited extent, there existed a rural peer subculture which was approving of delinquent exploits and whose members fairly regularly engaged in troublemaking behavior that could be termed delinquent. However, the percentage of rural adolescents who took part in this troublemaking youth culture was lower than in the urban case. This troublemaking rural youth culture was also predominantly male—rural females indicated very little involvement in acts of a delinquent nature.

It must be emphasized that there is no one factor which by itself can deter or encourage rural adolescent involvement in delinquent behavior. Instead, one can merely identify a progression of interrelated factors. Adolescents whose parents take a concerned interest in knowing whom their children associate with are also those youth who are happier with their home situation. This, in turn, tends to reduce the number of nights spent out with friends and the likelihood that those friends will be the type to engage in troublemaking capers. Adolescents with high home satisfaction and nondelinquent companions will also quite likely live up to internalized parental norms about appropriate behavior, even in the absence of specific parental directives.

On the other hand, rural adolescents from unsatisfying familial environments will be drawn into spending more time with delinquent companions in search of "kicks." Youth caught up in such a pattern will also be tempted to ignore the stirrings of conscience and parental admonitions when faced with opportunities for involvement in delinquent activities.

Notes

1. Data for the urban portion of the analysis stem from the "Female Delinquency" project directed by Peggy Giordano and Stephen Cernkovich at Bowling Green State University, Bowling Green, Ohio. Support for the project was provided by PHS Research Grant No. MH29095-01, National Institute of Mental Health, Center for Studies of Crime and Delinquency and by Bowling Green State University.
2. The fact that some rural sociologists have continued to deny the importance of delinquent peer groups among rural youth is well illustrated by the title of a somewhat later study, "The Myth of a Rebellious Adolescent Sub-

culture: Its Detrimental Effects for Understanding Rural Youth" (Bealer, et al., 1965).

3. However, some of the self-report studies comparing rural and urban behavior suffer from methodological flaws inasmuch as they only measure a limited number of rather minor offense behaviors. It is not out of keeping with the traditional conceptions to find little or no urban-rural difference in minor delinquent offenses.

4. In addition to attachment to conventional others, Hirschi posits three other elements of the bond: commitment to a conventional line of activity (specifically, high educational and/or occupational aspirations); involvement in conventional activities (which presumably leaves less time to get into trouble); and belief that conventional rules should be obeyed. However, he relates all three additional elements back to the home. The adolescent who is more attached to parents is more likely to be involved in and committed to conventional activities. Regarding belief, "Insofar as the child respects (loves and fears) his parents, and adults in general, he will accept their rules" (Hirschi, 1969:30).

5. Only white students are included in the data base because the number of non-white students in the rural schools proved insufficient for a valid interracial comparison. Additional information describing the sample and methodology are reported elsewhere (Natalino, 1979:66-72).

6. Separate scales were constructed to measure these offense patterns by summing respondents answers to the items included in each pattern. More detailed information regarding techniques of data analysis used in the study is reported elsewhere (Natalino, 1979).

7. Three offenses did not fit into any of the eight types of offense patterns: school probation, sex with same-sex partner, and sex for money. Responses to these items are, however, included in the measure of total delinquent behavior.

8. Respondents are classed as Low or High in delinquent behavior according to whether their scores of total delinquency ranked below or above the mean (average) delinquency score computed for all urban and rural cases.

9. Slightly less than 15 percent of the urban respondents reported having delinquent friends, with the same pattern of correspondence between peers and delinquency.

References

Bealer, Robert C., Fern K. Willits, and Peter R. Maida. 1965. "The Myth of a Rebellious Adolescent Subculture: Its Detrimental Effects for Understanding Rural Youth." In Lee G. Burchinal, ed. *Rural Youth in Crisis: Facts, Myths, and Social Change.* Washington, D.C.: U.S. Department of Health, Education and Welfare.

Clinard, Marshall B. 1942. "The Process of Urbanization and Criminal Behavior." *American Journal of Sociology* 48 (September):202-13.

————. 1944. "Rural Criminal Offenders." *American Journal of Sociology* 50 (July):38-45.

Cloward, Richard A. and Lloyd E. Ohlin. 1960. *Delinquency and Opportunity.* New York: Free Press.

Cohen, Albert K. 1955. *Delinquent Boys.* New York: Free Press.

Dentler, Robert A. and Lawrence J. Monroe. 1961. "Social Correlates of Early Adolescent Theft." *American Sociological Review* 26 (October):733-43.

Esselstyn, T.C. 1953. "The Social Role of a County Sheriff." *Journal of Criminal Law, Criminology and Police Science* 44 (August):177-84.

Glueck, Sheldon and Elnore T. Glueck. 1950. *Unraveling Juvenile Delinquency.* New York: Commonwealth Fund.

Hindelang, Michael J. 1973. "Causes of Delinquency: A Partial Replication and Extension." *Social Problems* 20 (Spring):471-87.

Hirschi, Travis. 1969. *Causes of Delinquency.* Berkeley: University of California Press.

Lentz, William P. 1956. "Rural-Urban Differentials and Juvenile Delinquency." *Journal of Criminal Law, Criminology and Police Science* 47 (October):331-39.

Lerman, Paul. 1967. "Gangs, Networks and Subcultural Delinquency." *American Journal of Sociology* 73 (July): 63-72.

Lowe, George D. and Charles W. Peek. 1974. "Location and Lifestyles: The Comparative Explanatory Ability of Urbanism and Rurality." *Rural Sociology* 39 (Fall):392-420.

Matza, David. 1964. *Delinquency and Drift.* New York: John Wiley and Sons.

McCord, Joan and William McCord. 1958. "The Effects of Parental Role Model on Criminality." *Journal of Social Issues* 14 (Fall):66-75.

Miller, Walter B. 1958. "Lower Class Culture as a Generating Milieu of Gang Delinquency." *Journal of Social Issues* 14 (Fall):5-19.

Natalino, Kathleen Weinberger. 1979. *Social Correlates of Rural and Urban Delinquency.* Ph.D. dissertation, Bowling Green State University.

Phillips, G. Howard. 1976. *Rural Crimes and Rural Offenders.* EB-613. Columbus, Ohio: The Department of Agricultural Economics and Rural Sociology, The Ohio State University.

Phillips, G. Howard and Kaye F. Bartlett. 1976. *Vandals and Vandalism in Rural Ohio.* Research Circular 222. Wooster, Ohio: Ohio Agricultural Research Development Center.

Polk, Kenneth. 1965. "An Exploration of Rural Juvenile Delinquency." In Lee G. Burchinal, ed. *Rural Youth in Crisis: Facts, Myths, and Social Change.* Washington, D.C.: U.S. Department of Health, Education, and Welfare.

Rodman, Hyman and Paul Grams. 1970. "Types of Delinquents." In Harwin L. Voss ed. *Society, Delinquency, and Delinquent Behavior.* Boston: Little, Brown and Company.

6

Delinquency Patterns of Farm Youth

MARTIN G. MILLER, ERIC O. HOIBERG,
and RODNEY F. GANEY

Introduction

In analyzing rural areas, a persistent theme in recent years has been to note the increasing similarity between the urban and rural segments of our society. For example, Sanders (1977:6) refers to the process of articulation whereby rural society has become more fully integrated into the larger society while still maintaining many of its distinctive institutions. Using this notion, the values, norms, roles, and behavior patterns of the rural population segment come to resemble increasingly those found in the dominant social order; but it is not a complete assimilation since differences continue to exist. This chapter focuses on the extent to which there are observable differences in juvenile delinquency rates between three population groups: rural farm, rural nonfarm, and urban. An effort will also be made to analyze the explanatory relationship between delinquency rates and certain structural and social psychological characteristics within the rural farm population segment.

Juvenile delinquency has been commonly treated as an urban phenomenon. The city, and especially the inner city, with its poverty, high population density, deteriorating neighborhoods, anonymity, and high unemployment rates has been seen as the typical breeding ground for the conditions that lead to delinquent behavior. Recent reports have tended to confirm the urban-rural differential in crime rates (Clinard 1974). This differential is evident in reported crimes as well as in juvenile court statistics (Jensen and Rojek 1980).

However, there is increasing recognition that the influence of the geographical variable is lessening. For example, using information from the FBI's *Uniform Crime Reports* of 1965 and 1976, Kratcoski and Kratcoski (1979:12) demonstrate that while the number of youths under 18 being arrested in urban areas increased by 85 percent, the number arrested in those areas classified as rural increased by 95 percent during the same time period. In addition, the nature of crime and delinquency appears to be roughly the same in rural and urban areas (Griffin and Griffin 1978: 68-69). Polk (1974), in fact, concluded from a study of rural Oregon youths that not only were the number of confrontations between youths and the law roughly equal for metropolitan and nonmetropolitan youths, but that the seriousness of the causes of these confrontations were also similar.

A common explanation for this convergence in crime and delinquency rates concerns the articulation process mentioned above. Because of increased sophistication in transportation and communication technology, rural and urban populations are similarly exposed to "mass culture" through the media channels and increased mobility potential. It has been assumed that this process has resulted in a leveling effect in the predominant values, norms, and behavior patterns of urban and rural dwellers. Another explanation for the convergence deals with the increasing tendency of law enforcement officials in rural areas to use formal means for reporting crimes and delinquent behavior. Bloch and Flynn (1956) argued that because of inadequate treatment and court facilities, juvenile offenders in rural areas were commonly handled through informal mechanisms such as friends, family, or local church officials and thus were not officially identified as delinquents in comparative statistics. It is a distinct possibility that many crimes in rural areas that would have been handled informally in the past are now finding their way into the official statistics through formalized reporting and treatment procedures.

Although there have been some exceptions (e.g., Clark and Wenninger 1962), studies that have used locational variables have tended to rely on the strict rural-urban dichotomy. This in part is because of the reliance of these studies on the *Uniform Crime Reports* which uses this classificatory scheme. The data for this chapter come from a comprehensive youth survey which allowed us to make finer distinctions, especially in the rural category. Consequently, the first part will deal with a comparison between self-reported delinquency rates of a sample of urban, rural nonfarm, and rural farm youths. The second part of the chapter will deal specifically with the rural farm population, a group that has received little research attention, and will explore the relationship between delinquency rates and selected structural and social psychological variables.

Procedures

The data for this study were collected from a statewide sample of 3,947 seventh through twelfth grade students. The purpose of the study was to assess the needs of the youth of Iowa. The sample was drawn with the goal of randomly selecting 32 of the 438 Iowa Public School Districts. Also, within these districts the intent was to sample students from each of the six grade levels with a minimum sample size of 25 children per grade level. In order to ensure a wide geographic distribution of school districts in the sample, the 438 districts were arranged geographically and sampled systematically with probabilities proportional to their sizes in terms of official total enrollment in grades seven through twelve during the 1975-76 school year.

DEVELOPMENT OF THE INSTRUMENT

In 1969, an agency called the "Youth Development and Delinquency Prevention Administration" was formed within the Department of Health, Education, and Welfare. In 1973, this federally funded agency became the Office of Youth Development (OYD). OYD employed the Behavioral Research and Evaluation Corporation (BREC) to develop a youth needs survey as part of a study of an intervention strategy for juvenile delinquency. The approach to this project was to assess why most youth turn out to be productive and contributing adults, and then attempt to foster these factors within the community. Hence, their intervention approach might be more accurately described as a prevention strategy.

The instrument employed in the collection of these data was the youth needs survey developed by the BREC. It was originally intended to be used as a program evaluation instrument for those treatment and prevention programs of the OYD. The scales were noted to have acceptable levels of reliability, homogeneity, and validity (Elliot et al. 1976:354).

These properties were reported to be similar for different age, sex, class, and ethnic groups. Also, these psychometric properties were unchanged whether the instruments were administered via personal interview or questionnaire form. A detailed description of the scales used in the present study is provided below.

ACCESS TO SOCIALLY DESIRABLE ROLES

Education. This scale was designed to assess perceptions regarding access to personally desirable educational roles. It was intended to be a direct measure of a youth's perceived ability to achieve a particular educational goal. The initial item asked the youth how far he would like to go in school. The subsequent items inquired as to the probability of achieving that goal. The scale was keyed so that a higher score indicated a greater perceived probability of reaching the desired goal.

Occupation. This scale assessed perceptions of the kind of employment to which youth aspire. The scale consisted of an initial item which asked what kind of job the respondent would like to have as an adult, followed by items which probed the perceived likelihood of reaching that level. The items were keyed such that a high summed score indicated a high level of perceived access to the desired occupational role.

Family acceptance. The intent of this scale was to assess the respondent's perception of the extent to which parents accept him. The range of access to desirable social roles in the home and within the family context is represented in this scale. The responses were scored in a direction so that a high summation of the items would indicate a high level of parental acceptance.

Normative pressure from peers. This scale was designed to measure the amount of pressure a youth feels from friendship groups to behave in either a conforming or deviant manner. The scoring was cumulative across all items and was keyed in such a direction so that a high score indicated perceived peer pressure to conform to society's norms.

YOUTH NEEDS

Several consensus problem areas were identified from the subject responses to the 65 item Youth Needs checklist. The consensus problem areas were problems or needs presented in the survey in which there were significantly larger proportions of youth subjects (30 percent or more) agreeing that these were issues of personal concern to them. These problem items were clustered, producing scalable need categories. The five need scales were: (1) *jobs*, i.e., concern about jobs not being available, no way to find out about jobs, jobs having no future, and lack of training for jobs; (2) *parents neglecting children*, i.e., parents do not understand kids' problems, no confidence in going to parents with problems, and parents not interacting with their children enough; (3) *schools*, i.e., no say in the running of their schools, no say in school free time, school personnel lack of understanding or an interest in students, lack of interesting and relevant classes, and student lack of power in affecting school programs and functions; (4) *police and youth*, i.e., police not interested in helping kids, police overreacting, police corruption, and police being unfair to male youths; and (5) *recreation and mobility*, i.e., not enough things to do, entertainment is too costly for kids, recreation and educational centers are not available at leisure time, and transportation is unavailable to get leisure time pursuits.

The scoring was cumulative across all items of each need scale and keyed in a direction that a high score indicated higher personal needs in the problem area.

NEGATIVE LABELING

By parents, teachers, and peers. These scales were intended to measure perceived negative or antisocial categorization by significant others. The scales employed a format modeled after the semantic differential. The same questions were asked of the three groups: parents, teachers, and peers. The scoring was designed so that a high score was indicative of more negative labeling.

Self-Esteem. This scale was designed to assess the extent to which a youth values, accepts, and respects himself. The scoring was cumulative across all items and keyed in a direction that a high score indicated higher positive self-esteem.

ALIENATION

Normlessness. The purpose of this scale was to assess the extent to which an individual believes that unapproved behaviors are required to achieve certain desirable goals. The scoring was cumulative across all items and higher scores implied greater normlessness.

Powerlessness. This scale was intended to measure a youth's perception of personal control over events in his life. Summing across all items gave an index of powerlessness in which a high score indicated a greater degree of societal estrangement.

SELF-REPORT JUVENILE DELINQUENCY

The dependent variable is *delinquent behavior* i.e., "norm violating behavior of a juvenile which, if detected by an appropriate authority, would expose the actor to legally prescribed sanctions" (Williams and Gold 1972:210). Delinquent behavior was measured through the self-reporting technique as initiated by Nye and Short (1957). The scale consists of 19 items covering a wide range of delinquent behaviors. A four-point continum scale was employed rating the frequency of behavior from "never" to "very often." The responses were summed across all items in which a high score indicated greater delinquent behavior. In order to suggest policies for delinquency prevention in noninstitutionalized populations, the present research was interested in all the respondents who committed delinquent acts, not only those who came before officials.

In an attempt to make the 19 items comprising the scale more manageable, the items were grouped into five categories. The grouping parallels the 1978 Iowa Criminal Code. The groups are: (1) status offenses/minor infractions which are inappropriate or illegal for a minor but not necessarily inappropriate or illegal for adults; (2) minor offenses against property and ownership/crimes against property in which the property involved was valued at $50 or less; (3) major offenses against property and ownership/crimes involving property valued at $50 or more; (4) offenses against persons/criminal physical acts perpetrated against other persons; and (5) drug offenses/crimes involving the use and sale of marijuana and hard drugs, glue sniffing, and the use of alcohol.

Analysis of Data

PROFILE ANALYSIS

The Youth Needs Assessment Survey had several items that asked simple descriptive questions about the socioeconomic background of the respondents. A profile of the three groups (rural farm, rural nonfarm, and urban) can be presented from the data obtained from these variables.

The junior high school (seventh through ninth grades) and senior high school (tenth through twelfth grades) portions of the groups were just about evenly split (total junior high school group N=1836, 47.9 percent and the senior high group N=1994, 52.1 percent). The rural farm and urban groups had slightly higher portions of senior high school subjects (rural farm junior high school, 46 percent and senior high school, 54 percent; urban junior high school, 47 percent and senior high school, 53 percent) than the rural nonfarm group (junior high school, 51.5 percent and senior high school, 48.5 percent).

The head of the farm families group was not as highly educated as the nonfarm rural and urban groups. Though a majority of the farm family heads were high school graduates (60 percent compared to 45 percent nonfarm rural and 41 percent urban), significantly fewer had one to three years of college (6.4 percent compared to 13.5 percent nonfarm rural and 15.3 percent urban) and significantly fewer had college degrees (3.3 percent compared to 17.3 percent nonfarm rural and 20 percent urban).

Size of family, measured here as the total number of children, demonstrates that the largest proportion in all three groups is three to four children (35.6 percent farm, 36.1 percent nonfarm rural, and 37.1 percent urban). There were more families in the farm and nonfarm rural samples than in the urban group that had five or more children (17.8 percent farm, 17.2 percent nonfarm, and 10.2 percent urban).

Most all the subjects in the groups lived with both parents (96 percent farm, 8.2 percent rural nonfarm, and 77 percent urban). More of the urban subjects reported they lived with their mother only (.8 percent farm, 7.1 percent rural nonfarm, and 13.4 percent urban) or with step parents (2.3 percent farm, 4.7 percent rural nonfarm, and 7.1 percent urban).

These data indicate that these groups differ somewhat on some key description variables such as family size and parents being present, but by and large the groups are similiar on most of these variables. The data also indicate that the divisions in the groups are generally representative of the total population in that group.

DESCRIPTION OF THE SELF-REPORTED DELINQUENCY OF THE GROUP

The degree of delinquency, from high to medium to low, of the three groups is presented in Table 6.1. It appears that the farm youths report less delinquency than the other groups. For example, in looking at the totals for each of the general offense categories, the lowest percentages in the high delinquency columns consistently appear in the farm category. The rural nonfarm group reported slightly more delinquency than the farm group while the urban group reported significantly more delinquency in all categories when compared with the other two groups. The only reversal of this trend appears in the minor offense category, "Taken

Table 6.1. Self-Reported Delinquency Rates By Type of Residence (In Percentages)

Offense Type	Rural Farm (N=364)			Rural Nonfarm (N=848)			Urban (N=2,633)		
	High	Medium	Low	High	Medium	Low	High	Medium	Low
Status offenses	11.8	33.1	55.0	13.3	33.6	53.1	21.2	36.2	42.6
Given Teachers Fake Excuse	9.7	25.5	64.8	9.7	29.2	61.1	16.0	31.2	52.7
Runaway From Home	0.9	6.3	92.9	1.1	7.5	91.4	3.2	9.3	87.4
Skipped School	7.4	20.3	72.3	8.2	18.6	73.0	14.8	24.6	60.5
Minor Offenses	9.2	42.7	48.1	12.6	42.6	44.8	14.1	35.8	50.1
Taken Little Things	6.9	31.5	61.6	7.9	32.7	59.5	11.1	32.2	56.8
Taken Something From Locker	5.8	23.4	70.9	5.5	26.0	68.6	3.3	17.8	79.0
Taken Something Worth $5-50	3.7	7.4	88.9	2.9	12.6	84.6	4.4	15.3	80.4
Major Offenses	6.6	15.6	67.7	8.8	29.0	62.3	11.5	29.4	59.2
Broken Into A Place	1.7	7.1	91.2	2.1	8.8	89.1	2.4	11.7	85.9
Taken Car For Drive Without Permission	2.0	5.7	92.3	2.4	7.1	90.6	2.7	8.0	89.4
Damage Property	4.5	23.7	71.7	7.3	22.8	70.9	8.4	23.9	67.6
Taken Something Worth $50	2.3	5.7	92.0	2.3	6.9	90.8	3.2	8.7	88.1

Personal Offenses	4.3	17.9	77.8	5.3	19.3	75.4	6.7	20.2	73.1
Used Force To Get Money	1.2	2.0	96.8	1.1	3.9	95.0	2.2	5.7	92.1
Beat Up Other Kids	4.0	13.7	82.3	3.7	15.5	80.7	4.5	13.9	81.6
Participated in Gang Fights	2.5	6.0	91.4	3.3	6.7	89.9	4.2	10.7	84.9
Drug Offenses	18.3	42.0	39.7	22.7	35.9	41.5	33.7	30.6	35.7
Used Marijuana	5.2	8.1	86.7	11.1	7.8	81.1	23.1	10.9	65.9
Sold Marijuana	2.2	1.7	96.0	3.1	3.7	93.0	7.6	7.6	84.8
Sniffed Glue	1.7	6.0	92.3	2.2	7.4	90.4	2.5	5.9	91.5
Used Hard Drugs	1.5	1.7	96.9	2.6	2.2	95.1	4.9	6.3	88.8
Sold Hard Drugs	1.2	0.0	98.9	1.1	0.9	98.0	2.6	2.7	94.7
Used Alcohol	31.2	25.1	43.7	31.5	22.7	45.6	37.5	24.2	38.3
Total Self-Reported Delinquency	11.4	38.9	49.7	14.9	41.3	43.7	24.1	37.3	38.5

a. Categories of high, medium, and low were established by using natural break points in the distribution of the offense types with a concern for ending up with approximately 1/3 of the population in each category. For the most part, the low category was somewhat higher than 1/3 of the sample and the high category was somewhat less than 1/3 the sample.

something from a kid's locker without asking him." Status offenses and drug offenses were the most often reported offenses by subjects in all three groups. Again, the farm youth group had the lowest percentages in the high category while the urban youth group obtained the highest percent.

The most reported offenses by all subjects were:

Status offense: "Given teacher a fake excuse for being absent."
Minor offense: "Taken little things worth $5 (or less) that didn't belong to me."
Major offense: "Damaged public or private property just for fun."
Personal offense: "Beat up on other kids or adults just for the heck of it."
Drug offense: "Used alcohol."

Note that alcohol use is predominant in all groups—over 30 percent of the respondents in each group reported high use of alcohol. Medium use of alcohol is higher for farm youths than rural nonfarm and urban youths. Though not nearly as high as alcohol use, high percentages of subjects from all three groups report the use of marijuana. Higher percentages of rural nonfarm youths (11.1 percent) and urban youth (23.1 percent) report that they have used marijuana than farm youth (5.2 percent).

In sum, our data are consistent with past findings on frequency of delinquency comparing rural and urban samples. We find the self-reported delinquency of rural farm youth to be lower than rural nonfarm and urban youths. Status offenses and drug offenses were reported most in all three types of groups.

Explanation of Delinquency Patterns of Rural Farm Youth

The following analysis focuses on the structural and social psychological correlates of rural farm youth delinquency.

The occurence of delinquency in the rural farm population must be attributed to a variety of factors. If solutions are to be found for the delinquency problem, relevant factors must be isolated and dealt with so as to break the cycle of delinquency. In isolating factors associated with delinquency, one approach is to generate a set of potential factors and test their association with occurences of self-reported delinquency.

STRUCTURAL FACTORS

Four major structural factors which may be related to delinquency concern the perceived access to socially desirable educational, occupa-

Table 6.2.   Correlation Matrix of Access to Desirable Social
Roles with Delinquency Categories for Rural Farm Youth.

	Status Offense	Minor Offense	Major Offense	Personal Offense	Drug Offense	Total Self-Reported Delinquency
Education	-.22[b]	-.26[b]	-.23[b]	-.23[b]	-.26[b]	-.33[b]
Occupation	-.02	-.05	.02	-.04	-.11[a]	.07
Family	-.25[b]	-.24[b]	-.24[b]	-.19[b]	-.31[b]	-.33[b]
Normative peer pressure	- 33[b]	-.33[b]	-.36[b]	-.31[b]	-.35[b]	-.42[b]

a.   Significant at the .05 level.
b.   Significant at the .01 level.

tional, family, and peer group roles. It can be anticipated that youths who feel they have ready access to these types of roles will feel less of a need to engage in delinquent acts (Merton 1938; Cohen 1955; Cloward and Ohin 1960). Table 6.2 contains the results of the analysis. Note the strong negative relationships between access to desirable educational roles and all types of self-reported delinquency. Educational roles are a primary source of personal evaluation for youths and clearly those who do not perceive that they will possess desirable roles in the future turn more frequently to delinquent acts. Occupational roles are not as strongly related to self-reported delinquency as are educational roles. This is probably a factor of the age of the respondents in that occupations are not as salient for youths at this stage. The only significant relationship is between occupation and drug offenses. This may indicate that a portion of the population has already turned to drug use as a source of income due to a perceived lack of future socially desirable occupational roles.

The degree of perceived familial acceptance tends to show significant negative relationships to the subcategories of delinquency. The magnitudes of these need areas were described earlier and their relationships to the subcategories of delinquency are listed in Table 6.3. The most significant relationships are found between the youth's perceptions of problems in their relations with police and all forms of delinquency. Note particularly the strong relationship (.38) between the perceived need for improvement in the police force and self-reported status offenses. Another way of putting this is that those youths who report high occurences of status offenses are also reporting a high need for improvements in police/youth relations. Also note that status offenses were the

Table 6.3. Correlation Matrix of Youth Needs with Delinquency Categories for Rural Farm Youth

	Status Offense	Minor Offense	Major Offense	Personal Offense	Drug Offense	Total Self-Reported Delinquency
Police and Youth	.38[b]	.29[b]	.32[b]	.22[b]	.28[b]	.36[b]
Schools	.21[b]	.15[b]	.14[b]	.00	.17[b]	.17[b]
Parental Neglect	.12[b]	.13[b]	.15[b]	.09	.14[b]	.15[b]
Recreational and Mobility	.11[a]	.11[a]	.08	-.08	.13[b]	.10[a]

a. Significant at the .05 level.
b. Significant at the .01 level.

most often reported forms of delinquency. Police are placed in an interesting position when it comes to status offenses. These types of offenses are only brought to the attention of the police due to the age of the offender. The officer, therefore, must treat these offenders differently from older offenders. It is no wonder that youths, who probably do not believe the police should be involved in these status offenses, have a difficult time understanding the officer's role. These first contacts with the police are very important in determining future police/youth interaction and therefore deserve a close analysis (Goldman 1963; Wattenberg and Bufe 1963). If youths do not feel that they are being treated fairly by police it can lead to frustration and a more personal rejection of normative behavior patterns. The high correlations with the other forms of self-reported delinquency indicate that police/youth interaction should be examined for the other offense categories as well.

The next strongest need area relative to self-reported delinquency is the need for a better school structure. Those youths who note a need for more interesting and relevant classes, more understanding by school personnel, and more say in the running of their schools also have high rates of self-reported delinquency. Again the highest relationship is with the status offenders. These offenses may be a direct reaction to a school system which is not responsive to the needs of the students. Of course no school system is perfect and these offenses will always exist, but improving the responsiveness of schools does appear to be one approach toward a possible reduction in these offenses.

Concern for jobs and a need for better parent/child relations show

Table 6.4.   Correlation Matrix of Negative Labeling and
             Self-Esteem with Delinquency Categories For
             Rural Farm Youth

	Status Offense	Minor Offense	Major Offense	Personal Offense	Drug Offense	Total Self-reported Delinquency
Parental Perceived Negative Labeling	.33[b]	.32[b]	.36[b]	.35[b]	.33[b]	.42[b]
Teacher Perceived Negative Labeling	.26[b]	.30[b]	.33[b]	.32[b]	.28[b]	.36[b]
Peer Perceived Negative Labeling	.32[b]	.36[b]	.45[b]	.40[b]	.32[b]	.45[b]
Self-Esteem	-.10[a]	-.06	-.08[b]	-.14[b]	-.12[a]	-.13[b]

a. Significant at the .05 level.
b. Significant at the .01 level.

significant but somewhat weak relationships to self-reported delinquency in all categories except personal offenses. The strongest of these relationships is between the concern over jobs and job training and status offenses. Here again, those youths who do not perceive an education as leading to worthwhile employment are the most likely to commit status offenses.

The need for better recreation facilities or facilities to which access is less costly shows only moderate relationships to self-reported delinquency. Contrary to what might be expected, it does not appear that a perceived lack of recreational facilities is related to overly high rates of delinquency.

SOCIAL PSYCHOLOGICAL FACTORS

There are a series of social psychological factors which may be related to delinquency in this population. These general areas which have been discussed at length in the literature are negative labeling, self-esteem and alienation.

The effect of negative labeling on youth has been shown to be detrimental. The label "delinquent" or "criminal" appears to produce a master status (Becker 1963) and therefore is difficult for a person to eliminate. This leads to a continued pattern of delinquency and further negative labeling. In this study, we have broken negative labeling into labeling from parents, teachers, and peers in order to show the differential impact of negative labeling from these sources. The results in Table 6.4 reveal a rather consistent and strong pattern of relationships, with the strongest relationship occurring in the correlation between peer labeling and both major and personal offenses. These data clearly support the notion that labeling can be a powerful correlate to delinquency. Self-esteem, on the other hand, does not correlate nearly as well with delinquency as do the labeling measures. This would indicate that it is not so much the young person's perception of himself that is related to delinquency, but rather it is his perception of other people's labeling of himself that is most related to delinquency.

Alienation is often conceptualized as a multidimensional concept (Seeman 1959). Three of the most often identified dimensions are normlessness, powerlessness, and social estrangement. The effect of alienation upon delinquency is different for each of these dimensions. Normlessness would intuitively seem to have the strongest relationship with delinquency since it represents the extent to which youths believe that socially unapproved behaviors are required to achieve their goals. As shown in Table 6.5, this dimension does indeed correlate strongly with all forms of delinquency. It appears that youths who report high levels of delinquency either have not developed appropriate normative attitudes or have adopted extranormative means of achieving their goals. In the latter case, inadequate opportunity structures might lead to the development of a heightened sense of normlessness and thus higher delinquency. In the former case, a lack of appropriate socialization may have resulted in high normlessness which resulted in higher delinquency.

Powerlessness is also strongly related to all forms of delinquency, although not as strongly as is normlessness. This indicates that those youths who report high delinquency feel that they can have little impact on their own lives. Similar relationships are found with social estrangement which indicates that those youths who report higher levels of delinquency also feel estranged from the larger society. They often feel lonely and that nobody cares about them.

In summary, the attitudinal factors that are examined above have generally strong relationships to self-reported delinquency. This is particularly true of negative labeling and normlessness.

Prevention of Delinquency

The previous data analysis sheds light on the rural-urban delinquency issue. Our study indicates that the rural-urban dichotomy persists. Fewer rural farm subjects fell in the high delinquency categories than rural nonfarm and urban groups. The urban group showed the highest delinquency percentages. Despite the eclipse or articulation of the rural community by the urban process, the institutions of rural society remain

Table 6.5.   Correlation Matrix of Alienation Dimensions
with Delinquency Categories for Rural Farm Youth

	Status Offense	Minor Offense	Major Offense	Personal Offense	Drug Offense	Total Self-reported Delinquency
Normlessness	.38[b]	.40[b]	.45[b]	.36[b]	.40	.49
Powerlessness	.19[b]	.19[b]	.22[b]	.25[b]	.23	.27
Social Estrangement	.17[b]	.13[b]	.18[b]	.18[b]	.24	.24

a.   Significant at the .05 level.
b.   Significant at the .01 level.

strong in surpressing delinquency. However, delinquency does occur among rural farm youth. What preventative stance does this study imply?

The study indicates strong relationships between several structural and social psychological variables and the delinquency of farm youth. We find that perceived lack of access to socially acceptable and meaningful roles of youth and feelings of alienation are associated with delinquency. These variables have long been identified as predictive of urban delinquency. But few have pointed out the importance of society giving farm youngsters the opportunity to take on socially acceptable roles as students, family members, peer group members, club members, or employees. This is essentially important to rural youth with the gradual disappearance of the family farm and the one-room school house. Successful performance of student, family member, peer group member, and employee roles leads to broader options for youth.

If increasingly responsible positions in society are denied a young person, delinquency becomes an increasingly attractive option. Meaningful roles lead to a positive development of an individual, that is:

A sense of competence—not only that the young person can do something but do it well.

A sense of usefulness—a feeling that the young person has something to contribute which is of value to others.

A sense of belonging—knowledge that the young person fits into a place, a group.

A sense of power or potency—the feeling that the young person's behavior will influence or determine the outcome of events.

Without the opportunity to develop meaningful roles and positive identity, young people can easily be labelled as failures, thus accelerating their alienation. It is clear, however, that alienation in and of itself does not account for the occurrence of delinquent behavior. Alienation is the result of the denial of socially acceptable roles and the application of negative labels. Once alienated, delinquent behavior is a way of expressing that alienation. If youth can be actively involved in the school, the family, the work world, and the community, delinquent behavior tends to diminish.

A tradition in American rural society has been the passing the work skills from father to son through a lengthy apprenticeship system. This is less true today. Many farm-raised youth are not planning to stay on the family farm or seek farming as a permanent livelihood. Such young-sters are seeking jobs in the factories, offices, and stores of the nearby communities and urban areas. Today's job market requires more complex and rapidly changing skills than those passed on from parent to child. Opportunities for learning within the family setting have been sharply reduced since father and mother often travel to the urban areas for employment. No single corresponding institution within our society has taken over this traditional role—instead, there are a variety of institutions (the schools, the welfare system, the church, the justice system, etc.) which have an impact on a young person and that individual's direction in life.

The opportunities to adopt meaningful roles in society are inextricably bound to a variety of institutions. It is necessary to look at those insti-tutions to determine how they might revise existing policies, procedures, and practices to allow different opportunities and experiences for all young people. The emphasis should be on ways to provide positive labels for young people, therefore reinforcing a positive self-image.

How does one go about changing institutions? Clearly, programs do not change institutions, people do. Young people must have access to meaningful roles such as meaningful work in the marketplace. In order for this to occur, employers must recognize and assume a primary role in the preparation and employment of the future generations of the work force. Young people must be brought from the sidelines into the main-stream of economic life. As young people enter the world of work, changes will occur in both the individual and the environment of which he is a part.

Young people, as an integral part of the institutions which have an impact on their lives, are in a strategic position to make constructive changes. Any school program or employment program must help young people to recognize their own skills and abilities to have an impact on the institutions of which they are a part. Hopefully, such a process will bring about an increase in individual feelings of self-worth which should in turn have an impact on the reduction of juvenile delinquency.

In sum, while the rates of juvenile delinquency observed for rural farm youth tend to be significantly lower than their rural nonfarm and urban counterparts, the structural and attitudinal correlates of delinquency appear to be quite similar.

References

Becker, Howard S. 1963. *Outsiders: Studies in the Sociology of Deviance*. New York: The Free Press.

Bloch, Herbert A. and Frank T. Flynn. 1956. *Delinquency: The Juvenile Offender in America Today*. New York: Random House.

Clark, John P. and Eugene P. Wenninger. 1962. "Socio-economic Class and Area as Correlates of Illegal Behavior Among Juveniles." *American Sociological Review* 27 (December): 826-34.

Clinard, Marshall. 1974. *Sociology of Deviant Behavior*. New York: Holt, Rinehart and Winston. 4th ed.

Cloward, Richard A. and Lloyd E. Ohlin. 1960. *Delinquency and Opportunity*. New York: Free Press.

Cohen, Albert K. 1955. *Delinquent Boys: The Culture of the Gang*. New York: Free Press.

Elliot, Delbert S., Suzanne S. Ageton, Margaret Hunter, and Brian Knowles. 1976. *Research Handbook for Community Planning and Feedback Instruments*. Boulder, Colorado: Behavioral Research and Evaluation Corporation.

Goldman, Nathan. 1963. *The Differential Selection of Juvenile Offenders for Court Appearance*. New York: National Research and Information Center, National Council on Crime and Delinquency.

Griffin, Brenda S. and Charles T. Griffin. 1978. *Juvenile Delinquency in Perspective*. New York: Harper and Row.

Jensen, Gary F. and Dean G. Roject. 1980. *Delinquency: A Sociological View*. Lexington, Massachusetts: D.C. Heath.

Kratcoski, Peter C. and Lucille Dun Kratcoski. 1979. *Juvenile Delinquency*. Englewood Cliffs, New Jersey: Prentice-Hall.

Merton, Robert. 1938. "Social Structure and Anomie." *American Sociological Review* 3 (October): 672-82.

Nye, F.I. and James F. Short, Jr. 1957. "Scaling Delinquent Behavior." *American Sociological Review* 22: 326-31.

Polk, Kenneth. 1974. *Teenage Delinquency in Small Town America*. Research Report 5. Rockville, Maryland: Center for Studies of Crime and Delinquency, National Institute of Mental Health.

Sanders, Irwin T. 1977. *Rural Society*. Englewood Cliffs, New Jersey: Prentice-Hall.

Seeman, Melvin. 1959. "On the Meaning of Alienation." *American Sociological Review* 24: 783-91.

Wattenberg, William W. and Noel Bufe. 1963. "The Effectiveness of Police Youth Bureau Officers." *Journal of Criminal Law, Criminology, and Police Science* 54(4): 470-75.

Williams, J.R. and Martin Gold. 1972. "From Delinquent Behavior to Official Delinquency." *Social Problems* 20 (Winter): 209-29.

7

Frequency of Drug Use Among Rural High School Students

TED L. NAPIER and
MARY CHRISTINE PRATT

Introduction

Drug abuse has emerged in recent years as a serious social problem within the United States. One of the major reasons for the concern expressed about drug use is the antisocial behavior often exhibited by illegal drug users. Not only is drug abuse[1] a criminal offense in and of itself but it also contributes to other criminal behavior since users frequently resort to criminal acts to secure money to buy drugs (McGlothlin et al., 1978; Cushman 1971; Inciardi and Chambers 1972).[2] Eckerman et al. (1971) observed, for example, that drug addicts composed 80 percent of all arrests for robbery in New York and 45 percent of such arrests in Washington, D.C. McGlothlin et al. (1978) demonstrated that during periods of high drug abuse individuals tended to be engaged in more criminal behavior to finance their drug use. Forslund (1977-78) revealed that rural youth also engaged in drug abuse, even though the extent of drug use was much lower than urban rates, and that users tended to be more frequently involved in criminal acts than nonusers.

These studies strongly suggest that a linkage exists between drug use and criminal acts. This implies that programs designed to prevent criminal behavior cannot ignore drug related crimes because one of the related factors associated with certain criminal acts is the need to finance drug use. To develop relevant preventive crime programs, however, requires knowledge of the extent, type, and frequency of drug use. Information is also required relative to the socio-demographic characteristics of the users so that preventive programs may be designed for a specific client group.

While it is reasonable to expect that information about drug users and drug use is necessary to develop effective preventive programs, the state of the art in drug abuse research is such that generation of additional research findings would be useful to program development. There are many areas of research which have received little or no attention. This is especially true for rural drug abuse. The relationship of drug use to the rural social milieu is not well known.

The purpose of this chapter is to report the findings of a drug abuse study conducted in a rural county located in the southwest portion of Ohio. The existing drug use literature is reviewed and the study findings are compared with findings from numerous national studies. The latter portion of the chapter is devoted to a discussion of the utility of the study findings for developing programs to reduce the extent of drug abuse in the study area.

The State of the Art In Drug Abuse Research

While some researchers argue that the rapid increase in drug abuse during the 1960s and 1970s is probably a short-lived fad (McGlothlin 1971), others take a less optimistic perspective by asserting that although drug use has plateaued, it will probably not decline (National Commission on Marijuana and Drug Abuse 1972:264-65). Still others contend that drug abuse is here to stay (Josephson 1974:178) and that some types of drug use are probably increasing. While consensus has not been achieved on the issue, there is considerable evidence supporting the position that significant increases have occurred in drug use over a relatively short time span, especially among youth and young adults (San Mateo County Department of Public Health and Welfare 1973; Abelson et al. 1973; National Commission on Marijuana and Drug Abuse, Second Report 1973:84; Groves 1974:252; Blum 1969; Imperi et al. 1968; Gallup Poll 1969; Solomon 1968). If recent trends are indicative of future drug use patterns, then it is probable that drug abuse will continue to increase, with the greatest increases observed among youth cohorts.

Drug use is not a recent social phenomenon that has emerged as a function of new technologies which have made it possible to produce new substances of abuse. Many drugs have been in existence for centuries and have been used and abused in practically every society of the world. Almost every society of the world, for example, has a documented history of fermented alcoholic beverages. The American Indian of the southwest and certain Mexican groups, for example, used mescal to develop hallucinogenic effects many years prior to the European settlement of North America. Opium use in Asia has been repeatedly documented and cocaine was used by the inhabitants of the Andes Mountains long before the European explorers discovered the New World (Bates and Crowther 1973).

While drug use has existed for centuries, all social groups have attempted to regulate drug use behavior. Social norms have emerged to define what is socially acceptable use of drugs and what constitutes abuse. Bates and Crowther (1973) correctly observe that all societies have defined several types of intoxicating substances as acceptable for use under certain conditions but not for others. Laws have been created to control the use of substances perceived to be dangerous to individual and group well-being.

This brief review of drug use history should demonstrate that the recent concern for drug use within the United States is not a function of the society being suddenly introduced to drugs for the first time, but rather is a function of the rapid increases in the illegal use of drugs by various segments of the population. Widespread violation of social norms used to control substances of abuse, antisocial behavior of users to finance their use, and concern for the social well being of the users have been primary factors for defining drug use as a social problem. This concern has spawned considerable research into the extent of drug use and the covariates of abuse.

One of the most frequently researched areas is the relationship between selected socio-demographic factors and the extent of drug use. The results of these research efforts show that many variables have been demonstrated to be significantly related to illegal drug use. While consensus has not been achieved in the drug related research, there are general patterns which have been identified. The existing research literature will be discussed in the context of specific variables which have been shown to covary with drug use.

Age. Age has been used as a predictive variable in drug use studies many times. The findings basically show that age is related in a positive manner to drug use for young people but inversely related for older age cohorts (Josephson 1974:195; Blum 1969; McGlothlin 1974:286-87; National Commission on Marijuana and Drug Abuse, Second Report 1973: 42-84; National Commission on Marijuana and Drug Abuse, First Report 1972:33-34). The only exception to this pattern appears to be alcohol use which tends to plateau in the later life with some considerable decline in consumption after middle age (McKee and Robertson, 1975: 564-65). The literature suggests that age is significantly related to frequency of drug use.

Sex. The consistency of the research findings for sex tend to suggest that males are more frequent users of most drugs (Pittel 1973: 886-87; McGlothlin 1974: 287-88; Josephson 1974: 195; National Commission on Marijuana and Drug Abuse, First Report 1972: 32; Lombrillo and Hain 1972; McKee and Robertson 1975: 564-65; Judd et al. 1973: 943; Solomon 1968; Blum 1969; National Commission on Marijuana and Drug Abuse, Second Report 1973: 48), but that the differences are probably diminishing over time. The major exception to this pattern is amphetamine use. The existing research indicates that females tend to be more frequent users of amphetamines due to stress and weight control (Ellinwood 1974: 305; Solomon 1968; National Commission on Marijuana and Drug Abuse, Second Report 1973: 48). These studies suggest that sex is significantly related to frequency of drug use and that males tend to be the most frequent users of most illegal drugs.

Socio-Economic Status. At one time, it was thought that drug use was a lower class behavioral pattern, but now people from all social classes have become extensive users. In fact, there are certain illegal drugs which have been shown to be more frequently used by higher socioeconomic groups than lower status people (National Commission on Marijuana and Drug Abuse, First Report 1972: 32; McKee and Robertson 1974: 565; Ianni 1973: 613; Josephson 1974: 195; Patch 1973: 1025-1040). Heroin users, however, tend to be from very poor socioeconomic situations (National Commission on Marijuana and Drug Abuse, Second Report 1973: 167-169). These research findings suggest that indicators of socioeconomic status is significantly related to frequency of drug use and that higher status people exhibit more frequent use of most illegal drugs since they have a higher probability of having the economic resources to purchase illegal drugs.

Parental Relationships. Several studies have revealed that drug use is significantly related to parental relationships. It has been observed that an unstable home life will increase the probability a person will become a drug user. When interpersonal relationships of parents are negative or have been severed by divorce or separation the probability is increased that children of that unit will abuse drugs (Johnson et al. 1972; National Commission on Marijuana and Drug Abuse, First Report 1972: 42; McGlothlin 1974: 289; Forslund 1977-78; Tolone and Dermott 1975; National Commission on Marijuana and Drug Abuse, Second Report 1973: 167-169). Apparently, drug use is perceived by users to be a means of coping with unhappy family situations. The only research report discovered which suggested that broken homes was not significantly related to drug use was a study reported by Judd et al. (1973) in which broken homes were shown not to be significantly related to marijuana use. The authors did note, however, that consideration of females alone demonstrated a significant difference between users and nonusers by marital status of parents (Judd et al. 1973: 943). These findings indicate that parents' marital status and parental relationships are significantly related to frequency of drug use and that stress within the family contributes to greater drug abuse.

Academic Performance. One of the most interesting findings produced by empirical research in the area of drug abuse among people is that drug users sometimes perform better in school than nonusers (Hogan et al. 1970; Patch 1973: 1055). This finding is especially true of marijuana users. Fischler (1975-76) and Forslund (1977-78), on the other hand, discovered that drug users usually do not perform as well academically as nonusers, even though Fischler (1975-76) observed no significant differences in academic performance for users and nonusers among junior high school students when they were considered separate from high school and college respondents. Regardless of the position one accepts, the implication of the findings is that the widely held position that drug users are poor students is now questionable. The literature suggests that academic performance is significantly related to frequency of drug use.

Personal Crises. It has been argued that personal stress will contribute to drug use and some literature tends to support the position. Ellinwood (1974: 307) indicates that people under stress tend to use amphetamines more frequently than people without personal stress. Judd et al. (1973: 944) also observed that marijuana use tended to increase with stress. These findings are logical since drugs may be used to escape reality. These findings suggest that personal stress is significantly related to frequency of drug use and that people with greater personal stress will tend to use drugs more frequently.

Age of First Use of Alcohol. Use of alcohol has been shown to be significantly related to other types of drug use (Josephson 1974: 197; Wechsler 1976; Groves 1974: 259; Goode 1971; McGlothlin 1974: 288-289; National Commission on Marijuana and Drug Abuse, Second Report 1973: 70-71, 92-93; National Commission on Marijuana and Drug Abuse, First Report 1972: 32-33; Ellinwood 1974: 308). Alcohol related research shows that individuals who use alcohol also have a much higher probability of using other drugs, especially marijuana, than nondrinkers. It should follow that earlier use of alcohol should increase the probability that the alcohol consumer will also experiment with other drugs at some time in his/her life. The literature suggests that age of first alcohol consumption is significantly related to frequency of drug use and that people who begin consuming alcohol at an earlier age tend to use other drugs more frequently than people who postpone alcohol use until later in life.

Study Methods

A drug use study was conducted within a rural county located in southwestern Ohio using freshmen and senior high school students as respondents. All high schools within the county were invited to participate in the study via communication with the executive officers of each school. One high school administrator refused to cooperate in the study which eliminated the school's student body from participation. The school which did not participate was one of the larger public schools in the county and was not significantly different from the other public schools included in the study. The exclusion of this school should not adversely affect the generalizability of the findings to the county. Four hundred and ninety-two usable questionnaires were completed which constitutes a response rate of 47.5 percent of all ninth and twelfth grade students in the county. Over 73 percent of all eligible students from the six cooperating high schools were included in the sample. The six cooperating schools consisted of one parochial, one vocational-technical, and four public schools.

The data were collected in the spring of 1979 at prearranged group sessions in the respective high schools. The questionnaires were administered by trained research personnel who explained the purpose of the study and instructed the students relative to proper procedure for responding to the questions. The interview situation was such that communication among the respondents was not possible, thus reducing the potential for inflation or deflation of drug use by the respondents due to attempts to impress or to hide their behavior from peers.

To ensure complete anonymity of the respondents, no names were required on the questionnaires. The students were instructed to place completed questionnaires in one of the unmarked envelopes which were located on the monitor's desk at the completion of the interviewing session. All of the students remained in the room until all of the questionnaires were completed and placed in the envelopes. The envelopes were sealed and delivered to the principal field investigator. With this procedure not even the researchers were able to identify individual questionnaires by respondent.

Measurement of Variables

Drug use was measured by a question which asked the respondents to indicate their frequency of drug use for ten types of drugs. The drugs evaluated were: barbiturates, amphetamines, opiates, marijuana, inhalants, hallucinogens, cocaine, heroin, methadone, and alcohol. Examples of each drug were given, both in technical and "street" terms, so the respondent would be able to associate the types of substances they were using or had used with the proper response category. The response categories for each drug were: "almost every day," "several times a week," "a few times a month," "a few times a year," "only once or twice ever," and "never used." Weighting values were assigned to each response category. The weighting values varied from six for "almost every day" to one for "never used." The predictive variables were measured as follows: Physical maturation as a concept was measured by two variables termed age and grade level. Socioeconomic status was measured by asking the students to classify their family's total income relative to other people within the community using the following categories: "very poor," "poor," "a little less than average," "about average," "a little more than average," "wealthy," and "very wealthy." Parental relationships were evaluated by two variables termed "marital status" and "parent interpersonal relations." "Parent interpersonal relations" were assessed by asking the respondent to choose the category that best described how his/her parents get along together: "very poorly," "somewhat below average," "about average," "somewhat above average," and "very well." Academic performance was measured by asking the respondents to indicate how their grades usually compared to other students in school. The possible responses were: "much worse," "somewhat worse," "about average," "somewhat better," and "much better." Personal crisis was measured with two variables termed "experience with serious problems" and "serious problems contributed to use." Experience with serious problems was measured by asking the respondents if they had ever been fired from a job, had trouble in school, had ever experienced a serious health problem, had experienced an emotional or psychological problem, or a death in their immediate family. The respondents were also asked if any of the problems mentioned contributed to their drug use. Age of first use of alcohol was measured by a question asking the students when they first began to use alcohol.

While the authors could not locate research which examines the relationship of perception of drug use as a problem and actual drug use behavior, such data were gathered to assess the perception of drug use in school and the community. It was reasoned that users should be in a state of consonance (Festinger 1957: 1-31) in terms of their perceptions and drug use. Drug users should view their drug behavior as socially acceptable and not constituting a problem within their school or community. The students were asked how serious the drug use was in their school and in the community. The possible responses to both questions were "no problem," "a very little problem," "a moderate problem," "a serious problem," and "a severe problem."

Study Findings

The findings are presented in a descriptive fashion with a brief discussion of the multivariate analyses conducted on the data set. Table 7.1 presents the frequency of responses to each drug evaluated and the mean age when drug use began.

These data show that alcohol and marijuana are the most widely used drugs among rural students who participated in this study. The inhalants, the hallucinogens, and the narcotics tend to be used much more infrequently. About 10 percent of the students report daily use of marijuana with an additional 12 percent using it several times a week. The table also shows that the respondents began to use drugs prior to or very early in their teens, which is consistent with other research (National Commission on Marijuana and Drug Abuse, Second Report 1973: 45; McKee and Robertson 1975: 564; Patch 1973: 1038-139).

The frequencies of drug use data presented in Table 7.1 were recombined into two categories which are those who have used the drug being evaluated and those who have never tried it. The percentage of respondents who have used each drug was compared with data presented by the National Commission on Marijuana and Drug Abuse in 1973. The na-

Table 7.1. Frequency of Drug Use and Age When Drug Was First Used Among High School Students In A Rural County of Ohio (Percentage of Respondents Who Have Used Drug: N=492)

Drug	Frequency of Use							Mean Age When Drug First Used (In Years)
	Almost Daily	Several Times A Week	A Few Times Per Month	A Few Times Per Year	Only Once Or Twice Ever	Never Used	No Data	
Barbiturates	1.2	3.3	7.7	8.7	7.1	69.3	2.7	14.4
Amphetamines	3.3	4.1	9.6	6.9	7.1	66.3	2.7	14.9
Opiates	0.8	2.6	5.5	18.7	8.9	60.0	3.5	10.3
Marijuana	10.4	11.8	9.8	7.1	12.2	46.5	2.2	13.9
Inhalants	0.4	0.8	1.4	1.0	3.7	89.4	3.3	11.3
Hallucinogens	0.8	1.0	2.0	2.4	1.8	88.6	3.4	14.0
Cocaine	0.2	0.6	2.4	3.9	3.7	85.8	3.4	14.3
Heroin	0.4	0.4	0.4	0.2	3.0	92.3	3.3	14.2
Methadone	0.6	0.6	0.8	1.0	1.4	91.9	3.7	14.8
Alcohol	5.5	15.9	25.8	31.1	N.A.	15.4	6.3	11.9

Table 7.2.   Comparison of Ohio Sample With National Drug
Use Data For High School Seniors (Percentage
Who Have Used Drug)

Drug	(1979) Ohio Data[a]	(1972) National Data[b]
Barbiturates	28.1	16
Amphetamines	30.9	19
Opiates[c]	36.5	5.2
Marijuana	51.3	40
Inhalants	7.3	9
Hallucinogens	8.1	14
Cocaine	10.7	N.A.
Heroin	4.4	N.A.
Methadone	4.4	N.A.
Alcohol	78.3	74

a. All missing data were treated as nonusers which
underestimates use slightly. The only figure that
clearly reflects the underestimation is hallucinogens
noted in Table 7.4. The figure 8.5 percent use with
friends is larger than the admitted use by respondents
(8.1 percent). There were 3.3 percent missing data for
hallucinogens which were treated as nonusers. The 8.5
percent is probably the true use of hallucinogens.

b. Source: Drug Use In America: Problem In Perspective,
second report of the National Commission on Marijuana
and Drug Abuse, U.S. Government Printing Office,
Washington, D.C., p. 82.

c. The high rate of opiate use can be partially explained
by the use of codeine-based cough medicine as an example
of the drug. There were no means available to the
researchers to identify individuals who were using the
drug illegally. The percentage is probably greatly
inflated by the inclusion of legitimate users. None
of the other categories of drugs used examples of
substances commonly employed for health purposes.

tional data are composed of mean values from all of the drug use studies
the Commission could locate for each drug evaluated. The comparison
of the Ohio data with the national data is presented in Table 7.2.

These data show that a higher percentage of the rural respondents
reported that they had tried drugs than the national studies indicated in
1972. For the exceptions of inhalants and hallucinogens, the rural students exceeded national use in 1972 for the drugs which could be com-

Table 7.3.   Reasons For Taking Drugs (Percentage of Respondents
Who Have Used Drugs: N=492)

Reason For Drug Use	Percentage Responding "Yes"
To Relieve Pain	88.2
To Control Weight	16.7
Out of Curiosity	24.2
To Cure or Prevent Illness	55.5
To Increase Pep	23.2
To Help You Get Through the Day or Night	15.4
For Enjoyment	30.3
To Calm Down	27.2
To Sleep	20.7

a.   Percentages do not sum to 100 percent since the
respondents could select several reasons.

pared. No data were available in 1972 for the narcotics which precluded comparisons being made for those drugs.

Table 7.3 presents the data relative to reasons for taking drugs. The overwhelming majority of respondents indicated they had used drugs for pain and a majority to cure or prevent illness. Many, however, used drugs for pleasure or to maintain some balance in their lives (speed up or calm down). Almost 25 percent used drugs out of curiosity.

The respondents were also asked about where they used drugs and with whom. These data are presented in Table 7.4.

A surprising finding is that many students used drugs at home. Other popular places for drug use are social gatherings, school, cars, and public places. Not surprising was the finding that drug use frequently occurred when friends were present, especially for marijuana, amphetamines, and barbiturates. Peer influence on drug use has been documented repeatedly (Goode 1979: 39; Kandel 1974: 207-209; National Commission on Marijuana and Drug Abuse, First Report 1972: 43; Ianni 1973: 613; Josephson 1974: 199) and the findings for the rural students is quite similar to the existing research literature.

The students were asked to indicate who they would seek to aid them if a friend with a drug problem needed help. These findings are presented in Table 7.5.

Table 7.4. Place Where Drug Was Used and With Whom Used (Percentage of Respondents Who Have Used Drug: N=492)

Drug Used	Place Where Drugs Are Used							With Whom Drugs Are Used			
	Home	Social Gatherings	School	Work	Public Places	Cars	Other Places	Alone	Friends	Family	Other
Barbiturates	19.1	8.9	10.0	2.6	8.7	8.9	2.6	11.0	19.3	8.7	0.8
Amphetamines	18.1	10.8	14.8	7.7	9.8	9.6	1.8	14.0	21.5	9.3	0.6
Opiates	34.1	2.8	4.5	1.6	2.0	2.4	1.4	9.3	7.7	25.8	1.0
Marijuana	20.5	25.8	22.6	11.0	19.5	36.6	2.2	16.9	49.8	8.9	0.6
Inhalants	4.3	1.0	1.4	1.0	1.4	3.0	0.6	2.2	3.3	2.6	0.6
Hallucinogens	4.1	4.3	4.7	1.6	4.5	4.9	1.0	3.9	8.5	1.8	1.0
Cocaine	3.7	5.5	2.6	1.6	3.9	5.3	0.6	3.3	9.3	2.6	0.4
Heroin	1.0	1.6	0.4	0.0	1.0	3.5	0.4	1.2	3.0	1.2	0.6
Methadone	2.0	1.0	0.6	0.2	1.4	2.6	1.8	1.8	2.8	2.2	2.6

a. Respondents frequently selected several places and different social conditions where drugs were used, therefore, the sum of the percentages will be greater than percentage of respondents indicating use of specific drugs noted in Table 7.2.

b. The data include legitimate users of codeine-based cough medication which inflates the percentage.

Table 7.5.   Where the Respondent Would Seek Aid For
Someone They Cared For Who Has A Drug
Problem (Percentage of Respondents:
N = 492)

Source of Aid	Percentage Seeking Aid For This Source
Medical Professional	9.8
Friend	36.4
Relative	19.7
Religious Leader	2.8
Teacher	1.6
Police	0.8
Social Worker	1.6
Telephone Hot Line	2.2
Drug Treatment Worker	8.5
Would Not Seek Help	13.4
Would Not Aid Friend With Drug Problem	2.0
No Data	1.0
Total	100.0

The student respondents revealed that they would seek aid most frequently from friends and family but many indicated that they would be hesitant to seek help from anyone. It is noteworthy that the people most frequently mentioned as the source of aid are probably the least qualified to help since a friend, especially a close friend, would probably be of the same age group and not be in a very good position to provide the type of aid needed to solve a drug-related problem. Unless the family members are sympathetic to the problems of the user and knowledgeable of drugs and drug use, they also may be of little help other than as a referral route to professional help.

A Test of the Research Expectations

Findings presented in Table 7.6 support in part the research expectations. Socioeconomic status indicators and perceived academic performance,

Table 7.6.   Zero Order Correlation For Selected Independent
Variables and Frequency of Drug Use (N=492)

Predictive Variable	Type of Drug Used					
	Barbiturates	Amphetamines	Opiates	Marijuana	Cocaine	Alcohol
Age	0.11	0.12	N.S.	0.19	N.S.	0.25
Grade Level	N.S.	N.S.	N.S.	0.15	N.S.	0.24
Sex	N.S.	0.10	N.S.	−0.11	−0.12	−0.11
Number of Siblings	N.S.	N.S.	N.S.	N.S.	N.S.	N.S.
Perceived Income	N.S.	N.S.	N.S.	N.S.	N.S.	N.S.
Parents' Marital Status	−0.11	−0.12	−0.11	−0.15	−0.12	−0.10
Parents' Inter Interpersonal Relations	N.S.	N.S.	N.S.	−0.14	N.S.	−0.17
Academic Performance	N.S.	N.S.	N.S.	N.S.	N.S.	N.S.
Experience With Serious Problems	0.17	0.18	0.14	0.19	0.10	0.22
Serious Problems Contribute to Use	0.27	0.20	0.17	0.25	0.20	0.21
Age of First Alcohol Use	−0.11	−0.12	−0.11	−0.13	N.S.	−0.09
Perception of Drug Problem in School	−0.18	−0.20	N.S.	−0.30	−0.13	−0.18
Perception of Orug Problem in Community	−0.14	−0.11	N.S.	−0.20	−0.12	−0.14

a. All missing data were assigned the variable mean and included in the analysis.

b. N.S. = Not Significant.

however, were not significantly correlated with frequency of drug use for any of the substances evaluated. Grade level was shown to be an insignificant predictor of drug use except for marijuana and alcohol. The same situation was noted for parents' interpersonal relations.

An important finding is the relative low correlations for all factors used as predictive variables. The amount of variance which can be explained in frequency of drug use is very small, thus, one must conclude that other variables are much better predictors of frequency of drug use than those included in this study. With few exceptions, the magnitude of the correlations is very low. This indicates that frequency of drug use for all drugs evaluated is basically randomly distributed. While general statements may be made relative to user characteristics within a specific class of drugs, it must be recognized that the predictive ability of the variables is quite low.

With this limitation stated, a summary of the findings from Table 7.6 is presented:

1. As age increases there is a slight tendency for drug use to increase. This finding is consistent with the literature noted and the research expectations.
2. Females tend to be more frequent users of amphetamines but less frequent users of marijuana, cocaine, and alcohol than males. Use of opiates and barbiturates are not differentiated by sex. These findings are basically similar to the national studies reported above and consistent with the research expectations.
3. Use of drugs was shown not to be a function of status indicators. Drug use was randomly distributed by class. This is contrary to the research expectations and the literature discussed above. These findings, however, demonstrate that drug use is no longer confined to lower class people but distributed throughout the socioeconomic classes.
4. Respondents with married parents who were living together in a harmonious manner tended to have a lower probability of being drug users than youngsters from broken homes. These findings are consistent with the research expectations and the reported drug use literature.
5. Academic performance was not significantly related to drug use. This is contrary to the research expectations derived from the existing literature but shows that drug users are not always the lowest achievers relative to academic performance.
6. Experience with serious problems was shown to be significantly related to greater drug use and to contribute to drug use. This is consistent with the research expectations and the existing research literature. It should be noted, however, that the relationship was relatively weak even though it was quite consistent.
7. Early use of alcohol tended to increase the probability that other drugs would be used more frequently. This finding is consistent with the research expectations and literature noted.
8. Perceptions of drug use as constituting a problem within the school and the community were significantly related to nearly all drug uses evaluated. Individuals who perceived drug use as constituting problems within the school and community tended not to use drugs as frequently as those who saw drugs as being of little consequence in the school and community.

Another finding of considerable interest is the frequency of multiple drug use among the study respondents. Almost 40 percent of the students who participated in the study indicated that they used drugs in combination. Of the drugs evaluated, alcohol was the most frequently mentioned drug used in combination with others. Slightly more than 26 percent of the respondents indicated that they used alcohol in combination with at least one other drug. The most frequently mentioned combination was alcohol and marijuana. Almost 39 percent of those persons reporting multiple drug use indicated that they used marijuana and alcohol on a regular basis. These findings are quite similar to those discovered in other youth related drug studies (Patch 1973: 977; Groves 1974: 259; Josephson 1974: 197; Goode 1971; McGlothlin 1974: 288-289; National Commission on Marijuana and Drug Abuse, First Report 1972: 32-33; National Commission on Marijuana and Drug Abuse, Second Report 1973: 70-71, 92-93; Ellinwood 1974: 308).

Summary and Conclusions

The study findings demonstrate that the percentage of rural high school students reporting drug use in 1979 was much higher for several drugs evaluated than comparable data from high school students in 1972 which were derived from averaging the findings from numerous studies conducted throughout the United States (many of the studies used to develop the 1972 drug abuse statistics were conducted in urban areas). Comparison of the Ohio findings with the 1972 data suggests that urban patterns of drug abuse have been diffused to rural areas and that drug use is probably increasing as noted in the introduction of this chapter. A similar conclusion was drawn by Bowker (1976) using data from a study conducted in the Pacific northwest using adult respondents. He observed that drug use among the rural respondents in his study were quite similar to findings generated in urban areas. While the extent of drug use noted in Bowker's study was low (Bowker 1976: 19), the pattern of use was similar to urban usage.

The magnitude of the drug use among rural youth is a very important finding in the research being reported here. Rural living has traditionally been perceived to be a major impediment to deviant behavior, especially drug abuse. Some evidence exists which supports the contention that rural areas have less of a drug problem than urban areas. The research findings reviewed by the National Commission on Marijuana and Drug Abuse (1972: 32, 1973: 66-67), for example, revealed that non-metropolitan areas had relatively low drug use prior to 1972. Research conducted by Forslund (1977-78), Heiligman (1973), Tolone and Dermott (1975), and Fischler (1975-76) demonstrated that rural drug use was relatively low when compared to national data. Heiligman (1973) did observe that the extent of drug use discovered among students in rural Minnesota indicates that drug abuse is no longer confined to the urban ghetto. While the Ohio study population may be atypical of rural areas in general, the findings raise serious questions about the validity of the belief that contemporary rural living still serves as a barrier to drug use influences for young people.

Several of the predictive variables selected for investigation (Table 7.6) were shown to be significantly related wfth frequency of drug use at the .05 level, but the strength of association was quite low. This finding indicates the nature of drug abuse among rural youth (probably urban as well) is much more complex than is commonly thought. Reliance upon existing theories and standard predictive variables will probably prove less fruitful than the development of new theoretical approaches and the identification and utilization of more relevant variables. These findings suggest that defining a "typical rural drug user" from the data is very difficult, if not impossible. Common stereotypes of the drug user as being a lower class male from a broken or strife ridden home, who is a low achiever in school, and subject to severe social and psychological stress is not true of the users in this study. While the patterns discovered within the data set are basically consistent with the existing literature in the field, all of the correlations with the frequency of drug use are quite low.

These findings also imply that urban oriented drug abuse prevention models cannot be applied easily to rural drug use. Apparently, drug use permeates the social fabric of the rural group under study to the extent that it affects people from all socioeconomic classes present with the county. Drug use is not confined to any identifiable socioeconomic subgroup, which implies that programs primarily designed for the urban ghetto poor will have little applicability to the rural study group. Innovative prevention programs designed to deal with rural social problems are sorely needed to address the rural drug issue.

The study findings should not be misconstrued as indicating that little can can be done to attack the drug problem discovered within the study county. The findings indicate that action programs do not have to be developed for a specific client group which can be identified by socioeconomic and psychological characteristics. Action programs designed primarily for youth and young adults should be appropriate. Educational modules designed for youth from differing social strata could conceivably be employed in school curricula to educate youth relative to the problems associated with drug use and to provide the students with information about how they could help a friend (or themselves) who developed a drug problem. Similar modules designed for parents would appear to be justified given the fact that family members would probably be sought out if a friend had a drug problem.

Any youth-oriented drug prevention program initiated in the county should incorporate some peer counseling since friends would be the people from whom they would seek help for a close associate with a drug problem. Peer counseling would probably function best in the initial contact stages with gradual substitution of adult professional help.

Notes

1. Drug abuse is defined as the use of illegal drugs. Use of a legal definition reflects the value structure of the society in terms of how the substance being used is perceived by the group. Many substances have both beneficial and negative effects and a legal definition provides a means of assessing the legitimacy of substance use (Josephson and Carroll 1974:xx).
2. The authors have no reason to believe that the county selected for study is atypical of other agriculturally oriented counties of the state but do not claim generalizability of the findings. Additional research must be undertaken to verify the findings in other counties before generalizability is claimed.

References

Abelson, H., Cahn, R., Schrayer, D., and Rappeport, M. 1973. *Drug Experiences, Attitudes, and Related Behavior among Adolescents and Adults*. Princeton, N.J.: National Commission on Marijuana and Drug Abuse, Response Analysis Corporation.

Bates, W., and Crowther, B. 1973. *Drugs: Causes, Circumstances, and Effects of Their Use*. Morristown, N.J.: General Learning Press.

Blum, R. 1969. *Students and Drugs*. Jossey Bass Publishers.

Bowker, L.H. 1976. "The Incidence of Drug Use and Associated Factors in Two Small Towns: A Community Survey." *Bulletin on Narcotics* 28 (4):17-25.

Calahan, D., Cisin, I., and Crossley, H. 1969. *American Drinking Practices: A National Study of Drinking Behavior and Attitudes*. Rutgers, New Jersey: Rutgers Center For Alcohol Studies, Rutgers University.

Cushman, P. 1971. "Methadone Maintenance in Hard-Core Criminal Addicts: Economic Effects." *New York State Journal of Medicine* 71:1768-74.

Eckerman, W.C., Bates, J.D., Rachal, J.V., and Poole, W.K. 1971. In *Drug Usage and Arrest Charges, A Study of Drug Usage and Arrest Charges among Arrestees in Six Metropolitan Areas of the United States*. Washington, D.C.: Drug Enforcement Administration.

Ellinwood, E. 1974. "The Epidemiology of Stimulant Abuse." In F. Josephson and E. Carroll, eds. *Drug Use: Epidemiological and Sociological Approaches*. Washington, D.C.: Hemisphere Publishing Corporation.

Festinger, L. 1957. *The Theory of Cognitive Dissonance*. Stanford, California: The Stanford University Press.

Forslund, M.A. 1977-78. "Drug Use and Delinquent Behavior of Small Town and Rural Youth." *Journal of Drug Education* 7 (3):219-24.

Fort, J. 1969. *The Pleasure Seekers: The Drug Crisis, Youth and Society*. New York: Bobbs-Merrill.

Goode, E. 1971. "The Use of Marijuana and Other Illegal Drugs on a College Campus." *The British Journal of Addiction* 66:213-15.

Groves, W. 1974. "Patterns of College Student Drug Use and Lifestyles." In E. Josephson and E. Carroll, eds. *Drug Use: Epidemiological and Sociological Approaches*. Washington, D.C.: Hemisphere Publishing Corporation.

Heiligman, A.C. 1973. "A Survey of Drug Use in a Rural Minnesota Senior High School." *Drug Forum* 2 (2):173-77.

Hogan, R., Mankin, O., Conway, J., and Fox, F. 1970. "Personality Correlates of Undergraduate Marijuana Use." *Journal of Consulting and Clinical Psychology* 35:58-63.

Ianni, F.A. 1973. "Attitudes towards the Relationship among Stress-Relief, Advertising and Youthful Drug Abuse in Two Recent Field Studies." In *Drug Use in America: Problem in Perspective* Vol. 2. National Commission on Marijuana and Drug Abuse. Washington, D.C.: U.S. Government Printing Office.

Inciardi, J.A., and Chambers, C.D. 1972. "Unreported Criminal Involvement of Narcotic Addicts." *Journal of Drug Issues* 2:57-64.

Johnson, K., Abbey, H., Scheble, R., and Weitman, M. 1972. "Survey of Adolescent Drug Use." *American Journal of Public Health*.

Josephson, E. 1974. "Trends in Adolescent Marijuana Use." In E. Josephson and E. Carroll, eds. *Drug Use: Epidemiological and Sociological Approaches*. Washington, D.C.: Hemisphere Publishing Corporation.

Judd, L., Gunderson, E., Alexander, G., Attewell, P., Buckingham, B., Blau, E., Crichton, J., Mandell, A., and Schuckit, J. 1973. "Youth Drug Survey." In *Drug Use in America: Problem in Perspective*, Vol. 2, National Commission on Marijuana and Drug Abuse. Washington D.C.: U.S. Government Printing Office.

Kandel, D. 1974. "Interpersonal Influences on Adolescent Illegal Drug Use." In E. Josephson and E. Carroll, eds. *Drug Use: Epidemiological and Sociological Approaches*. Washington, D.C. Hemisphere Publishing Company.

Lombrillo, J.R. and Hain, J.D. 1972. "Patterns of Drug Use in a High School Population." *American Journal of Psychiatry* 128:836-41.

McGlothlin, W., Anglin, M.D., and Wilson, B.D. 1978. "Narcotic Addiction and Crime." *Criminology* 16 (3):293-315.

McGlothlin, W. 1971. *Marijuana: An Analysis of Use Distribution and Control*. U.S. Bureau of Narcotics and Dangerous Drugs. Washington, D.C.: U.S. Government Printing Office.

National Commission on Marijuana and Drug Abuse. 1972. *Marijuana: A Signal of Misunderstanding*. Washington, D.C.: U.S. Government Printing Office (First Report).

————. 1973. *Drug Use in America: Problem in Perspective*. Washington, D.C.: U.S. Government Printing Office (Second Report).

O'Donnell, J., and Ball, J. 1966. *Narcotic Addiction*. New York: Harper and Row.

Patch, Vernon D. 1973. "Public Health Aspects of Adolescent Drug Use." In *Drug Use in America: Problem in Perspective*, Vol. 1, National Commission on Marijuana and Drug Abuse. Washington, D.C.: U.S. Government Printing Office.

Rainwater, L. 1967. *And the Poor Get Children*. Chicago, Illinois: Quadrangle Books.

San Mateo County Department of Public Health and Welfare. 1971. *Five Mind Altering Drugs*. San Mateo, California.

————. 1973. *Preliminary Summary, 1973.* San Mateo, California.

Solomon, D., ed. 1968. *The Marijuana Papers.* New York: Bobbs-Merrill Publishers.

Tolone, W.L., and Dermott, D. 1975. "Some Correlates of Drug Use among High School Youth in a Midwestern Rural Community." *The International Journal of the Addictions* 10 (5):761-77.

Wechsler, H. 1976. "Alcohol Intoxication and Drug Use among Teen-Agers." *Journal of Studies on Alcohol* 37 (11): 1672-77.

8

The Nature of Vandalism Among Rural Youth

JOSEPH F. DONNERMEYER
and G. HOWARD PHILLIPS

Introduction

A recent newspaper article described vandalism in the United States as a "$2 Billion-a-Year Tantrum" (Shannon 1979:1). Schools alone were reported vandalized to the amount of $600 million annually. Homes and automotive vehicles were also frequent targets of a growing and costly form of criminal behavior. The findings reported in a more rcent study suggest that the problem may be far greater than the newspaper headline quoted. The study, summarized by *U.S. News and World Report* (1979:59), estimated that the crime of vandalism to commercial establishments alone exceeded $2.5 billion per year.

The FBI (U.S. Department of Justice 1979:320) defines vandalism as:

> ... the willful or malicious destruction, injury, disfigurement or defacement of any public or private property, real or personal, without consent of the owner or person having custody or control, by cutting, tearing, breaking,

marking, painting, drawing, covering with filth, or any other means as may be specified by local law.

In 1978, 223,391 persons were arrested for committing acts of vandalism (U.S. Department of Justice 1978:187).

The reader may initially assume that vandalism is more extensive in the larger cities of the United States. However, several recent rural crime studies have documented that vandalism is an extensive problem in rural areas as well. A 1975 investigation of the types of crimes occurring to open-country households in Ohio found that nearly one in every six households were the victims of at least one act of vandalism annually (Phillips 1976). Similar research was undertaken in a rural farm community in Northwest Indiana in 1977-78, and in a coal county in Southwest Indiana in 1978-79. Findings indicated that nearly 10 percent of the open-country and small town households had an act of vandalism committed against them (Smith 1979; Donnermeyer et al. 1981).

Rural businesses also appear to be frequent targets for vandalism. The Northwest Indiana rural crime study extended its analysis to include local commercial establishments. Vandalism was one of the most frequently mentioned crimes occurring to commercial establishments, accounting for nearly 30 percent of all criminal incidents reported. The average cost of an act of vandalism was calculated to be about $80 (Smith 1979). Results from a study of crimes committed against farm retail outlets, including both roadside markets and pick-your-own operations, indicated that vandalism was the most serious problem in both volume of incidents occurring and average cost per incident. Nearly one-half of the farm retail outlets had experienced at least one act of vandalism annually. Average cost per incident was $83 (Donnermeyer et al. 1980).

Vandalism to rural public property likewise has become a multimillion dollar problem. Research on the expense for repair or replacement of vandalized road signs located on county roads in rural Ohio found an annual cost figure of $20.27 per mile (Donnermeyer et al. 1980).

The findings from these research projects clearly indicate that vandalism is a costly crime. Who commits vandalism in rural areas? Arrest records of Sheriff departments from the rural Ohio crime study found the offender to be most often a teenager (Phillips, 1976). Whether it occurs in urban or rural areas, vandalism has long been considered a "youth crime." One conception of vandalism is that of the "boys-will-be-boys" variety. Vandalism committed by rural youth in particular is perceived as a "traditional" act associated, for example, with Halloween. Acts such as turning over outhouses are tolerated by property owners in their attempts to cooperate with the spirit of the holiday. Having sustained nothing more than minor damage, the outhouse is merely put back in place the next day.

A second conception is that destructive and malicious acts of vandalism are committed by only a small proportion of young persons, and that generally it is the result of a poor family environment or some other form of social malaise which causes the vandal to exhibit "abnormal" behavioral patterns. Therefore, if rural youth engage in vandalistic behavior of a destructive nature, it must somehow be "abnormal" or "atypical," and is caused by idiosyncratic or circumstantial characteristics associated with the social environment of the individual vandal. However, conceptions are one thing, reality is another.

The purpose of this chapter is to examine the pattern of rural vandalism. This discussion is based upon evidence reviewed from two studies of self-reported vandalistic behavior among rural high school students. An attempt is made to answer four basic questions. First, how widespread is involvement in vandalistic behavior among rural youth? Second, what are the situational characteristics associated with the commission of vandalism by rural youth? Third, what motivates rural youth to commit acts of vandalism? Finally, are there differences between the vandal and nonvandal by their age, sex, family background, attendance at church, and participation in extra-curricular activities? Before moving to a discussion of the research findings, a brief description of the two vandalism studies is presented.

Study Areas

THE OHIO STUDY

The Ohio vandalism study was part of a broader research project on the phenomenon of rural crime.[1] The larger project had randomly selected one cluster of three contiguous counties from each of three substate regions of Ohio. These substate regions included the Industrial Northeast, Appalachia (Southeast), and the Corn Belt (Central and Western Ohio). The sample consisted of all sophomore level students from one high school within each of the three clusters. The high schools from which the sample was selected were predominantly rural in nature. The three high schools were within local county school districts. High schools from city and village school districts were not considered as part of the universe from which the samples were selected because of the possibility that a larger proportion of the student body would be from urban areas.

The sophomore level was selected because this grade level contains mostly 15- and 16-year-olds. Students in this age group become licensed drivers and this phenomenon was hypothesized to be related to a marked increase in vandalistic behavior.

The total number of sophomores from the three high schools was 634. The survey instrument was administered at the high schools in March 1975. The instrument was distributed to 599 sophomores, of whom 572 returned usable responses. The absentee rate among sophomores during the day on which the survey was administered at each high school averaged 5.5 percent.

The questionnaires were group-administered. Students were instructed not to put their name or any other form of identification on the questionnaire. Upon completion, each student inserted his own survey instrument through a slot into a sealed box.

The content of the survey instrument relied upon self-reports by the respondent with respect to committing acts of vandalism. The instrument included questionnaire items on the number of acts of vandalism engaged in by the respondent. In addition, for the most recent act of vandalism, more detailed information surrounding the event was asked, such as when the act was committed, number of persons present, type of property which was damaged or destroyed, how the respondent became involved, and self-perceptions of his own vandalistic behavior. The instrument also included questions pertaining to the social, economic, and family background of the respondent.

THE INDIANA STUDY

The Indiana vandalism study was conducted in an effort to replicate the results of the Ohio study.[2] Following some minor changes in wording and format, the same survey instrument was employed. In addition, the survey instrument was supplemented with a series of items on participation in extra-curricular activities, both those associated with the local high school, and out-of-school activities. These items were included in an effort to examine the relationship between the likelihood of committing vandalism and participation in extra-curricular activities.

The survey instrument was administered to 354 junior level (eleventh grade) high school students from two school districts in a rural county of Southwestern Indiana. The largest city in the county had a population of about 2,700 persons, according to the 1979 Census estimate of the population. The economy of the county is dominated by the coal industry, with agriculture also important.

The survey instrument was administered to the junior class in May 1979. At both high schools, the survey was group-administered. School personnel were available to monitor the process. However, in order to assure students complete anonymity for their responses, at no time were school officials allowed to handle the survey forms. The average absentee rate on the days the instruments were administered to both junior classes was about 4 percent.

Both the Ohio and Indiana samples represented a large segment of youth growing up in the contemporary social and cultural environment of rural areas in the Midwest. The purpose of both studies was to examine vandalistic behavior among typical young persons from rural areas. Neither study was designed to measure the vandalistic behavior of high school drop-outs or chronic truants. These individuals comprise only a small proportion of the total rural youth population.

Committing Vandalism

What proportion of the students engaged in vandalism? The FBI definition of vandalism as "malicious destruction" was utilized in both studies in order to define vandalistic behavior for the respondents. Based upon the FBI definition of vandalism, nearly 52 percent of the Ohio and Indiana respondents admitted to committing one or more acts of vandalism during their lifetime (Table 8.1). The similarity in results of the studies was so striking, given that both were administered independently in different states.

Table 8.1 also indicates that vandalism was a recurring form of behavior. Among those who had participated in vandalism, nearly three quarters of the Ohio respondents, and three-fifths of the Indiana respondents, had committed at least three acts of vandalism.

Types and Severity of Vandalism

These results suggest that vandalism among rural youth may be a very normal form of behavior, given that a slight majority of rural youth did actually commit vandalism. However, it is important to ask: (1) what were the types of vandalism in which rural youth engaged? and (2) what were the levels of destruction? The Indiana study expanded the analysis of rural vandalism by soliciting a brief narrative description of the most recent act of vandalism in which the respondents had engaged. Each description was classified into one of four categories, according to the severity of the vandalistic act. Severity was defined as the degree of damage or destruction to the vandalized property. Damage or destruction was designated as referring to either the dollar value of the effected object and/or to the amount of work or effort necessary for the victim to

Table 8.1.   Frequency of Participation in Acts of Vandalism
Among Rural Youth

| Number of | Study Area | | | |
| Vandalistic Acts | Ohio | | Indiana | |
Committed	Number	Percent	Number	Percent
None	277	48.4	169	47.7
One or Two	76	13.3	75	21.2
Three or More	219	38.3	110	31.1
Total	572	100.0	354	100.0

repair, clean up, or in some way correct the damage. The four categories included: (1) minor; (2) somewhat serious; (3) serious; and (4) very serious.[3]

Types of vandalism which fell into the minor category included such "traditional" activities as soaping car or house windows and draping toilet paper over trees, shrubs, houses, and other objects. Minor acts of vandalism composed 26.2 percent of all acts described by respondents to the Indiana study.

The "somewhat serious" category exhibited more malicious examples of vandalism. Typical of the vandalistic acts at this level included throwing eggs at cars and houses, damaging or attempting to crush trashcans, spray painting road signs, and digging up bushes in yards. What may perhaps be a unique form of rural vandalism was the practice by one respondent of filling the purses of female students at his high school with fresh cow manure.

These examples of vandalism from the "somewhat serious" category generally manifested either a modest dollar cost or some inconveniences to the victim to clean up or repair the damage. This level of vandalism represented 29.6 percent of the total acts described by the Indiana sample.

The type of vandalism classified as "serious" included such acts as breaking street lights or house windows, shooting out road signs, and spray painting automotive vehicles. Two particular types of vandalism included in this category required access to a car or truck. These were "driving a 4-wheel drive vehicle" through a recreation area in order to rip up the sod on the baseball and other playing fields and driving through a graveyard for the purpose of damaging gravestones. Acts of vandalism within the "serious" category made up 35.3 percent of all acts described in the Indiana study.

Within the "very serious" category were included the most malicious forms of property destruction and defacement. Examples of the type of vandalistic acts at this level of severity were breaking out car windows, ripping out drive-in theater speakers from their stands, burning down a barn, and "destroying" the interior of a hotel room. These examples of vandalistic behavior, accounting for 8.9 percent of the total, generally represented a high dollar cost to the victim.

In summary, the patterns which emerge about vandalism by rural youth from the Ohio and Indiana studies revealed several major points. First, vandalism was not an activity restricted to only a few so-called bad apples. A slight majority of the respondents from both studies had committed at least one act of vandalism in their lifetime. Second, vandalism by rural youth was not a "one time" action. Most of the rural high school students from the Ohio and Indiana studies admitted to having committed three or more acts of vandalism. Third, nearly three-quarters of the vandalism represented a level of severity which, from the point of view of the victim, generally would be considered as more than a simple Halloween prank. Descriptions of vandalism provided by respondents in the Indiana study indicated extensive property damage, and in only one-quarter of the cases could the act of vandalism be viewed as a "Halloween style" prank.

Circumstances Associated with the Commission of Vandalism

Respondents to both the Ohio and Indiana studies were asked a series of follow-up questions on the situation and circumstances related to the most recent act of vandalism in which they had participated. Explored here are several specific patterns of vandalism by rural youth, such as the location and type of property vandalized, when acts of vandalism were committed, whether or not vandalism was an individual behavior or if it occurred in a group setting, the mode of transportation to the site where the vandalism took place, and the use of alcohol and drugs in association with the commission of the act.

LOCATION AND TYPE OF PROPERTY VANDALIZED

Where did the vandalism committed by the rural youth take place? Did it only occur in rural areas? Or, was it restricted to the Main Street of nearby small towns? Or instead, did it tend to occur in larger cities outside the rural young person's county of residence?

Forty-three percent of the most recent acts of vandalism committed by the respondents from the Ohio study and 49 percent from the Indiana study, were located exclusively in rural areas. The type of property most frequently vandalized in rural areas was the nonfarm residence. Public property located in rural areas was vandalized nearly as often.

An urban location was the site for vandalism in 35 percent of the time in the Ohio study and approximately 40 percent of the time in the Indiana study. A residence was the most frequent target for vandalism in an urban area. As in the pattern of vandalism committed in rural locations, public property was the second most frequent target in urban locations.

Most of the vandalism committed by rural youth occurred in the county of residence. Nearly 83 percent of the most recent acts of vandalism described in the Ohio study, and about 70 percent from the Indiana study, occurred in the county of residence of the perpetrator. If the site for vandalism was located outside of the county of residence, it tended to be within the boundary of a nearby city or town that was easily accessible by car. However, the most important insight which emerged was that vandalism within small town and rural communities was "local" and not due to "outsiders."

WHEN VANDALISM OCCURRED

It has long been assumed that there is a temporal pattern to vandalism. One such assumption is that vandalism is an activity which manifests itself most often during the autumn months, while another is that vandalism was made for weekends. In both studies, the three autumn months of September, October, and November were most likely to be the time in which vandalism occurred. Thirty-one percent of the most recent acts of vandalism from the Ohio study and 49 percent from the Indiana study were committed during the fall months. However in Ohio, it was nearly as likely for the vandalism to have occurred during the winter months of December, January, and February (28 percent). Only 10 percent of the vandalism committed by rural youth from the Indiana study took place in the winter. In the Ohio study, 18 percent of the vandalism was committed during the spring (March, April, and May), and 23 percent during the summer (June, July, and August). In the Indiana study, 29 percent of the vandalism was committed during the spring months, and 12 percent during the summer months.

Despite the differences in the distribution of vandalism by season of the year between the Ohio and Indiana studies, both demonstrate two things. First, the greatest proportion of vandalism committed by rural youth occurred during the autumn season (i.e., the Halloween season).

Second, despite this fact, in both studies over one-half of the incidents of vandalism took place during the other nine months of the year. This indicates that vandalism was spread throughout the full year. These findings strongly support the contention that vandalism is no longer prankism associated with Halloween, but a year-round problem.

According to the day of the week, nearly three out of every five acts of vandalism committed by students in the Ohio study, and over two-thirds of those perpetrated by the students in the Indiana study, took place during the weekend (Friday, Saturday, and Sunday). The remaining proportion of vandalism in both studies was evenly spread throughout the other four days of the week. In addition, the Ohio study found that a majority of the vandalism occurred in the early evening hours, from 5 P.M. to 8 P.M.

These results indicate that vandalism among rural youth was a leisure time activity. Weekdays, for nine or ten months of the year, are "open" and less structured with respect to the use of non-school hours. This has largely been due to the fact that there is a reduced need for youth in work-related roles in contemporary rural society. As a result, this free time is often filled with activities, such as vandalism, which are in violation of the behavioral prescriptions of society.

VANDALISM AS A GROUP ACTIVITY

One of the most powerful social forces influencing the behavior of high school-age youth is the peer group. Peer group pressure may be translated in many ways, but very often it means a set of norms and values which deviate from the larger culture. As a result, a young person must often choose between conflicting loyalties, that is, between what his friends of the same age want him to do, and what his family and other authority figures define as proper.

Generally, vandalism has been recognized as a "group activity." The Ohio and Indiana studies confirm a similar pattern among rural youth. In both studies, between 90 to 95 percent of the most recent acts of vandalism described by the respondents were committed in association with one or more other individuals. About one-quarter of the vandalistic acts involved a group with only two persons, and about one-quarter included three persons. Approximately two out of every five acts of vandalism were committed in groups of four or more persons.

MODE OF TRANSPORTATION AND VANDALISM

In both studies, the predominant mode of transportation was a motor vehicle. Forty-seven percent of the most recent acts of vandalism in Ohio and 60 percent in Indiana involved the use of a motor vehicle. Most of the time the motor vehicle was a car. Only in about 20 percent of the cases was the motor vehicle a truck or motorcycle. Walking was the second most popular means of travel in both studies, representing 35 percent of the total in Ohio and 28 percent in Indiana. The remaining cases of vandalism involved other modes of transportation, such as a bicycle or a combination of walking and a motor vehicle.

ALCOHOL AND DRUGS

In the description of their most recent act of vandalism, the respondents from the Ohio and Indiana studies were asked if they or other persons in the group were drinking alcoholic beverages or using drugs prior to the time at which the vandalism took place. Nearly 40 percent of rural youth in the Ohio study and 46 percent from Indiana said that alcohol was being consumed. Beer and whiskey were the most often mentioned types of alcohol from the Ohio youth. While beer was also popular among the Indiana youth, whiskey was barely mentioned.

About 12 percent of the respondents from the Ohio study said that either themselves or someone in the group had been using drugs near the time that the vandalism was committed. Among those from the Indiana study, about 18 percent mentioned the use of drugs. In both cases, marijuana was the most popular drug in use.

Perception of Vandalism by Rural Youth

How did rural youth who committed vandalism perceive their own actions? Was vandalism viewed as a game or joke? Or, was it viewed as something more serious? The Ohio study found that a majority of those who had committed an act of vandalism became involved because they "just happened to be there," "were bored," "playing around," or "pressured by others." Significantly, less than one in ten described their involvement in vandalism as a "Halloween prank" or "practical joke." In essence, involvement was unplanned and, in many cases, even spontaneous.

Table 8.2 summarizes the self-perceptions of respondents in both the Ohio and Indiana studies about their vandalistic behavior. It is readily apparent that a large majority of the respondents viewed their most recent act of vandalism as a game, joke, or contest. In other words, the commission of vandalism was perceived as "just for fun." Less than one out of every five acts of vandalism was viewed as "getting even" or revenge, and fewer than 10 percent were perceived as the consequences of other reasons, such as seeking to draw attention to a problem or issue,

Table 8.2. Self-perceptions of Vandalistic Behavior
            by Rural Youth

| | Study Area | | | |
| | Ohio | | Indiana | |
Behavior	Number	Percent	Number	Percent
A Game, Fun, Contest, etc.	164	64.3	102	67.5
Getting Even, Revenge	32	12.5	29	19.2
Side Effect of Committing a More Serious Offense	20	7.8	10	6.6
An Expression of Rage	11	4.3	0	0.0
To Draw Attention to an Issue or Grievance	10	3.9	5	3.3
Other Reasons	18	7.1	5	3.3
Total	255	100.0	151	100.0
No Information	40	---	34	---

expressing rage, or associated with the commission of some other crime. The Ohio study expanded analysis of self-perception of vandalism to include whether or not the respondents viewed their own vandalistic behavior as a criminal act. Nearly 71 percent did not view their behavior as in any way constituting a crime or as wrong.

Clinard and Quinney (1967) likewise found that most vandals did not perceive their behavior as criminal. The concensus among social scientists who have studied vandalistic behavior is that in general it is motivated by competitive and status-seeking opportunities within the peer group setting. As evidenced by the results from the Ohio and Indiana studies, these same social forces appear to be operative among rural youth.

Who Committed Vandalism Among Rural Youth

The results from the Ohio and Indiana studies have indicated that a slight majority of rural youth had engaged in acts of vandalism at least once in their lifetime. Furthermore, among a great majority of these individuals, vandalism was a recurring form of behavior. Who among rural youth participated in vandalistic behavior? Was there a profile of what the typical rural vandal looked like with respect to such characteristics as sex, age, family background, and participation in organized youth activities?

AGE AND SEX

It is generally assumed that among younger persons, males would be far more prone to engage in vandalistic behavior than females. The results from both studies confirm that a greater proportion of males were involved in vandalism than their female counterparts. Slightly over 68 percent of the male respondents in the Ohio study and 62 percent of the males from the Indiana study participated in vandalism. In contrast, only about 37 percent of the female students in the Ohio study and nearly 43 percent of the females from the Indiana study engaged in vandalistic behavior. Although there was a considerable difference between the male and female respondents, it is noteworthy that among the female group, nearly two out of every five had committed an act of vandalism. While males tended to be the major perpetrators, vandalism was certainly not a behavior engaged in exclusively by the male sex.

Was there a difference in the proportion of rural youth who committed acts of vandalism according to their age? The Ohio study indicated that among sophomore students, there was no difference in the proportion of youth 15 years of age and under who had committed vandalism when compared with sophomores 16 years and over. In fact, there was a slightly higher proportion of the 15 and under age group (53.2 percent) who had engaged in vandalistic behavior than among those 16 and over (50.4 percent). In stark contrast, the results from the Indiana study of junior students indicated a significant difference by age, and in the opposite direction from the Ohio findings. Only about 43 percent of the juniors 16 years of age and younger had been involved in vandalism compared to slightly over 56 percent of those 17 years and over. This may suggest a marked rise in participation as young persons achieve or approach their seventeenth year. Additional research, however, is necessary in order to further clarify the relationship between age and vandalism.

MARITAL STATUS OF HOUSEHOLD HEAD

One common image of the teenage vandal is that he or she is likely to come from a "broken home," which generally means a one parent household. Information on the relationship between marital status and participation in vandalism is shown in Table 8.3. The findings from the Ohio study indicate a significant difference according to involvement in vandalism between those youth who were from a situation in which the household head was married and those in which the household head was divorced, separated, or widowed. There was a similar pattern found in the results from the Indiana study, although the difference was not statistically significant.

Table 8.3.   Involvement of Rural Youth in Acts of Vandalism
and Marital Status of Household Head

| Study Area | Involvement in Acts of Vandalism | | | | | |
| | Yes | | No | | Total | |
	Number	Percent	Number	Percent	Number	Percent
OHIO						
Married	236	49.4	242	50.6	478	100.0
Divorced, Separated, or Widowed	37	69.8	16	30.2	53	100.0
Total	273	51.4	278	46.6	531	100.0

$$x^2 \leq .01, \quad C=S.$$

INDIANA						
Married	156	51.5	147	48.5	303	100.0
Divorced, Separated, or Widowed	22	61.1	14	38.9	36	100.0
Total	178	52.5	161	47.5	339	100.0

$$x^2 > .05, \quad C = N.S.$$

In an earlier discussion about the temporal occurrence of vandalism committed by rural youth, it was suggested that vandalism is a consequence of how free time is used. The results from Table 8.3 further suggest that degree of parental supervision, as measured by the marital status of the household head, does have something to do with whether or not rural youth engage in vandalistic behavior. The Ohio study extended analysis of the relationship between vandalism and family background by examining the young person's orientation toward participation in family activities. The respondent was asked to indicate the degree to which he "liked" or "disliked" doing things with his family. The relationship between involvement in vandalism and both of these factors is summarized in Table 8.4. There was a significant difference between feelings about participating in family activities and involvement in vandalism. Only 39 percent of those who indicated that they "very much" liked to do things with their family had committed acts of vandalism. Comparatively, slightly over 57 percent of those who "disliked" participating in family activities had engaged in vandalistic behavior.

Most explanations of delinquent behavior consider the strength of the bond between the adolescent and the parents to be a critical factor (Natalino 1979:3-6). For instance, Hirschi (1969) has found that an

Table 8.4.   Involvement of Rural Ohio High School Sophomores
             in Acts of Vandalism and Self-perception about
             Participation in Family Activities

Feelings About Being With and Doing Things With the Family	Involvement in Vandalism					
	Yes		No		Total	
	Number	Percent	Number	Percent	Number	Percent
Like to Very Much	57	39.0	89	61.0	146	100.0
Like to Somewhat	188	56.0	148	44.0	336	100.0
Dislike	42	57.5	31	42.5	73	100.0
Total	287	51.7	268	48.3	555	100.0

$$X^2 \leq .01, \; C=S.$$

effective deterrent to delinquent behavior in general is the internalization of parental norms and conformity to parental expectations. The findings in Table 8.4 show a similar pattern with respect to the commission of vandalism. Rural youth who perceived themselves as negatively oriented toward participation in family activities manifested a greater tendency to become involved in vandalism. In contrast, rural youth who perceived themselves as positively oriented toward participation in family activities were less prone to engage in vandalistic behavior.

RELIGIOUS AFFILIATION

In addition to the family, a second important institution in rural society is the church. Did affiliation with and participation in church-related activities differentiate the vandal from the nonvandal among rural youth? Table 8.5 summarizes the results from the Ohio and Indiana studies on this question. In both cases, membership alone had little effect on involvement in vandalistic behavior. Nearly 52 percent of the rural youth from the Ohio study who had committed an act of vandalism were formally affiliated with a church. This compared to about 53 percent of those from the vandal group who had no religious affiliation whatsoever. There was a somewhat greater difference between vandals and nonvandals according to the proportion who were affiliated with a church in the Indiana study. The differential, however, was not statistically significant.

In addition to religious affiliation, both studies also collected information on the frequency of participation in religious and church-related activities. The findings in Table 8.5 do indicate that rural youth from both studies who participated frequently in church-related activities had

Table 8.5   Involvement of Rural Youth in Acts of Vandalism
and Membership and Participation in Church
Activities

| Study Area | Involvement in Acts of Vandalism | | | | | |
| | Yes | | No | | Total | |
	Number	Percent	Number	Percent	Number	Percent
OHIO						
Church Membership						
Yes	212	51.9	203	48.9	415	100.0
No	73	52.9	65	47.1	138	100.0
Total	285	51.5	268	48.5	553	100.0

$$x^2 > .05, \text{ C=N.S.}$$

Frequency of Participation						
Weekly	44	42.0	58	58.0	100	100.0
Several Times Per Month	102	52.3	93	47.9	195	100.0
Rarely/Never	147	54.6	122	45.4	269	100.0
Total	291	51.6	273	48.4	564	100.0

$$x^2 \leq .05, \text{ C=N.S.}$$

INDIANA						
Church Membership						
Yes	139	50.4	137	49.6	276	100.0
No	34	57.6	25	42.4	59	100.0
Total	173	51.6	162	48.4	335	100.0

$$x^2 > .05, \text{ C=N.S.}$$

Frequency						
Weekly	86	46.0	101	54.0	187	100.0
Several Times Per Month	23	57.5	17	42.5	40	100.0
Rarely/Never	63	58.9	44	41.1	107	100.0
Total	172	51.5	162	48.5	334	100.0

$$x^2 \leq .05, \text{ C=N.S.}$$

a.   Chi-square was computed with 1 degree of freedom based upon weekly vs.
non-weekly participation in religious activities.

a lesser tendency to have engaged in acts of vandalism. For instance, 42 percent of the sophomores from the Ohio study who participated in religious activities weekly had committed an act of vandalism compared to nearly 55 percent who "rarely" or "never" got involved in church-related affairs. Likewise, 46 percent of the juniors from the Indiana study who participated in church-related activities had been involved in the commission of an act of vandalism, compared to nearly 59 percent who participated "rarely" or "never."

These findings suggest that religious affiliation does not differentiate the vandal from the nonvandal among rural youth. However, when viewed from degree of participation in church-related activities, there was a significant difference. A social control theory of delinquent be-

Table 8.6.   Involvement of Rural Indiana High School Juniors
              in Acts of Vandalism and Participation in
              Extra-Curricular Activities

Participation in Extra-Curricular Activities	Involvement in Acts of Vandalism					
	Yes		No		Total	
	Number	Percent	Number	Percent	Number	Percent
School-Related Activities						
One or More	102	49.5	104	50.5	206	100.0
None	73	53.7	63	46.3	136	100.0
Total	175	51.2	167	48.8	342	100.0

$$x^2 > .05, \text{ C=N.S.}$$

Out of School Activities						
One or More	81	47.6	89	52.4	170	100.0
None	96	55.5	77	44.5	173	100.0
Total	177	51.6	166	48.4	343	100.0

$$x^2 > .05, \text{ C=N.S.}$$

havior "holds that non-delinquent youth are insulated from delinquency by strong ties to the conventional order" (Natalino 1979:2). The role of the family is one important aspect of this, and the results from the Ohio study (Table 8.4) indicate the effect of family life on involvement in vandalism. This pattern was equally reinforced by the relationship regarding participation in church activities and vandalism.

PARTICIPATION IN EXTRA-CURRICULAR ACTIVITIES

Since participation in church-related activities did distinguish the vandal from the nonvandal, what was the relationship between participation in extra-curricular activities, both in and out of school, and vandalism? In an attempt to examine this question, the Indiana study included a series of questions on participation in clubs, organized sporting events, and other associations, either affiliated with the school or sponsored by other organizations (i.e., 4-H, Rural Youth, softball leagues, senior scouts, etc.). As the results summarized in Table 8.6 indicate, there was at best a weak association between participation in extra-curricular activities and involvement in vandalism. There was a slight tendency for those with no extra-curricular activities to have engaged in vandalistic behavior. However, the percentage difference was not statistically significant.

These results did not support the common sense notion that participation in organized activities outside of regular school hours reduces the likelihood that the young person will engage in vandalistic behavior. It appears that there is a qualitative dimension to participation in organized activities that needs to be examined more fully before a complete understanding of its relationship to deviant behavior can be attained.

Vandalism Among Rural Youth: Summary of Findings

The Ohio and Indiana studies highlight several important patterns about vandalism among rural youth. First, contrary to popular belief, most acts of vandalism were not "harmless pranks." Based upon descriptions provided by the junior high school students from the Indiana study, nearly three out of every four acts of vandalism involved either a direct economic cost to the victim or an indirect cost in terms of the victim's time to repair or clean up damage. Second, slightly over one-half of the rural youth in the two samples had participated in at least one act of vandalism, and a majority had been repeatedly involved three or more times. Third, evidence from both the Ohio and Indiana studies indicated that vandalism was "normatively acceptable" behavior. Not only had a majority of the respondents engaged in vandalistic behavior three or more times, but nearly two-thirds in both study areas perceived vandalism as a "game" or "joke." Additional analysis of the self-perceptions of their own vandalistic behavior among the Ohio sample indicated that very few viewed their action as in any way criminal. Further evidence that vandalism was normatively acceptable came from the fact that over nine out of every ten vandals in both samples committed their act while with one or more persons, that is, in a "group" setting.

A fourth important pattern that emerged from the data was that vandalistic behavior was likely to occur in the county of residence of the vandal. The most likely target was a private residence, although public property was only slightly less likely to be involved. In addition, a rural location had a slightly greater chance of being selected for the vandalistic act.

Fifth, vandalism occurred during all times of the year, further dispelling the notion that vandalism in rural areas is associated with the "Halloween spirit." However, the fall months still remained the most likely time for vandalism to be committed by rural youth. Sixth, vandalism was found to be largely a weekend activity. Seventh, in less than half of the cases was it mentioned by those who were involved in vandalism that someone in the group had recently consumed alcohol or were on drugs.

Figure 8.1:

Conditions Affecting Involvement in Vandalism
Among Rural Youth

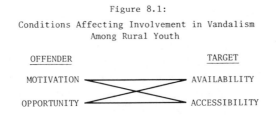

Eighth, there were several important distinguishing characteristics of the type of rural youth who had been involved in vandalism. The vandal was more likely to be male, although a sizeable minority of the female respondents from both studies had engaged in vandalistic behavior. Also, the head of the household at which the vandal resided was more likely to be divorced, separated, or widowed than the nonvandal. In addition, among the respondents from the Ohio study, positive feelings about participation in family-related activities were more likely to be exhibited by the nonvandal than by the vandal. This indicates that the quality of the relationship between the young person and his parents (or guardians) may be important to the final determination of who among rural youth commit vandalism. It is primarily through the parents that the normative prescriptions of what is right and wrong are learned.

Finally, perhaps the most surprising finding from the Ohio and Indiana studies was the fact that although participation in religious activities was related to nonparticipation in vandalistic behavior, participation in neither school-related or out-of-school related organized activities failed to significantly distinguish the vandal from the nonvandal.

Implications For Prevention Programs

It appears the commission of vandalism by rural youth is conditional upon four basic factors. These factors are summarized in Figure 8.1. On the left side are two factors associated with the offender: motivation and opportunity. On the right side are two factors associated with the target of the vandal: availability and accessibility. Each will be discussed below.

MOTIVATION

Vandalism is a group activity. The majority of vandals do not perceive the act as anything more serious than a "game" or "joke." Vandalism is normatively acceptable and this is reinforced by the fact that a majority of rural youth have committed at least one act of vandalism, and most have repeatedly engaged in such behavior.

This suggests that one primary method to reduce the commission of vandalism is through the "socialization" process, that is, during the acquisition of the values and norms that guide everyday behavior. This is no easy task, given the powerful influence of the peer group, especially during the teen years. A further obstacle arises from the fact that in rural as well as urban areas, there is an increased tendency for both parents to work, which means less time for the young person to be involved in family activities and to be supervised by parents.

Educational institutions, particularly at the primary and junior high school levels, have been targeted as appropriate settings in which such attitude- and behavior-change strategies could prove effective. One such approach is the "Crime Prevention Course for Young People" (Wursch-midt and Phillips 1978; Miller Productions Incorporated 1976; Hamrick 1979). Generally, a course of this nature is designed for the total student body and not simply for the "exceptional" cases, (i.e., the "bad apples"). The basic goals of these courses are to introduce the student to what the law defines as criminal behavior, to indicate the cost of crime to the victim, including those crimes which are considered relatively minor (i.e., vandalism); and to provide instruction on the basic principles of crime prevention, especially with respect to the personal property of the student and his family members.

The general orientation of a crime prevention "curriculum" is not to "lecture" directly to the student that certain forms of behavior are inappropriate, but rather to illustrate why society has codified a set of rules or laws that define some actions as legally wrong. This type of strategy, being geared toward the potential offender, is a longer-run and more "curative" approach than many other types of "prevention" and "deterrent" strategies which are proposed as solutions to reduce crime. Given the extensiveness of involvement in vandalism among rural youth, these strategies may prove effective, especially if they train the young person to be more assertive and less willing to "bow" to peer group pressure.

It is necessary at this point to initiate research designed to test the effectiveness of strategies which are directed toward modifying the mo-tivational structure that creates an atmosphere in which vandalism is generally viewed as a "game" or "joke." Although this type of approach has a great deal of common sense appeal, it is too premature to accu-rately gauge its viability.

OPPORTUNITY

According to the results of the Ohio and Indiana studies, the opportunity to commit vandalism was not significantly decreased by the degree to which rural youth participated in activities beyond regular school hours. Opportunity in terms of availability of time to commit vandalism will always be present to some degree, no matter how many sports, clubs, and other organizations to which a young person may belong.

However, opportunity has a second dimension which goes beyond the mere availability of time. Opportunity also refers to the availability of situations in which vandalism is a likely outcome due to "peer" influence within the group. Evidence from the Ohio study demonstrated the countervailing nature of positive feelings toward involvement in family activities and whether or not rural youth engaged in vandalistic behavior. In addition, frequency of participation in church-related activities also influenced involvement in vandalism. In both rural studies, evidence indicated that it was not participation in mere quantitative terms that operated as an effective preventive strategy by restructuring the young person's utilization of free time after school and on weekends (i.e., opportunity), but instead it was the quality of such activities. As mentioned previously, Hirschi (1969) has stressed as important influences in creating nondelinquent behavior the internalization of normative prescriptions through such socialization mechanisms as the family, church, and school. Also of importance in contemporary American society, with the large amounts of time available beyond what is necessary for work or, in the case of the adolescent, for school, is the orientation toward and utilization of leisure time.

Prevention strategies which seek to reduce the commission of vandalism by rural youth must be cognizant that how leisure time is used, (that is, the quality of utilization) is important. The old adage that "idle hands are the devil's workshop" may not be sufficient for designing of strategies to reduce vandalism among rural youth. Although youth recreation programs may be necessary for some rural communities, especially where such facilities or programs are not presently available, their mere existence may have little effect on the reduction of vandalism or other forms of deviant behavior among youth. Such programs may even be counterproductive if they serve to strengthen the influence of the peer group beyond regular school hours. For instance, the commission of vandalism by rural youth may increase while commuting to and from a particular recreational activity.

AVAILABILITY

Availability refers to the degree to which a particular object is perceived as a likely target for the vandal. As the findings from the Ohio and Indiana studies indicated, the target may be in either a rural or urban location and may be either private or public property. In contrast to the longer-run, offender-oriented strategies which attempt to modify the motivational and opportunity structure conducive to the commission of vandalism, prevention strategies here would be oriented toward making the potential target less inviting. Law enforcement has for some time called this type of strategy "target-hardening."

The target-hardening approach may be especially effective in deterring a substantial proportion of rural youth from committing a vandalistic act against a specific target. For instance, the isolated farm and nonfarm residences in the open-country may lead the potential vandal to believe there is little chance of being seen committing an act of vandalism, and therefore of being caught. Proper lighting may prove to be an effective method for the owner to reduce the probability that his property may end up as the target. Public property, such as in a park or recreation area, often become the target for vandalistic behavior. One method to curb the recurrence of damage is by fixing the vandalized property as soon as possible after its occurrence. It has been found that allowing vandalized property to remain unrepaired encourages additional vandalism in the same general area (Bennett 1969).

Against those youth who perceive vandalism as a game or joke and are not motivated by revenge or in association with the commission of more serious crimes, the target-hardening approach does provide a viable deterrence strategy. This type of vandal is likely to define the risk as too great. However, target-hardening techniques tend to displace the problem from the property which has been "hardened" to property which remains "vulnerable." Its major limitation is that it is site-specific.

ACCESSIBILITY

Accessibility may be defined as the degree to which the vandal is able to get to, reach, or in some way make contact with the potential target. The primary mode of transportation for rural youth from the Ohio and Indiana studies who were involved in vandalism was a motor vehicle. The car, pick-up truck, four-wheel drive jeep, etc., allow young persons to have ready accessibility over a wide geographic area. It is a fairly simple matter to travel to a location where the potential vandal feels unknown (i.e., feels anonymous) and thereby decreases the probability that he/she will be recognized and subsequently caught.

Oscar Newman (1972) has demonstrated that spatial lay-out is an important situational factor in explaining why some places manifest higher crime rates than others. Rural areas are especially vulnerable because of low population density and relatively longer distances between neighbors than in towns and cities. This factor, coupled with the ability of motor vehicles to make potential targets easily accessible, creates situations in which the commission of vandalism is inviting to the potential vandal in the rural environment.

Summary Remarks

Vandalism is widespread in rural areas of the United States. The results from the data presented in this chapter indicates that more than half of rural youth have actively engaged in vandalism. The evidence also shows that vandalism is not perceived as "unacceptable" behavior by rural youth. Its root cause may be found in motivational factors which determine whether or not rural youth will choose to engage in vandalistic behavior. Preventive strategies which may prove most effective on a long-run basis are those attitude and behavior approaches oriented to the potential offender.

Notes

1. More detailed information about the methodological procedures employed in the Ohio vandalism study may be found in Bartlett (1976).
2. More detailed information about the methodological procedures of the Indiana vandalism study may be found in Donnermeyer and Phillips, 1980.
3. Levels of severity were developed through a rating system. A panel of four judges independently were instructed to read each description of vandalistic behavior and assign a score from 1 (minor) to 4 (very serious). A specific incident was classified only upon receiving a minimum of three identical rankings. Only a few incidents did not receive identical rankings by at least three judges. These incidents formed a second list which was then given to a fifth judge in order to "break the tie."

References

Bartlett, Kaye F. 1976. *A Self-Reported Study of Participation in Vandalism by the Sophomore Classes of Three Selected Rural Ohio High Schools.* Ph.D. dissertation, The Ohio State University.

Bennett, Joseph H. 1969. *Vandals Wild.* Portland, Oregon: Bennett Publishing Company.

Clinard, Marshall B. and Richard Buinney. 1967. *Criminal Behavior Systems.* New York: Holt, Rinehart, and Winston.

Donnermeyer, Joseph F. and G. Howard Phillips. 1980. "The Nature of Vandalism Among Rural Youth." Paper presented at the annual meeting of the Rural Sociological Society, Ithaca, New York. August.

Donnermeyer, Joseph F., Robin D. Cox and Todd N. Wurschmidt. 1980. *Road Sign Vandalism and Theft Along County Roads in Ohio.* Socioeconomic Information

No. 624, Columbus, Ohio: Department of Agricultural Economics and Rural Sociology, The Ohio State University.

Donnermeyer, Joseph F., G. Howard Phillips and Mary Jo Steiner. 1981. "Age, Fear of Crime and Victimization in Rural Areas." Paper presented at the annual meeting of the North Central Sociological Association, Cleveland, Ohio. April.

Hamrick, Scott. 1979. *The Charlottesville/Albermarle Crime Resistance Program.* Charlottesville, Virginia: Charlottesville/Albermarle Public Schools.

Hirschi, Travis. 1969. *Causes of Delinquency.* Berkeley and Los Angeles: University of California Press.

Miller Productions Incorporated. 1976. *The Child's Keys to Crime Prevention.* Wichita Falls, Texas: Education Support Services.

Natalino, Kathleen W. 1979. "A Rural-Urban Comparison of Delinquency, Home Factors, and Peer Group Involvement." Paper presented at annual meeting of the North Central Sociological Association Meeting, Akron, Ohio. April.

Newman, Oscar. 1972. *Defensible Space: Crime Prevention Through Urban Design.* New York: Macmillan.

Phillips, G. Howard. 1976. *Rural Crimes and Rural Offenders.* Extension Bulletin 613. Columbus, Ohio: Cooperative Extension Service and Department of Agricultural Economics and Rural Sociology, The Ohio State University.

Shannon, Don. 1979. "Vandalism: A $2-Billion-A-Year Tantrum." *The Indiana Star.* April 1.

Smith, Brent L. 1979. *Criminal Victimization in Rural Areas: An Analysis of Victimization Patterns and Reporting Trends.* Ph.D. dissertation, Purdue University.

U.S. Department of Justice, Federal Bureau of Investigation. 1979. *Uniform Crime Reports.* Washington, D.C.: U.S. Government Printing Office.

U.S. News and World Report. 1979. "In Hot Pursuit of Business Criminals." July 23.

Wurschmidt, Todd N. and G. Howard Phillips. 1977. *Teachers' Guide: Rural Crime Prevention for Young People.* ESO-486. Columbus, Ohio: Department of Agricultural Economics and Rural Sociology, Ohio Cooperative Extension Service, The Ohio State University.

The Prevention of Rural Crime

Introduction

As the sub-title suggests, the theme of this book is "Integrating Research and Prevention." At this time, a healthy partnership is more hope than reality. One reason may be found in the repeated comments of every reading in Part One—that there has been very little research conducted on the extent and nature of crime in the rural United States. A second reason will be voiced often in the readings within Part Two—that crime prevention has only recently emerged as a constructive and respectable approach to addressing today's crime problems.

Given the steadily rising level of rural crime, the need for viable crime reduction strategies for rural areas likewise increases. The readings in Part Two are devoted to the theme of crime prevention.

Similar to Part One, the second half of this book is divided into two sections. The first section concerns the application of knowledge and presents three readings whose major themes center on the implications of theory and research for the development of crime prevention programs. The second section concerns approaches to rural crime prevention and includes a series of readings which address the planning and implementation of specific crime prevention programs for rural areas.

The Application of Knowledge

Chapter 9, by Robert O'Block, Todd N. Wurschmidt, and Joseph F. Donnermeyer, reviews various theoretical approaches for crime reduction strategies. The authors find significance in the analogy that "both crime and disease have many causes and require various methods of treatment." They emphasize the need for a multi-theory approach in which a given theoretical framework focuses upon a specific type of crime. Chapter 9 concludes by laying the foundation for the development of crime prevention theories targeted to rural areas.

In Chapter 10, R. Paul McCauley specifies the functions of "crime analysis" in providing a sound base of information on which to design crime prevention programs. McCauley also outlines the minimal ingredients for valid crime analyses, including specification of the volume of crime occurring by crime type, delineation of time of occurrence and geographic location, identification of victim and suspect characteristics, and detailed descriptions of property loss. McCauley concludes by considering the administrative complexities and resource problems of carrying out detailed crime analyses within law enforcement and suggests the use of volunteer and other community resources to assist in the vital stages of information-gathering, data analysis, and prevention program planning.

The final chapter in this section is by George Sunderland. Sunderland critically examines a series of contemporary strategies suggested for use in combatting the rising rural crime problem including crime causation theories, criminal justice and law enforcement, juvenile justice, and rehabilitation each from the perspective of the crime prevention practitioner who is "confronted with the day-today workability of crime reduction proposals." Sunderland concludes Chapter 11 with a discussion of the application of opportunity-reduction programs to the prevention of crime. His examples of their effectiveness are derived from his experience as a crime prevention specialist for the National Retired Teachers' Association/American Association of Retired Persons.

Approaches to Rural Crime Prevention

The second section of Part Two begins with a chapter by B.M. Gray II on "Crime Prevention Philosophy and Practice." In Chapter 12, Gray reviews the history of crime prevention and defines the basic objectives of primary prevention within the total context of the criminal justice system. Gray devotes much of the chapter to a discussion of crime risk management for rural farms and homes and re-emphasizes the need for "management decisions . . . based upon analysis, not simply hunches."

Chapter 13, by Edmund G. James and Steven D. Gladman, continues the major themes developed in the previous chapter. Contrasting the "operative" and "curative" approaches to crime prevention, the authors examine the effectiveness of opportunity-reduction strategies in terms of the need for both an accurate and localized assessment of the crime situation, and the positive functions of community involvement.

In Chapter 14, Gwen Hall focuses upon the utilization of community resources and support for local crime prevention programs. The theme of Hall's chapter is summarized by her statement that on-going crime prevention programs "can only remain supportive through cooperative efforts" within the local community. Hall outlines the major advantages and disadvantages of rural police-community relations in the planning and implementation of crime prevention programs, and predicts the increased need for rural law enforcement to develop community organization skills in light of the continued and growing "shortage of law enforcement manpower" and resources.

Todd N. Wurschmidt and G. Howard Phillips, in Chapter 15, discuss the role of prevention from a different perspective than the preceding authors. They argue that a large proportion of the rural crime problem can be attributed to the increased involvement by young persons in unlawful behavior. The authors note that this involvement is due to an increase in opportunities for peer centered activities, concomitant with a decrease in the influence of family and other socializing institutions within rural society. The authors then outline two primary long-range approaches to crime prevention that require the involvement of the family and school. Both aim at strengthening the responsibility and capability of young persons to function effectively in their social environment.

In the final chapter of the book, by Gary R. Wilson, the future role of rural law enforcement in the development of crime prevention programs is addressed. Wilson argues strongly for the need of a change in the policing style of rural enforcement, away from a "reactive" pattern to a "proactive" stance. The latter half of the Wilson chapter focuses on the "steps" to implementing this "proactive" approach for rural sheriffs' and police departments.

9

The Role of Theory in Rural Crime Prevention

ROBERT L. O'BLOCK, TODD N. WURSCHMIDT
and JOSEPH F. DONNERMEYER

Introduction

One of the most important aspects of rural crime prevention, if indeed not the most important, is the development of a sound theoretical base. This is particularly important because rural crime has increased rapidly during the sixties and seventies. The result of this increase has been a growing search for solutions among rural law enforcement agencies, community groups, and farm organizations.

Too often crime prevention programs are implemented without prior thought as to their appropriateness to a given community. The reason to implement may be based solely on availability of funds, limited knowledge of programs from other communities, or an inaccurate assessment of the local crime problem. For example, in a small midwestern community, the chief of police's decision to implement an auto theft program was founded largely on the fact that his wife's car recently had been stolen.

Such efforts are too often doomed to failure, the result of which is an inaccurate assessment that crime prevention is not an effective crime control strategy. The truth of the matter may be that the program was inappropriate, given the nature of the local crime problem, or because insufficient attention was given to the details of implementing the prevention program.

However, for many rural communities across the United States, crime prevention is proving to be an effective addition to their crime control arsenals. In response to the growing need for model strategies, several theories of crime prevention have been articulated in the past decade. As such theoretical developments continue, they need to include not only consideration of the extent and pattern of crime, but also of how prevention programs can best be implemented in the local community.

This chapter is intended to accomplish three objectives. First, it will examine the role of theory in rural crime prevention. Second, five theories concerned with the design of crime prevention programs are described, along with their application to small towns and open-country environments. Third, issues related to the application of theory for rural crime prevention are addressed.

The Role of Theory in Rural Crime Prevention

Theory, simply stated, is an attempt to describe and understand how and why events occur. It represents an interrelated set of statements about a particular issue or problem. For example, Sutherland's theory of differential association sought to explain criminal behavior as learned or acquired through contact within an intimate, personal, group setting (Sutherland 1937).

Due to income level, location of residence, and other factors, individuals have varying opportunities to associate with particular subgroups within society. Sutherland's theory stated that those individuals who had greater opportunity to interact with criminal sub-groups were more likely to internalize criminal norms and learn criminal behavior.

However, even a theory as well established as Sutherland's represents but one attempt to explain the complex phenomenon of crime. Crime is a problem so complicated that the elusive search for one general theory, capable of explaining the entire spectrum of criminal behavior, has been equated to the alchemist's magical quest for gold. Given the many different types of crime, from homicide to vandalism, and the numerous variables which interact to influence the commission of any given crime, theory construction becomes a complex matter.

Crime and its theoretical development is comparable to the problem of disease. Both crime and disease have many causes and require various methods of treatment. It has long been recognized, for example, that infections, mental illnesses, cancer, broken arms, and so on, stem from different causes, and therefore require different theoretical frameworks. We know it would be ridiculous to expect the same theory to explain diabetes and schizophrenia, for this would be like saying that if one has diabetes, he should also be schizophrenic.

By the same token, all crimes cannot be explained by the same theory. Perhaps the following paragraph best summarizes the intricacies involved in explaining crime:

> Each single crime is a response to a specific situation by a person with an infinitely complicated psychological and emotional makeup who is subject to infinitely complicated external pressures. Crime as a whole is millions of such responses. To seek the "causes" of crime in human motivations alone is to risk losing one's way in the impenetrable thickets of the human psyche. Compulsive gambling was the cause of an embezzlement, one may say, or drug addiction the cause of a burglary or madness the cause of a homicide; but what caused the compulsion, the addiction, the madness? Why did they manifest themselves in those ways at those times? (U.S. Department of Justice 1967:17).

As can be seen from the analogy of crime and disease, it is unlikely that any single theory will be sophisticated enough to explain the multifaceted problem of crime.

The role of theory in crime prevention has two distinct but interrelated aspects. The first aspect has to do with crime causation. Whether one is a theoretician or practitioner, when an attempt is made to deal with solutions to a problem, assumptions are posited about the extent of the problem, the nature of the problem, and why the problem has occurred.

Theory for crime prevention is important because a misunderstanding of the nature of the problem, or the reasons it has occurred, will lead to misdirected programs. The crime prevention practitioner either implicitly or explicitly has a "working" theory of crime causation which is utilized to evaluate the relative effectiveness of various prevention strategies. Often, assumptions about cause are prefaced by the crime prevention practitioner with such phrases as "I know it will work." or "It's only common sense."

The second aspect of theory for crime prevention refers to the actual design of preventive programs. Crime prevention practitioners make assumptions about strategies which deter or reduce the opportunity for crime to occur. For instance, it is assumed that the installation of deadbolt locks will deter home burglaries. This assumption rests on the logic that deadbolt locks, being of sturdier construction than the key-in-knob type, will prolong a burglar's attempt to illegally enter a home. This often appears in the crime prevention literature as the "four minute" rule. Most burglars will take no more than four minutes to break into a house. If more than four minutes is required, the risk level becomes unacceptable, and the burglar will search for an easier target.

In addition to considering the deterrent effect of security measures, crime prevention theories involve assumptions about how security information can be effectively communicated to the general public. For example, crime prevention practitioners may assume that the audience to whom prevention programs are targeted adhere to the same explanations on crime causation and deterrence as they do. If the prevailing opinion in the community is that the crime problem can be solved only through stricter sentencing, then the practitioner will likely experience failure in educating the community to the benefits of such alternatives as better home security measures.

Most people do, in fact, perceive some value in securing their own property. However, an often expressed comment, and one that is almost sure to bedevil the crime prevention practitioner at public meetings is: "Why bother to lock my doors or waste my money on deadbolt locks? Nothing can stop a burglar from breaking into a house, if he really wants to get in!" This statement represents a negative assessment of the relative effectiveness of home security measures. The crime prevention practitioner who is sensitive to the attitudes of his audience will more likely perceive the need to discuss the merits of home security practices before proceeding on to any technical discussion of lights, locks or alarms.

Theory for crime prevention as related to the design of educational programs therefore aids the practitioner in two ways. First, theory helps delineate rationales as to the deterrent value of specific prevention strategies. Second, theory assists in the identification of effective strategies for disseminating crime prevention information.

Crime Prevention Theories for Rural Areas

Crime prevention for rural areas is only now beginning to be recognized as an effective approach to dealing with the rapidly emerging problem (O'Block 1981). In the past, the major emphasis in attempting to control crime in urban, as well as in rural areas, was to punish and rehabilitate, an after-the-fact approach. It has taken many years to recognize the importance of crime prevention as a distinct approach.

However, some scholars and researchers argue that at present, there are no theories of crime prevention, only of crime causation. Admittedly, crime prevention is in a state of theoretical infancy. Despite this, there are several models, described below, which do seem to reflect valid crime prevention strategies.

Only theories relevant to the design of crime prevention strategies are discussed here. Although crime causation theories are important to the development of crime prevention programs, such theories are more properly the domain of criminology. Crime causation theories deal directly with understanding how and why crime occurs. In contrast, theories relevant to the design of crime prevention strategies concentrate more on the situation of the victim.

ENVIRONMENTAL DESIGN THEORY

The major theorists linking crime with the physical environment have been Newman (1972), Jeffery (1977), and Gardiner (1978). According to Gardiner, the concept of territoriality is the primary connection between the physical environment and criminal activity. The territoriality concept must involve at least three conditions: (1) a resident must take a genuine interest in and feel a certain amount of responsibility, along with his neighbors, for an area which goes beyond that of their own front doors; (2) residents must be willing to take action when they believe this territory to be threatened by intruders; and (3) the above two factors must be strong enough so that potential offenders realize if they intrude, their intrusion is likely to be detected. In all of its various forms, territoriality is a desired condition or goal in achieving environmental security (Gardiner 1978).

Architectural criteria for constructing or remodeling the physical environment should be established to allow and encourage the development of individual and group territoriality. In order for this to be accomplished, a number of peripheral factors, including the residence of the victim, the residence or source of the offender, and the location of the offense, must be examined. This will determine both the geographic area of the environment in which the crime took place and the reason why the victim and offender came into contact.

Many elements within an environment may be responsible for bringing victim and offender together, and these are referred to as crime generators. There are basically three categories of crime generators within an environment which must be considered as affecting the level of security: (1) known crime generators, such as "hot spots" or areas at which crime is known to occur frequently (eg., bars, drug dealing points, and parks); (2) service generators, such as public or private facilities which attract potential victims as well as potential offenders (eg., open spaces, parks, public facilities, hospitals, high schools, and commercial locations; and (3) movement generators, such as public conveyances which attract potential victims/offenders (eg. bus stops, walkways, and parking lots). As interaction between people take place within an environment, identification of crime generators plays a major role in analyzing the cause and effect phenomena. By relating the location of the crime generators with the structure of the environment, and with how and by whom the environment is used, it is possible to speculate on a probable cause-and-effect relationship between certain patterns of crime.

Rural environments exhibit unique sets of crime generators, different from those associated with urban areas: low visibility and the relative isolation of farm property and rural homes, minimal police resources available for patrol and surveillance functions, and the geographic relationship of barns, garages, and other outbuildings to the homestead represent crime generators in the rural setting. For instance, Phillips et al. (1976) found that barns and other outbuildings located behind the home rather than between the home and a public road were less vulnerable to theft and burglary because the former arrangement offered greater visibility.

Practitioners faced with the task of developing preventive strategies for rural areas can benefit from the territoriality concept contained within the environmental design theory. Traditionally, rural people maintain stronger informal social interaction patterns. They are more familiar than urban dwellers with other members of the neighborhood and community. Yet at the same time, rural people are more independent and individualistic. Both of these elements suggest that the rural population will display a greater sense of territoriality and will more likely take action in response to a crime threat. Prevention programs, such as neighborhood watch and CB patrol, which emphasize rural people's independent nature and their informal network of interaction, tie into the basic tenets of environmental design theory.

More generally, many rural areas are now in a period of population increase, and environmental design theory suggests issues related to the planning of growth. Decisions to locate industry, recreational facilities, and commercial developments in rural areas should consider the interactional patterns of persons who will be using the environment and how these factors contribute to increased crime levels.

INFORMATION THEORY

According to information theory, crime deterrence can be achieved by reducing the level of payoffs for committing the crime, or by increasing the strength of cues (i.e., suspicious behavior or unusual activity) the criminal has to emit in order to carry out the criminal act (Willmer 1970). Requiring the criminal to use more skill or time, or making him change his usual method of operation through target-hardening might result in a reduction in the expected level of payoffs and an increase in the strength of cues emitted.

In management terms, the level of payoff can be thought of as the point of cost effectiveness of committing a crime. In other words, the criminal has to ask himself, is the risk of getting caught worth the risk involved in committing the crime? An example of decreasing payoffs is provided by the all-night convenience stores that advertise the fact that no more than fifty dollars is kept in the safe during the night, or that the safe requires two keys to be unlocked. An example of detecting cues displayed by criminals is the ability of airport security personnel to recognize behavior of passengers who typify "skyjacker profiles."

Studies of arrests made by sheriffs (Phillips 1976) and of youth participation in illegal activities (Polk 1969; Natalino 1979; Donnermeyer and Phillips 1980) found that rural crime is perpetrated largely by the amateur criminal (i.e., males, 15-21 years old). Information theory suggests that increased target-hardening by rural residents may prove very effective in reducing crime levels, especially the types of incidents committed by young amateurs.

Phillips (1975) has found that rural people exhibit lax attitudes toward practicing crime prevention, in part due to the historically low level of crime in rural areas. Now that rural crime is increasing rapidly, information theory suggests that attitude-change programs aimed at developing positive attitudes toward home and farm security may prove beneficial.

However, the assumptions underlying information theory, as with nearly all theories of crime prevention, remain largely untested. For example, there has been only minimal empirical work accomplished on the extent to which specific target-hardening strategies reduce victimization probabilities (Steiner 1981). Donnermeyer (1981) suggests that in the rural environment, there may be many situational factors which "override" the intended purpose of locks and other security paraphernalia. Some of these factors were suggested earlier in the discussion of environmental design theory. Visibility, the isolation of rural homes, and longer response times of law enforcement may neutralize the effectiveness of exterior lighting, alarm systems, and other security hardware, which according to information theory, are intended to increase risk.

Information theory is based on the principle that deterrence is possible if the risk level is raised (ie., payoffs are lowered). As such, it may prove useful in developing researchable hypotheses aimed at evaluating the conditions under which target-hardening measures reduce crime levels in both the rural and the urban environment.

TAP THEORY (TIME OF ARRIVAL OF POLICE)

Response time, or the amount of time it takes the police to respond to a crime, is dependent upon three distinct timing activities: (1) detection time, that is, the beginning of the commission of the crime until it is detected and an alert sounded; (2) reporting time, which is the time interval between the activation of an alarm or detection by other means (passerby, guards, etc.), and the receipt of the information by police; and (3) response time, or the interval from the receipt of the information by the police dispatcher until the police patrol arrives at the scene of the crime. The culmination of these three responses, or the total interval between the detection of the criminal act and the arrival of police officers at the scene, is known as time of arrival of police (TAP). As stated by Mandelbaum (1973:49), "TAP includes the time of arrival of other counterforce elements, such as guards and watchmen, as well as the police; however, because the great majority of responses to criminal alarms are by the police, TAP is used as the basic criterion."

A key concept is to increase the time of both intrusion and escape of the intruder. The complexity and length of time needed to gain unauthorized entry are crucial in determining whether a criminal will accept the risk. If the criminal decides to accept the risk and enters successfully, the next most important factor affecting TAP becomes detection and capture. Utilizing detection and transmission devices at the site, communication lines to commercial central stations and/or the police, and opportunities for the passersby to observe and report criminal activity will increase the probability that police will arrive while the crime is in progress.

Results of recent studies indicate that the most critical factor is the reporting time of the crime. If this is done automatically by electronic detection devices, the response of the police can begin more quickly. However, rural and urban law enforcement agencies become aware of crime largely through citizens' reports. Unfortunately, victims and witnesses have been known to wait twenty minutes or more before calling police.

Reporting time is a particularly important point to consider in the prevention of rural crime since minimal law enforcement resources and the geographic scope of police jurisdictions increase police response time.

Educational programs aimed at teaching citizens to be good witnesses and to encourage the immediate reporting of suspicious activity are basic to the successful application of TAP theory.

RANDOM AREA SEARCH THEORY

Random search, or "patrol," is based on the probability that a patrol which is moving continuously in a random manner within a given area, will detect a crime in progress (Elliot and Sardino 1971:13).

Although patrol is one of the oldest types of police service, its effectiveness in preventing crime is now being seriously questioned as a result of the Kansas City preventive patrol experiment (Kelling 1974). Patrol seems more appropriately oriented towards detection of criminal activity and serves as a rapid means of reacting to criminal attack rather than actually deterring any attempts to commit a crime. In addition, the large geographic areas under the jurisdiction of rural police agencies suggest that resources may never be increased to a level sufficient to make the random area search theory work as a crime deterrent in the rural environment.

DISPLACEMENT THEORY

Displacement theory postulates that, while crime may be prevented in one neighborhood by the use of Neighborhood Watch and other target-hardening procedures, the nearest neighborhood not so protected will experience an increase in crime as criminals simply move to easier targets. Crime prevention through target-hardening tactics is therefore seen by displacement theory as only displacing crime from one neighborhood to the next.

This viewpoint is somewhat plausible since crime is largely a matter of opportunity and, if crime prevention is to be successful for an entire community, it will be necessary for all areas within the community to employ strategies for reducing crime. However, two points should be made with respect to displacement theory.

First, it can be argued that displacement theory is not really a critical theory of crime prevention, but rather, a proof that crime prevention and target-hardening strategies can be effective. Rather than helping to establish the interrelationship between how and why crime occurs, and using this knowledge to design crime control programs, the displacement phenomenon surfaces because home security measures have effectively deterred potential offenders from challenging security barriers at specific locales.

The three minimal elements which must be present in order for a crime to occur are a motivated offender, an opportunity, and a suitable target or victim. If crimes are to be prevented, the practitioner needs to put in place programs which remove the effects of at least one of these three elements. Supporters of environmental design theory or information theory, for example, would suggest the merits of concentrating on lessening the opportunities for crimes to occur. Rehabilitation programs, as another example, are targeted at the offender population.

Displacement theory, on the other hand, merely postulates that the deterrent effect of security measures serves to shift the operation of offenders. The theory may aid in explaining crime increases in adjacent neighborhoods or communities, but does not lend assistance in the design or implementation of crime prevention programs.

Second, Reppetto (1976) has argued that the displacement phenomenon is not nearly as pervasive as often contended. Reppetto develops his argument by challenging the assumptions on which displacement theory is based. The two principle assumptions are (1) offenders are "totally deterministic and inelastic," meaning they do not evaluate opportunities to commit crimes and likelihood of apprehension, but are instead driven to commit a predetermined number of offenses per day, week or month; and (2) offenders have access to resources and the knowledge which will allow them freedom to shift their operations, at will, from one locale to another.

Phillips (1976) found that offenders most often arrested by Ohio sheriffs were young males. Additionally, accumulating evidence (Donnermeyer and Phillips 1980; Phillips 1976) suggests that young offenders commit offenses in the company of peers, as a result of peer challenge, and without prior planning. Such amateur and unsophisticated offenders are unlikely to change their modus operandi, shift their location of operation, or begin commiting more serious offenses as a result of a community's crime prevention effort.

Theoretical Considerations for Rural Crime Prevention

Any theoretical framework for crime prevention must give consideration to factors which appear to influence the growing crime problem. Believed to be primary contributors to the rural crime problem are the following (Phillips et al. 1980):

Relative isolation of rural homes, together with increasing accessibility to country areas

Increasing rural population

Limited or minimal police protection and longer police response times

Need by farmers to maintain extensive equipment inventories

Growing affluency of rural residents

Remoteness of recreational facilities in rural areas

Belief on the part of the public that rural areas are immune from urban crime problems

Rural crime prevention theory must also take into account the following:

Nature of crime problems affecting rural areas. This is of paramount importance to any crime prevention campaign, since this information signifies specific areas to which anticrime strategies should be targeted. For example, Phillips found that vandalism and larceny respectively were the two leading crimes committed in rural Ohio (Phillips 1975). Further analyses of Phillips' work revealed that mailboxes were the property most often affected by vandalism, and that 20 percent of rural thefts involved gasoline. Information such as this is basic to the wide-scale prevention of crime, rural or urban.

Differences, if any, between crimes reported and crimes committed. These data are essential to theory construction, since the crime problem itself is distorted without accurate statistics. Research on rural crime by Phillips found that of 842 Ohio Farm Bureau Councils, 46 percent were aware of unreported crimes. Data obtained from this study further indicated that reasons for not reporting crimes most frequently included that it was "no use" to report known crimes and there was an "unwillingness to get involved" (Phillips 1974:27).

Public's attitude toward rural law enforcement. Many rural residents perceive enforcing or getting convictions for rural crimes to be increasingly difficult.

Profile of individuals committing crimes in rural areas. This information will help determine who the offenders are in terms of age, sex, race, or whether they are rural residents or migrating urbanites.

Patterns, if any, in the commission of crimes in rural areas. These data pertain to established patterns of crime according to times of the day, seasonal changes, location, and type of community.

Variations, if any between crime rates and criminal behavior in different rural areas. This information will allow law enforcement to determine if different rural areas within a state experience greater or lesser amounts of crime and if the criminal behavior expressed is significantly different.

Communicating crime prevention information. Crime prevention theory should also consider a proper educational framework, since the exchange of information is vital to a successful crime prevention program. As Donnermeyer (1979:3) stated:

> Crime prevention is basically education, and the nature of the educational process is the exchange of information (i.e., facts ideas, opinions) between people.

Traditionally, delivering crime prevention information within an educational framework has not been a priority among most law enforcement agencies. The tendency is still to provide education to victims after the fact, rather than before they become victimized. In addition, once the exchange of information has taken place, measuring its effectiveness in reducing crime becomes a challenge. Perhaps the following statement best reflects this problem:

> We cannot directly see the benefits of using crime prevention measures for we will not know if practicing crime prevention is the cause for our not becoming a victim of crime (Wurschmidt and Phillips 1979).

It would seem that the success of any program can be inferred by comparisons of statistical data, collected before and after the program's initiation, as long as all variables affecting the results are properly identified and taken into consideration.

Conclusion

At present there are numerous theories of crime prevention, but there is no one theoretical base which can prevent crime. There will perhaps need to be an integration of existing theories since crime, being a complex problem, will require a complex theory of prevention. In addition, there are interrelationships between crime causation and crime prevention which need further exploration.

We must not be too eager to accept certain proposals as theories or as fact until they have been validated. Research and evaluation of present theories must be intensified as well as continuing the search for new theories. The theories that have been presented in this chapter all have strengths and weaknesses, as well as advocates and opponents. At present, none of these theories can answer all of our questions, but serve only as our best attempts to deal with the prevention of crime.

References

Asbury, George B. 1906. *The Cure and Prevention of Crime.* Jeffersonville, Indiana: Indiana Reformatory Trade School Press.

Donnermeyer, Joseph F. 1979. "Community Development and Crime Prevention for Rural Areas." Paper presented at the annual meeting of the Community Development Society, Kansas City, Missouri. August.

————. 1981. "Crime Prevention Programming for Rural Environments: A Systematic Approach." Paper to be presented at the annual meeting of the Academy of Criminal Justice Sciences, Philadelphia, Pennsylvania. March.

————. and G. Howard Phillips. 1980. "The Nature of Vandalism Among Rural Youth." Paper presented at the annual meeting of the Rural Sociological Society, Ithaca, New York. August.

Elliott, J.F. and Thomas J. Sardino. 1971. *Crime Control Team.* Springfield, Illinois: Charles C. Thomas, Publisher.

Gardiner, Richard A. 1978. *Design for Safe Neighborhoods.* Washington, D.C.: National Institute of Law Enforcement and Criminal Justice, Law Enforcement Assistance Administration, U.S. Department of Justice.

Jeffrey, Ray C. 1977. *Crime Prevention Through Environmental Design.* Beverly Hills: Sage Publications, Inc.

Kelling, George L. et al. 1974. *The Kansas City Preventive Patrol Experiment.* Washington D.C.: Police Foundation.

Mandelbaum, Albert J. 1973. *Fundamentals of Protective Systems.* Springfield, Illinois: Charles C. Thomas, Publisher.

Natalino, Kathleen W. 1979. "A Rural-Urban Comparison of Delinquency, Home Factors, and Peer Group Involvement." Paper presented at the annual meeting of the North Central Sociological Society, Akron, Ohio. April.

National Crime Prevention Institute. 1978. *The Practice of Crime Prevention.* Louisville, Kentucky: National Crime Prevention Institute Press.

Newman, Oscar. 1972. *Defensible Space.* New York: The Macmillan Company.

O'Block, Robert. 1981. *Security and Crime Prevention.* St. Louis: The C. U. Mosby Company.

Phillips, G. Howard. 1974. *Rural Crime in Ohio As Perceived by Members of Farm Bureau Councils.* ESO 362. Columbus, Ohio: Department of Agricultural Economics and Rural Sociology, The Ohio State University.

————. 1975. *Crime in Rural Ohio.* ESO 363. Columbus, Ohio: Department of Agricultural Economics and Rural Sociology, The Ohio State University.

————. 1976. *Rural Crime and Rural Offenders.* EB 613. Columbus, Ohio: Department of Agricultural Economics and Rural Sociology, Ohio Cooperative Extension Service, and The Ohio State University.

————. , Todd N. Wurschmidt, and Joseph F. Donnermeyer. 1980. "The Ohio Rural Victimization Study." Newsline, Rural Sociological Society 8 (January):26-31.

————, George M. Kreps and Cathy Wright Moody. 1976. *Selected Environmental Factors in Rural Crime.* Research Circular 224. Wooster, Ohio: Ohio Agricultural Research and Development Center.

Polk, Kenneth. 1969. "Delinquency and Community Action in Nonmetropolitan Areas." In Donald R. Cressey and David A. Ward, eds. *Delinquency, Crime, and Social Process.* New York: Harper and Row, Publishers.

Reppetto, Thomas A. 1976. "Crime Prevention and the Displacement Phenomenon." *Crime and Delinquency* 22(2): 166-77.

Steiner, Mary Jo. 1981. *The Adoption and Diffusion of Crime Prevention Practices and Behaviors Among Rural Residents.* Ph.D. dissertation, The Ohio State University.

Sutherland, Edwin H. 1937. *The Professional Thief.* Chicago: University of Chicago Press.

U.S. Department of Justice. 1967. *The Challenge of Crime in a Free Society.* Washington, D.C.: U.S. Government Printing Office.

Wurschmidt, Todd N. and G. Howard Phillips. 1979. *Rural Crime Prevention Workshop—A Sharing of Ideas.* NRCPC 1. Columbus, Ohio: The National Rural Crime Prevention Center, The Ohio State University.

10

The Role of Crime Analysis in Developing Rural Crime Prevention Programs

R. PAUL McCAULEY

Crime prevention programs have become quite popular in recent years in the United States. Law enforcement agencies began to formalize their prevention function with the coming of the 1970s. Law enforcement, however, learned quickly that crime prevention was not solely their responsibility; that the responsibility had to be shared with the citizenry and interest groups if success was to be realized.

Understanding this period of time—post-1960 urban violence era—is important for those concerned with rural crime prevention. The most obvious aspect is that the 1960s brought attention to the *issue* of urban crime. Robbery, burglary, homicide, rape, assault, arson, and skyjacking were the primary crime issues crying out for relief in the cities. Law enforcement agencies responded in numerous ways to these issues. One response was crime prevention. Now rural areas are getting attention in dealing with some of the same crimes (i.e., larceny, vandalism, and burglary). The task in part is to adapt and modify the urban crime prevention techniques of the 1970s to the rural needs of the 1980s. Additionally, new prevention strategies need to be devised to address crimes unique to rural areas (i.e., livestock and farm equipment theft).

The success of crime prevention activities by law enforcement agencies is open to debate since community involvement has been a part of the crime prevention effort virtually from the beginning. Therefore, it is quite difficult to assign credit totally to law enforcement or to community activities for achievements in crime prevention.

To some observers the success of crime prevention activities, in general, is suspect. Those who doubt the success claims of crime prevention programs do so for a variety of reasons, both general and specific. However, the most critical reason to doubt the appropriateness of a crime prevention program, is the lack of data necessary to evaluate effectiveness.

Since 1973, the author has taught at the National Crime Prevention Institute at the University of Louisville. The students have included police chiefs and sheriffs, mayors, state representatives and other elected officials, governors' aides, detectives, patrol officers, and community leaders. The vast majority are police crime prevention officers. These students represent just about every state in the United States and reflect a cross-section of the various types of crime prevention operations including large and small city police departments (from New York City Police with 30,000 officers to numerous villages, towns, townships, and boroughs with one-man departments), county police and county sheriffs' departments, the FBI, the U.S. Army, the U.S. Navy, housing authority police, industrial security firms, and others.

The first question asked of every class is, "How many of you have a crime analyst or someone assigned in your organization to analyze crime data for the purpose of establishing crime prevention priorities?" Although an exact record of their responses has never been kept, the author estimates that 90 percent of the crime prevention operations do not have benefit of systematic crime analysis.

To many observers the absence of crime analysis in the prevention of crime is ridiculous. Without it, crime prevention programs can be based on erroneous information with subsequent priorities being inaccurate—even counterproductive. This chapter is designed to stress the importance of data analysis for crime prevention.

Rural Crime Needs Analyzed

Recognizing that the categories of crime remain constant whether urban or rural crime is being discussed, it must be understood, however, that urban and rural crime characteristics may vary greatly as to cultural patterns, lifestyles, and law enforcement models. These variations in crime characteristics must be identified and appropriate community and enforcement responses developed. The immediate concern here is rural crime. The critical point is that different crime characteristics require different responses and the things that are appropriate in urban settings may or may not be appropriate in the rural setting.

Of course, a burglary, by law, is the same in the city as it is in the country. The same is true of theft, vandalism, and so on. But the differences in what is taken, how it is taken, when it is taken, and how the taker disposes of the items are crucial both to the prevention and apprehension of the law breaker. A cursory examination of the things which could be taken from rural homes, farms, and businesses include most things that could be taken from the urban areas. These items include televisions, money, clothing, jewelry, C.B. radios, furniture, automobiles, etc. However, there is evidence to suggest that "collectibles" (miniatures, chinaware, silver, crystal, antiques) are a pastime for "country folk" and often are displayed on low window sills. These visible collectibles may be inviting to the potential burglar.

Analysis of the rural crime situation must be refined to meet the special needs unique to the rural area. It is inadequate simply to have the local news media report an increase in rural crime. It is insufficient to have the sheriff's department or the farm/ranch organizations indicate an increase in property theft. In practice, crime prevention does not mean that a community will prevent all crimes. Rather, efforts should be made to prevent or reduce crimes that have priority. For example, it would be senseless to develop an arson prevention program when arson has not been identified as a local problem. An arson program would be absurd if it were developed at the expense of a timber theft prevention program in an area where timber is being taken unlawfully. Crime analysis is the key to setting these priorities.

What is it that is to be prevented in a given rural area? The following list may help find this out:

1. Arson (a) house (b) barn (c) shed (d) timber (e) other
2. Burglary (a) T.V. (b) furniture (c) money (d) jewelry (e) typewriter (f) equipment (g) other
3. Theft (a) tractors (b) livestock (1) cattle (2) horses (3) chickens (4) hogs (5) other (c) trucks (d) automobiles (e) vehicular equipment (f) equipment attachments and accessories (g) grain (h) fruit (i) timber (j) tree seedlings (k) fuel (1) gasoline (2) diesel (l) tools (m) chemicals (n) antiques (o) other
4. Vandalism (a) land/fields (b) timber (c) schools (d) school buses (e) equipment (f) lawns and structures (g) other

The list could be extended even further. But the real question in any crime analysis is not necessarily what the politically influential farmer, businessman, or rancher has experienced, or only what is reported to the sheriff, but what *in fact* is the crime profile in the area.

The basic crime profile will include the crime type and classification. In addition, rural crime prevention programs will have to be based on information which considers the following (for more detail, see Table 10.1):

- geographic factors
- time factors
- victim target descriptors
- suspect descriptors
- property loss descriptors
- physical evidence factors
- specific M.O. (modus operandi) factors
- suspect vehicle descriptors.

In Support of Crime Analysis

It has been said that a journey of a thousand miles begins with a single step. The crime prevention participant (police officer, citizen volunteer, etc.) is very much aware that developing crime prevention programs in a community is indeed a difficult and long journey. The journey should begin with the logical first step forward—crime analysis. However, for many, the first step may not have been forward, but instead was sideways or even backwards.

The National Crime Prevention Institute has defined crime prevention as "the anticipation, recognition, and appraisal of a crime risk, and the initiation of some action to remove or reduce that risk. This definition has been accepted virtually across the United States as the basic operational definition of the crime prevention function. Crime analysis is an integral part of this definition. It is the analysis of crime data that enables a law enforcement agency or citizens' group to anticipate, recognize, and appraise crime risks.

Crime analysis is the essential ingredient upon which all other actions are developed. Without first having the crime data analysis framework, crime prevention programs almost certainly will go off in a haphazard direction and will not achieve the established objectives. Crime analysis, therefore, becomes the compass before the first step is taken to insure that the direction or objectives are properly established and that appropriate strategies are implemented to achieve those objectives. Unfortunately, many crime prevention programs have been established without direction and often, the results are an endless journey to nowhere.

Perhaps one of the best analogies that can be drawn is of a sailor with a sextant lost at sea. His first task is not to determine where he wants to go, but to determine where he is. Once he uses his sextant and shoots his location, then he can set sail for his objective. Crime analysis provides

Table 10.1. Universal Factors For Crime Analysis

* CRIME TYPE	Burglary (class: business-commercial, residential, other) Robbery (class: armed vs. not armed) Auto Theft (automobile, commercial vehicle, motorcycle, etc.) General Larceny (thefts from autos, auto scrap metal, dock, etc.) Fraud (forgery, credit cards, confidence games, etc.) Rape and Sex Crimes (forcible rape, child molesting, indecent exposure) Aggravated Assault and Murder
* GEOGRAPHICAL	Location offense occurred Street address or intersection Block Sub-reporting area or census tract Reporting area, patrol area or beat Zone, precinct, or district
* CHRONOLOGICAL	Specific time offense occurred Time span in which offense occurred (day-night) Day of week Week of year Month of year
* VICTIM TARGET	Victim person (sex, age, race, etc. of victim) Type victim structure (single dwelling house, apartment, high rise, etc.) Type victim premise (commercial, industrial, public, etc.) Victim purpose (sales, service, manufacturing, etc.) Victim knowledge of suspect
* SUSPECT	Name of responsible Age of responsible Race of responsible Height of responsible Weight of responsible Clothing and unusual characteristics
* SUSPECT VEHICLE DESCRIPTIVE	Specific license number Make of vehicle Model and year of vehicle Color of vehicle Damage to vehicle
* PROPERTY LOSS DESCRIPTIVE	Serial number of property loss Make of property loss (brand name, etc.) Model of property loss Type of property loss Purpose property used for

Source: Police Crime Analysis Handbook, U.S. Department of Justice, Law Enforcement Assistance Administration, November, 1973, p. 33.

the same basic tool for crime prevention as the sextant does for a lost sailor.

Who Should Do Crime Analysis?

In some police departments, part-time and full-time crime analysts operate at a broad range of organizational levels. These levels range from the analysis of data for only one specific crime—burglary, for example—for the exclusive use of the crime prevention unit, all the way to a departmental analyst who is responsible for analyzing crime and management data for all divisions, bureaus, and units within the department including crime prevention.

The decision that crime prevention practitioners must make is how crime data can be used to the best advantage of the crime prevention mission. If the crime prevention program is receiving adequate data from the law enforcement agency(ies) or community organizations and agencies, there may be little need for a specialized crime prevention analyst. Unfortunately, however, the departmental crime data collected by most rural and urban law enforcement agencies generally are not specific enough to take the prevention function beyond traditional police patrol. Therefore, it becomes essential that crime analysis be refined for the specific purpose of crime prevention, especially in rural areas. This means an assessment is needed to determine if the local department and/or community agency is collecting the kinds of information essential for rural crime prevention activities. The first part of this assessment is determining if the crime reports, incident reports, and activity reports provided by the patrol officer solicit the specific crime prevention information that is required. Once this is achieved, crime prevention managers (police or citizen) know that the local department is in need of additional reporting forms (or a modification of the existing reporting forms) to include the essential information upon which crime prevention can build its strategies.

Once the proper information is collected, it has to be organized and translated so it means something in terms of crime prevention operations. If someone in the local law enforcement agency can do it, fine. Or if a citizen volunteer can do it, fine. Both are perfectly legitimate. Basically, broadbase information should be collected by the law enforcement agency and then each operating unit within the department—whether it is patrol, investigation, traffic, or crime prevention—should take these data and make them into something that is meaningful. Appropriate data should also be shared with civic groups having crime prevention programs. This helps to legitimize the crime prevention function with

FIGURE 10.1:

CRIME ANALYSIS PROCESS

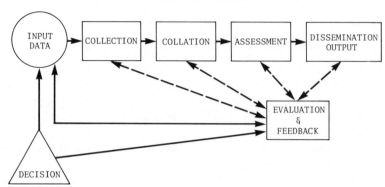

the total community. It is not incorrect for a central analysis unit to collect all the raw data and distribute specific reports to investigation, patrol, traffic, crime prevention or citizen groups. On the other hand, it may be better in some departments for the raw data to be distributed to each of these units for analysis.

The crime analysis process is diagrammed in more detail in Figure 10.1. Very simply, the entire process requires that crime data (input) are collected, collated, or organized in meaningful ways for assessment. The results of the assessed data are then evaluated and fed back either for adjustment in one or more phases of the process or for managerial decisions.

It must be remembered that crime analysis is a planning function regardless of the organizational unit in which it is placed. The primary purpose of crime analysis is to study daily crime activities in order to determine the location, time, and special features. Also, crime analysis increases objectivity, enables better coordination between operational units in law enforcement, facilitates intra- and interagency communication, reduces time required to determine crime patterns, and improves the capability to identify trends. Figure 10.2 illustrates the key role crime analysis plays in the overall crime prevention planning process.

Police officials have long recognized that one of their primary management weaknesses is their inability to be proactive (anticipatory), rather than reactive or crisis-oriented. Crime analysis is a primary element in transforming policing and crime prevention into proactive rather than a crisis operation.

Crime analysis has often been dismissed on the premise that it is too complicated, too sophisticated, and, therefore, the results are meaning-

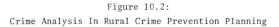
Figure 10.2:
Crime Analysis In Rural Crime Prevention Planning

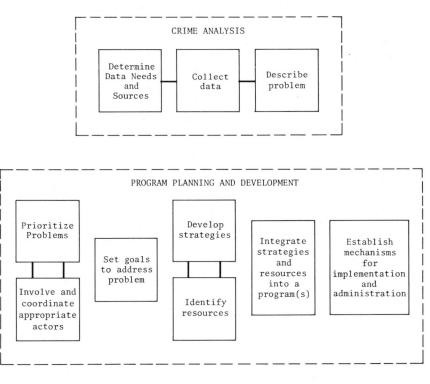

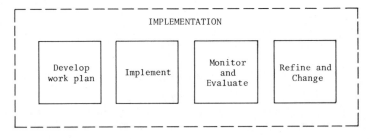

Source: Minnesota Crime Prevention Center, <u>Crime Analysis For Crime Prevention</u>
(Minneapolis, Minnesota, 1978), pp. 1-2.

less. That point is well taken and the author is not advocating the use of super-sophisticated, analytical techniques. In the monograph *Crime Analysis In Support Of Patrol: Phase I Report,* which was published by the U.S. Department of Justice (1977), the foreword made this point very clear:

> Although some form of crime analysis has been ongoing in police departments for many years, in the last decade the function has been greatly enlarged. To ascertain the present status of crime analysis, this research assessed both the literature and current practices in twenty-three police departments around the country.
>
> The message of the study is clear: Better understanding and coordination between the analyst and the departments that use the analysis is essential. The police officials polled in this survey acknowledged the value of crime analysis. At the same time, they were not convinced that the more sophisticated mathematical analysis techniques—such as response force modeling and crime event predictions—are superior to less sophisticated formulas. In fact, the study found that the more formal the analysis program, the more remote it becomes to practitioners and the less likely it is that the information it produces will be used.

The message is clear: crime analysis must be useful to practitioners. Perhaps this is a generalization, but many of the most successful crime prevention programs have recognized this years ago and developed crime analysis as a simplistic but useful activity. The techniques that are most often used are based on the notion of refined simplicity; that is, getting a high rate of analytic accuracy using the basic and most simplistic techniques. The pinmap and modified MO file (i.e., modus operandi or method of operating) analyses are two techniques that have been used for years.

Crime prevention has a very definite responsibility to determine patterns and trends in crime. Crime analysis also is the basic operation that yields substantive data for effectiveness measures of specific programs, policies, and procedures. Without crime data which has been analyzed and presented clearly, the crime prevention function cannot provide supporting data for their recommended crime prevention programs. Furthermore, it will be impossible to furnish trend data for crime prevention planning, targeting, budgeting, and allocation of our resources. Crime analysis is the first step of the journey toward productive crime prevention activities.

Rural Crime Prevention Program Building

Each comprehensive rural crime prevention program ultimately must address the following elements:

- Problems—or needs assessment
- Capabilities—or resources assessment
- Strategies—or delineation of proposed actions to be taken
- Management—or allocation of responsibilities for the proposed actions, including their scheduling, supervision, and coordination
- Evaluation—or design for determining at least the *what* and the *how* of the program's process and impact

PROBLEMS OR NEEDS ASSESSMENT

It was stated above that crime prevention is a planning function. To emphasize the importance of crime analysis in planning for a comprehensive rural crime prevention program, it must be understood that crime analysis is the first phase of planning. In planning jargon, the first phase is called problem identification or needs assessment. Since planning is a sequential process with each step building upon the preceding steps, it is quite clear that if the first step is weak, all subsequent steps will build upon this weakness.

There are two special problems confronting the proper needs assessment of rural crime patterns. Small community police departments and county sheriff departments may not be in the best position to collect data. Limited personnel and budgetary resources are probably universal constraints. Second, rural response time (time for a law enforcement officer to answer a call from the time a citizen calls the department until the time an officer arrives at the scene) may be quite long because of a large geographical area patrolled. In addition, the crime—grain theft, for example, may not be discovered for several weeks i.e., until the crop is transported for sale. As a result, many criminal incidents may go unreported to law enforcement agencies.

Law enforcement data must be used carefully because it is based on crimes *reported*, rather than on crimes experienced by rural residents. Real crime is all crimes reported *plus* the crimes which have occurred but which have not been reported.

Because of the experiences of urban areas, rural areas should look at crime prevention rationally and not with the emotional urgency which demands the immediate implementation of a crime prevention program. The first crime prevention project in every community should focus on the collection of real crime data (victimology data) rather than relying solely on crime data reported to the law enforcement agencies. This suggestion does not advocate a sit-back-and-wait attitude. It can be achieved if engaged in as a cooperative effort. For example, rural areas have organizations as do urban population centers. These organizations have a variety of purposes but in the final analysis they all contribute to the quality of rural life one way or another. Crime prevention can easily become a part of any organization which is engaged in activities to improve rural life. The 4-H, Farm Bureau, cooperative groups, citizen's band radio clubs, volunteer fire departments, ladies' clubs or ladies' auxiliaries, church groups, and garden clubs are a few organizations existing in many rural areas. One or more of these groups could contact the entire county by telephone and conduct a basic crime inventory. Management responsibility, scheduling, and supervision of the county-wide crime inventory could rest with the organization's president or the crime prevention committee chairman. Remember someone must be responsible if results are to be achieved.

The first question in such a telephone crime inventory probably would be, "Have you been a victim of a crime?" In order to insure the validity of response, one would ask this question only for the past six or twelve months and repeat the question for each specific crime type. One would also make sure the respondent can at least specify the month in which the crime occurred. Second, the interviewer would ask whether or not each criminal incident mentioned by the respondent was reported to law enforcement officials. Then more specific information would be solicited. Experience indicates that many rural dwellers, primarily farmers-ranchers, will not know if they have been a crime victim unless the crime is of some magnitude. They may not have the proper checks and controls to know on a daily basis if small tools, machine accessories, grain, even livestock, are missing.

If the telephone crime survey indicates the rural dwellers, farm and residential, need better inventory controls because they really do not know if they are being victimized, then the need for a second project is brought to light: a property inventory analysis. Techniques and procedures other than telephone surveys may be used. Which type depends upon resources and expertise available to collect the data.

CAPABILITIES OR RESOURCE ASSESSMENT

Once the problem has been assessed, the amount of resources (money, people, equipment) needed to implement crime prevention programs can be determined. Without first determining the nature of the problem, no one can say what resources are needed. However, a general resource availability assessment may be conducted concurrent with a needs assessment. One must recognize that these elements are sequential but time limitations may require concurrent activities.

STRATEGIES

Once the preliminary steps are completed strategies can be developed. These strategies must be organized on broad-based government and citizen participation. Each community will have its own unique differences which will require different strategies.

MANAGEMENT

Whatever strategies are developed, their implementation and operation must be managed. People have to be assigned tasks and schedules for activities have to be maintained. Workers must be taught their tasks and

Table 10.2 Planning and Implementing a Comprehensive Rural Crime Prevention Program

Planning and Implementation Stages:	Actions to be Taken by Policymakers and Program Implementers:
I. Description--Critical conditions in need of changes are detailed	Continuously assess degree of fit between goals and accomplishments with respect to crime and fear of crime
II. Diagnosis--Analysis plus prescription (problems analyzed, possible remedial alternatives prescribed)	Assess innovative approaches, appraise existing opportunities for support, evaluate potential contributions of ongoing programs, seek inputs from local informants and outside consultants, identify program advocates who can develop consensus among community and agency leaders.
III. Initiation--Steps taken that will facilitate implementation of the proposed strategies	Lay groundwork for proposed strategies (e.g., reallocate or seek new resources, recruit new personnel, delegate responsibilities for the several components)
IV. Introduction--Sitewide dissemination of information about the imminent activities	See that the details of the strategies--including the reasons for them and the benefits expected--are clearly explained to all members/residents who will be affected by them.
V. Transition--Occurrence of first moves towards activation of strategies	Closely monitor the activities of the members/residents to make certain that the program directives are being activated.
VI. Routinization--Crime prevention activities become generalized or widespread	Actively promote feedback about the results of the stragies being implemented in order to alleviate difficulties and sustain and enhance support.
VII. Stabilization--Crime prevention activities become institutionalized	Periodically assess degree of fit between changed crime and fear conditions and other needs of the members/residents to minimize the social pressures to revert to old patterns and to optimize their commitment to the new patterns.

supervision provided. But anyone who has participated in a church bazaar, county fair, or a chicken barbecue for the volunteer fire department is an old hand at this element. Of course, a government agency (police, sheriff, state police) may be willing and able to assume this role. But if not, the management of rural crime prevention programs is not restricted to law enforcement or other units of government. Citizen volunteer groups can assume many leadership roles.

EVALUATION

Evaluation is not simplistic. On the contrary, evaluation is a sophisticated on-going process in any program. The programming process Evaluate, Plan, Implement, Evaluate, (EPIE), attempts to illustrate the importance of evaluation by including it as an element prior to program planning. This effort is needed to build into every rural crime prevention program, for example, a process by which the program's effectiveness can be measured. In simplistic terms, evaluation is asking those involved in rural crime prevention: To what extent has the crime prevention program(s) you developed and implemented had impact on the crime(s) you targeted for reduction? To respond to this question, one must do an initial crime data analysis to measure crime prior to the time the crime prevention program was implemented, and again after the program has been implemented for a sufficient time period. Ironically, the crime analysis which was the crucial first step to determine "needs" is the important final step by which the crime prevention programs' worth will be measured.

Program Stages

A comprehensive rural crime prevention program is an attempt to cause major alterations in the routines of the citizens, business people, law enforcement personnel, public and private agencies and associations, and a variety of other groups in each rural area. In short, such a program seeks to create major community and organizational changes. Effective management of such a program requires that adequate attention be given to each of the program's planning and implementation stages. Table 10.2 outlines the activities associated with each of seven stages: Description, Diagnosis, Initiation, Introduction, Transition, Routinization, and Stabilization.

The following discussion highlights the management issues for each stage. They fall into two categories:

1. Actions to be taken by policymakers and program coordinators/implementers; and
2. roles and responsibilities to be assumed by the other site members and users, e.g., community residents, agencies, and associations.

For the policymakers and program coordinators/implementers, the issues include the following:

1. Detail the level or extent of the target crimes and fear of such crimes; specify their relevant characteristics, e.g., predominant victim groups, offender groups, MOs, and locations (description).
2. Analyze the patterns and apparent sources of such crimes, the environmental characteristics, and the existing resources (including influential advocates) and ongoing programs to propose the approaches/solutions (diagnosis).
3. Lay the groundwork for the prescribed approaches (e.g., reorganize, authorize, generate/commit necessary resources, hire/reassign key personnel) (initiation).
4. Announce, inform, prepare (introduction).
5. Implement the strategies by directing, coordinating, or directly supervising the initial actions/moves (transition).
6. Promote and monitor widespread acceptance of, and involvement in, the ongoing and emerging crime and fear reduction activities; optimize feedback-responsiveness loops (routinization).
7. Institutionalize the crime/fear prevention concepts and strategies by promoting expansion of the network of agencies, groups, and projects which expect crime prevention approaches to be part of their day-to-day target crimes and fear of such crimes (stabilization).

For the other site members and users, there are the following related issues during the first three stages:

1. Community involvement—Problems are raised and redefined; issues are proclaimed, solutions are requested (description).
2. Community involvement—Solutions are suggested, reoriented, and placed in context (diagnosis).
3. Community involvement—Approaches and strategies are suggested; pragmatic details are input to help refine the approaches and strategies authorized by the policymakers (initiation).

During the final four stages, when the prescribed changes are actually being implemented and institutionalized, these community members and agencies are called upon to react in ways appropriate to each stage:

1. To become sufficiently aware (introduction).
2. To respond on schedule to specific strategies (transition).
3. To promote and reinforce changed behavior and expectations of the other community members and users (routinization).
4. To view and respond to the climate of reduced crime and fear not as a transitional situation but as the new status quo (stabilization).

While the management structure for each rural crime prevention program does include all of the above concerns, the primary focus should be on the initial stage. It is here that the actual requirements for carrying out a realistic work program must be confronted. It is here that the success of most programs will be determined.

Conclusions

The goal of crime prevention programs is to initiate and implement crime prevention activities which successfully reduce crime and the fear of crime. As indicated in this chapter, the crime prevention planning process has three major components and involves a variety of resources and participants at various stages throughout the process.

Crime analysis is a critical first step in determining the need for crime prevention programs. It is also an essential element in planning and implementing programs once this need is determined. Crime analysis comes into play again in the evaluation of crime prevention programs, e.g., What was a program's impact? Was crime reduced? etc. Because of the key role which crime analysis plays throughout the planning process, a good deal of attention should be given by an agency to the development of a crime analysis process and capability.

Effective crime prevention programs can begin only as a result of relevant and reliable information. Basic to preventing crime is understanding how and when it occurs. Programs often fail because the problem has not been adequately identified. As a result, good programs are sometimes matched with the wrong problem. For example, a burglary prevention program directed at single family dwellings would be misdirected if most burglaries occurred in apartment units. And, because the nature and extent of the problem changes, it is necessary that crime analysis be done on an ongoing basis.

The difficulty of selecting appropriate crime prevention strategies is compounded by the diversity of crimes, offender methods, victim characteristics, and the environmental settings in which crimes occur. Further compounding the difficulty is the profusion of inconsistent opinions about which strategies are best. However, crime patterns can be analyzed to determine the causes of fear and the major threats against security. By knowing the nature and extent of the crime problem and integrating this with other relevant data, priorities can be set, areas targeted, strategies tailored, and resources allocated for programs to reduce crime and fear.

A combination of factors must be studied—including victim characteristics, the community and physical setting, suspect characteristics, and the suspect's modus operandi. With this information it is possible to define more clearly the crime problem. The availability of this information will facilitate the determination of strategies most appropriate for preventing and controlling crime.

A description of crime county-wide cannot substitute for further analysis at the "rural neighborhoods" level in preparing localized crime prevention programs. Different "rural neighborhoods" have different crime problems. Only through the use of citizen and police knowledge coupled with localized statistics can the problems in a "neighborhood" be articulated and appropriate strategies developed and implemented.

Notes

* Taken in part from *Comprehensive Crime Prevention Program*, Office of Anti-Crime Programs, Law Enforcement Assistance Administration, (updated).

Selected Bibliography

Johnson, Thomas E., and Joel B. DeKraker. 1976. *Planning for Prevention: A Comprehensive Approach*. Lansing, Michigan: Office of Criminal Justice Programs, 1976.

McCauley, R. Paul. 1975. *Crime Analysis*. Louisville, Kentucky: National Crime Prevention Institute.

———. 1978. "Crime Analysis: The Important First Step." *NCPI Hotline*. February/March. Louisville, Kentucky: National Crime Prevention Institute.

U.S. Department of Justice Law Enforcement Assistance Administration. Undated. *Comprehensive Crime Prevention Program*. Washington: U.S. Government Printing Office.

———. *Crime Analysis for Crime Prevention*. South Minneapolis, Minnesota: Minnesota Crime Prevention Center.

———. 1977. *Crime Analysis in Support of Patrol*. National Evaluation Program, Phase I Report, Series A, Volume 17. Washington: U.S. Government Printing Office.

———. *The Crime Process: A Training Workbook*. LEAA Grant 75TN-99-0002. Sacramento, California: The California Crime Technological Research Foundation.

———. 1978. *Introduction to Analysis and the Criminal Justice System*. Washington: U.S. Government Printing Office.

———. 1973. *Police Crime Analysis Unit Handbook*. Washington: U.S. Government Printing Office.

11

A Practitioner's View of Combatting Crime: With Special Reference to Programs for the Elderly

GEORGE SUNDERLAND

Introduction

Over the last two decades the crime explosion has focused much attention upon the kinds of criminal incidents that affect persons in their everyday lives. Crimes such as robbery, rape, burglary, assault, purse-snatching, and others have enormously debilitating effects upon society and its quality of life. Nowhere is the impact of crime more serious than among the elderly. The economic, psychological, and physical harm caused by victimization has been found to be greater among the elderly than among any other age group (Conklin 1975; Clemente and Kleiman 1976; Lebowitz 1978). Although most sources of official crime data indicate that overall the elderly are less likely to be victimized than other age groups, this is not true for particular types of offenses, including con and fraud, strong-armed robbery, purse-snatch and pick-pocket (National Retired Teachers Association/American Association of Retired Persons 1979). In addition, the negative psychological impact resulting from fear of crime among older persons is especially serious (Clemente and Kleiman 1976).

Crime is now on the increase in rural America. Given the fact that nonmetropolitan areas of the United States generally have higher proportions of older citizens than metropolitan areas (U.S. Department of Health, Education, and Welfare 1978:130), what will be the effects of crime on the rural elderly? Perhaps even more important, what are the solutions available to rural areas for the crime problem in general, and specifically for one important part of rural society—the elderly?

The purpose of this chapter is two-fold. First, it will examine the various alternatives which have been proposed as so-called solutions to crime. It will look critically at these solutions from the viewpoint of the crime prevention practitioner. The crime prevention practitioner, whether he is a law enforcement officer working for a nonlaw enforcement agency such as the National Retired Teachers' Association/American Association of Retired Persons, is confronted with the day-to-day workability of crime reduction proposals. However, what seems to work in theory does not always work in reality.

The second purpose of the chapter is to review the effectiveness of programs which teach law-abiding citizens to prevent crime and to illustrate the need for thorough analyses of the local pattern of crime before planning these programs. Special reference will be given to crime prevention programs for the elderly population. Before proceeding to the examination of various crime prevention efforts, the next section will make a few general statements about the recent growth in crime.

Some Observations about the Growing Problem of Crime

In 1968, for the first time, a national poll reported that crime—meaning the fear-provoking and bothersome types referred to as "street crime"— was the highest concern of the people (Gallup 1968). This high level of concern continued through the decade of the 1970s and into the 1980s. Some factors contributing to this appear to be:

A. The rapid increase in fear-provoking or worrisome crimes. These crimes included rape, robbery, purse-snatching, burglary, larceny from person, fraud, vandalism, and others. During the past two decades, a period during which our population increased approximately 22 percent:

1. Reported robbery increased 426 percent
2. Reported larceny increased 1,216 percent
3. Reported residential burglary increased 288 percent
4. Reported murder, rape, and aggravated assault increased 302 percent (U.S. Department of Justice 1959-80).

B. The as yet unexplained growth of unprovoked violence in stranger-to-stranger crimes. More persons were assaulted even though such actions were entirely unnecessary to the completion of the criminal acts.

C. A general rise in those crimes touching the victims directly. This rise increased personal alarm.

D. A greatly expanding number of studies and surveys which brought about a still imperfect, but better, understanding of criminal activity. Their more accurate definitions of crime patterns and frequencies focus attention on the crime crisis.

E. The rapid rise in actual crime introduced the factor of vastly more perceived fear caused, in part, by vicarious victimization.

F. An increase in the public's general disillusionment with the criminal justice system's ability to protect society, and the admission within the system itself of its inability, leading to searches for alternatives to the conventional avenues of crime control.

An exposition of just a few of the reported crime increases warrants this rise in public fear and concern. However, all of these increases are in *reported* crime which must be adjusted to postulate for the *actual* volume of crime being committed. Reported-to-actual crime relationships vary widely by crime types, age and sex of victims, locality, and other factors. The National Crime Survey (U.S. Department of Justice 1979:65) produces reasonably reliable bases for extrapolation. The percentage of reported-to-actual crime in the types just noted are: rape, 58.4 percent; robbery, 55.5 percent; aggravated assault, 51.5 percent; burglary, 48.8 percent; purse snatch, 46.4 percent; crimes of theft, 24.8 percent.

Solutions to the Crime Problem:
A Practitioner's Viewpoint

Merely relating a particular strategy to the problem of criminal victimization without an in-depth examination of that strategy's operational potential is unwise. Any response position should be discounted as a superficial, "band-aid" approach unless other alternatives also are examined in the light of their practicality. In this section, the operational effectiveness of several alternatives will be examined. These solutions include the causative approach, the court system and law enforcement, juvenile justice, and rehabilitation.

CRIME CAUSATION—THE SEARCH FOR THE ELUSIVE "ROOTS"

The most natural and frequent question people ask about crime is "why." They ask it about individual crimes, and about crime as a whole. In either case it is an almost impossible question to answer. Each single crime is a response to a specific situation by a person with infinitely complicated psychological and emotional makeup, who is subject to infinitely complicated external pressures. Crime, as' a whole, is millions of such responses. To seek the causes of crime in human motivation alone is to risk losing one's way in the impenetrable thickets of the human psyche.

This statement is taken verbatim from the Report of The President's Commission on Law Enforcement and the Administration of Justice (1967). This massive study reaffirmed findings announced over and over again by other studies.

It is generally believed by many judges, law enforcement officials, and criminologists that crime cannot be reduced unless its "root" causes are known. However, from the viewpoint of many crime prevention practitioners, the persistent demand for finding the "roots" of crime is the most frequent obstacle they face in formulating operationally sound crime reduction efforts. However, the causative solution must be seriously considered before being rejected in favor of other strategies.

While some crime causation theories may apply to specific individuals, none yet have general or even widespread application. Most popular theories of causation cite "poverty" and "income inequality" as important factors.

It is tempting to follow a course of "pure reason" and believe that a person who is not poor and lives amid plenty has no reason to steal or commit crime for monetary gain. Following this line of reasoning, if poverty is eliminated, crime will "go away." This is attractive to consider, but a few facts soon dispel this notion. First, most poor people are not committing serious crime. In the past 20 years, a period of great affluence, crimes have increased dramatically. In the history of this country, many poor people living under the most destitute conditions and performing the most menial tasks have committed very little crime. One example was the immigrant Jewish population coming into New York City in the 1800s. Another was the poor Chinese who came to this country in the last century. The Chinese lived under such abominable conditions and suffered such affronts by society that the saying, "He doesn't have a Chinaman's chance," became popular and widespread. Yet these immigrant Chinese committed very little serious crime. And until they became Americanized in recent years, their progeny committed very little crime.

Charles E. Silberman (1978:169) writes in *Criminal Violence, Criminal Justice* that "poverty, inequality and racial discrimination" cause crime. Yet, in another chapter, the author cites case after case of bank presidents, politicians, wealthy businessmen, lawyers, doctors, and many others committing a great deal of crime, but who certainly are not suffering from poverty, inequality, or racial discrimination.

Dr. Richard Blum (1972), of Stanford University, after an exhaustive inquiry searching for the predictors of crime, observed that many youngsters get into trouble from having too much too soon, from lack of religiosity, from parents who are contemptuous of authority and transmit this contempt to their children, from lack of discipline, and from too much permissiveness. His inquiries covered a period of more than a decade and resulted in significant findings for crime prevention practitioners.

Practitioners of crime prevention are often thwarted by the "crime causation" proponents who decry any effort other than the pursuit of the elusive "roots" of crime. However, crime prevention practitioners may seek some solace in the knowledge that expedient alternatives are gradually coming into grace. To quote from the publication, *Crime* (Adams 1976:59): "But if causes cannot be pinned down and better understood, much about crime can be, with potentially useful results. Many criminologists now bend their major efforts toward learning how criminals operate and how those operations might be prevented."

THE COURTS AND THE COPS—PERFORMANCE AND PROBLEMS

If the factors which motivate criminals are not fully known, can it at least be assumed that lawbreakers can be caught, convicted, and incarcerated? Let us take a look at the performance of law enforcement and the courts in reducing crime.

One obstacle to evaluating performance is the lack of system-wide information. The criminal justice system is not really a system, but is made up of independent components. Not until such organizations as the Institute for Law and Social Research (INSLAW) conducted studies was a true system-wide picture available. In a series of revealing reports by INSLAW, it was found that, from "Ashtabula to Washington, D.C." the proficiency of the criminal justice system is dismal (INSLAW 1977). Examples to confirm this conclusion are limitless. For instance, in Washington, D.C., for a crime type that should have a very high conviction rate, commercial robbery, in one year there were 2,070 reported incidents, which projects to approximately 2,300 actual incidents. There were 86 juvenile arrests. Information on their disposition in the juvenile justice system is nearly impossible to obtain. Of the 220 adult arrests, there were 108 convictions. A review of post-conviction disposition reveals that, of these, about 20 percent were released immediately to probation or were given suspended sentences.

Examining INSLAW's (1977) performance perspectives for commercial burglary in Washington, D.C., the conviction rate was found to be about 1 percent. Again, the post-conviction disposition reveals about one-third were immediately released to probation or given suspended sentences.

Arson is one of the fastest growing crimes in the country. Because of the nature of the crime, it is difficult to determine its extent. Experts estimate arson has increased more than 500 percent in the past 15 years. About three-quarters of all school fires are arson, and about one-third of all fires are arson. The arsonist is rarely arrested and even less often imprisoned. In fact, the conviction rate has been less than 1 percent.

Vandalism damage exceeds $2,000,000,000 annually, of which about $600,000,000 occurs in the schools. This crime is usually committed by very young people. Few are apprehended and, because they are juveniles, the extent of action against the offender is the "inconvenience" of a hearing, rarely anything more.

In one recent year, national statistics revealed over 3 million burglaries were reported to the police (U.S. Department of Justice 1978). For that year, nearly 7 million actual burglaries occurred in the 76.5 million households of this country. In one representative major city, more than 19,000 burglaries were reported (an estimated 41,000 burglaries actually occurred). This "typical" city assigned 11 full-time detectives to the investigation of these burglaries. This represents one officer for each 1,727 burglaries "known to the police." With such a crushing caseload, how effective can the police be? Or expected to be?

Only about 15 to 20 percent of total police personnel time is directed toward crime control efforts. Doubling or tripling police agencies, an impossible dream under current trends toward fiscal austerity, would have but a minute effect.

As difficult as it may be to accept, the courts and the police cannot cope with the present magnitude of criminal activity. Criminals are not easy to apprehend and are becoming even more difficult to convict.

In some metropolitan jurisdictions, 1 percent of the criminal cases will fully occupy 15 to 18 judges. Given that the police "clearance" rates are low, the police arrest far more persons than the courts can handle. Were the police to increase their efficiency even a minute amount, the court system would collapse.

JUVENILE JUSTICE

Statistics show that most bothersome street crimes are committed by young males (U.S. Department of Justice 1978: 194-97). It is a problem that has been long observed and it has been of crisis proportions for a number of years. The handling of juvenile offenders is a clear example of the too often experienced chasm between idealism and realism. With good intentions, the juvenile system is operated to avoid stigmatizing the offender with a criminal record and to afford a "second chance." As many studies have disclosed, the second chance has extended into hundreds and even thousands of chances. There is seldom a "first offender;" it is nearly always the first time caught for an offense. Depending on the location, a juvenile may commit from hundreds of burglaries before being caught, and many more before the system imposes sanctions. Numerous other crimes, such as vandalism, theft, shoplifting, and many lesser crimes, are sprinkled between the crimes of burglary, purse-snatch, and strong-arm robbery. It is believed at the present time that criminal patterns of behavior begin between 10 and 12 years of age. However, until the youthful offender reaches adulthood, meaningful sanctions are seldom imposed by the juvenile justice judges. It is incredible to believe that the youthful offender will suddenly cease criminal activity upon reaching adulthood after a number of years of satisfying and rewarding youthful criminal activity. The instant rewards, together with little or no sanctions, actually encourages juvenile criminal activity.

There are some alternatives in dealing with young criminals which avoid the "stigmatization" process. Restitution in the form of work to repay the offended is certainly nonstigmatizing, while being efficacious. This has proved to be a deterrent to criminal conduct where it has been tried (U.S. Department of Justice 1979).

Restitution also has the advantage of bringing the victim back into the system "out of the cold" so to speak by forcing the offender personally to witness the damage or injury inflicted. In addition, too often juvenile judges see only the dramatics displayed by the offender and fail to see the havoc wreaked upon the victim.

This author has had numerous conversations with law enforcement officers who are critical of the court's handling of juvenile offenders. Until a number of apprehensions are made (often three or more), the juvenile offender is not punished. Restitution is one of many forms of punishment which seek to return the responsibility for the young offender's behavior on himself and to change his attitude toward committing crime before it becomes a career choice.

REHABILITATION—DOES IT WORK?

What are the other avenues which, theoretically, should lead to crime reduction? One is the long and deep-felt idealism that reform is the answer and that rehabilitation is the only salvation. This makes sense; a cure is better than symptomatic treatment. The Jacksonian reformers of the 1820s and 1830s shared these innovative and grandiose ambitions. They would not merely deter but eliminate crime. They would not punish, but would reform the criminal. Prisons should be places of rehabilitation.

It is only reasonable to give new therapies an opportunity to develop and mature. After one hundred and fifty years and mountains of money, how does rehabilitation work? Not very well, according to the experts in the field.

Mr. Norman Carlson (1976) as Director of the Federal Bureau of Prisons, a man with long experience and considerable responsibility, has stated that "most persons in the corrections field are now willing to admit that no one knows how to rehabilitate a criminal and that crime is a disease for which society has no cure." Robert Martinson (1977) made an exhaustive investigation of 231 rehabilitative programs covering the period from 1945 through 1967 and concluded that the programs had had no appreciable effect on recidivism.

Increasingly, practitioners and scholars of national repute have admitted our inability to change criminal to noncriminal behavior against the will of the offender. Sociologist Gwynn Nettler (1974:50) writes in *Explaining Crime*:

> A first fact is that arrest "reforms" some offenders, in the sense that their behavior is "corrected." The offensive behavior stops. Despite this fact, many observers do not regard a change of conduct after arrest and upon the threat of additional penalty as rehabilitation. What they seek is not just a change in behavior, but a change of heart that leads to the change in behavior. Whether or not one requires that a change of character accompany a change in conduct before a person can be deemed to have been rehabilitated a second fact deserves reporting. Efforts to rehabilitate offenders do not work well. There is no science of personality change which has yet been verified or which in its experimental phases has proved successful.

Dr. Marvin Wolfgang (1978) notes that within the past two decades, careful studies have begun to evaluate the efficacy of the rehabilitation model, employing increased statistical sophistication and arriving at negative conclusions. Yochelson and Samenow, a psychiatrist and a psychologist respectively, in a study lasting more than 15 years, concluded with such statements as, "Psychiatric concepts and techniques don't work with criminals because most diagnoses of mental illness result from the criminal's fabrication" (Methvin 1978: 121).

These failures do not result from a lack of good will, of good intentions, of professional experience or of funds allocated. Observable failures are everywhere and they have long been noted by police. Police see the same offender committing crime repeatedly. In a Nashville, Tennessee "sting" operation, of 304 persons arrested, 88 percent had prior arrest records. This 88 percent, or 269 offenders, had 2,155 total prior arrests (*Crime Control Digest* 1978). Since many crimes are committed for each arrest, the actual number of crimes committed would be astronomical, if known. These criminals have been the subject of much study in recent years. In a National Institute of Law Enforcement and Criminal Justice (1978) study, 49 habitual offenders were reported as having committed 10,500 crimes, all of a serious nature. What has been long observed by police is now being confirmed by studies.

At this stage it may appear to be overkill to marshal additional authorities who have concluded that rehabilitation has not been effective in diverting the criminally inclined to noncriminal behavior. Although the belief in the reform movement is deeply entrenched, the words punishment, deterrence, retribution, and incapacitation are achieving new respectability. They occur frequently in the writings of such esteemed scholars as James Q. Wilson (1975), Norval Morris and Gordon Hawkins (1970), as well as in the speeches of major Presidential candidates. The penal system in the United States is now going through an extensive re-examination of its purpose, which may eventually result in new and effective ideas.

Practitioner's Appraisal—Crime Does Pay

Crime does pay and crime prevention practitioners have long observed this. Crime is an exciting career. Most of the risks have been removed. It is profitable, working hours are set by the criminal, aggressions can be vented, power exercised, the "establishment" flouted, the chains of oppressive work routine cast off, and the rewards of private entrepreneurship enjoyed. Crime does not require much training or very high skill levels as opposed to the long periods of training to be an electrician, a technician, a teacher, a lawyer, or about any other occupation that can be mentioned. The criminal receives encouragement and support from his peers. Rewards are instant and not deferred. Crime is an occupational choice that offers more rewards for the investment than most other lines of work.

As a wage earner, even the common street junkie moves immediately into the executive level. As an experiment try the following. Obtain the statistics on male and female wage earners in this country broken down as to age groups and salary levels. Then canvas your local police to determine the amount of money a doper must acquire each day to support his habit. The author did this in Washington, D.C., and found the ordinary street drug addict was acquiring an amount of money exceeding the top 0.1 percent of the female wage earners and in the top 8 percent of male wage earners.

Criminals are not often caught and, if caught, often not convicted. When convicted, a good one-third or more do not go to prison and the few who are imprisoned are seldom deterred by the experience. Sociologist Gwynn Nettler (1974) writes, "Given the low risk of penalty and the high probability of reward, given the absence of pangs of guilt and the presence of hedonistic preferences, crime is a rational occupational choice for such individuals."

In summary, if the proposed approaches to reducing crime—the causative, the courts and law enforcement, the juvenile justice system, and prisoner rehabilitation—do not work and if crime is increasingly becoming an attractive career choice, then what other alternatives are available to the crime prevention practitioner? The final part of this chapter will discuss programs designed to assist the law-abiding public in reducing the opportunity for crime to occur. Special focus will be given to programs which assist the elderly protect their person and property.

Crime Prevention for Older Persons: An Active Involvement

In a way, it is fortunate that the crime types most frequently committed against older citizens are so "opportunistic" in nature that crime prevention techniques will reduce criminal activity by reducing opportunity. These crimes, with the exception of con games, are largely committed by young males having low skill levels and attacking easy targets. Unfortunately, the elderly are often perceived as "easy targets" by the young offender.

According to the National Crime Study (1979), older persons have lower victimization rates for the violent crimes of murder, rape, and aggravated assault. However, older persons are more frequently the targets for fraud and swindles by con artists, and older persons also have higher-than-average victimization rates for strong-arm robbery, purse-snatch and pickpocket.

The impact of crime on older persons is often much worse than when committed against younger persons. Many older persons, for example, must live on fixed incomes; the income of some depends entirely upon the regular arrival of monthly pension or social security checks, which are especially vulnerable to criminal thievery. Unexpected losses resulting from criminal activity can create severe economic hardship for an older person.

Physical injuries, too, suffered during criminal assault can seriously impair an older person's health and mobility for a long time. Moreover, the fear of crime can increase the isolation of many older persons, not only eroding the quality of their daily lives but also increasing their vulnerability to criminal attack.

Effective crime prevention, for the general public as well as for more specific target population such as the elderly, must be based upon the total commitment of the community in support of well-structured programs—programs based upon in-depth analyses of the problem and that allow the public to participate in their design.

The Need for Crime Analysis

While it may be useful (even necessary in some cases) to build victim profiles and to develop crime type correlation to age, time, location and other factors on a national basis, it is more desirable to conduct crime analyses for particular localities, and for specific crimes. This is necessary for program development, tactical counter-measures, budgetary considerations, and other valid reasons.

The need for a location-specific analysis in particular localities is illustrated in the few examples that follow. The city of Wilmington, Delaware initiated a program in response to the high level of concern about street crimes committed against older persons. These crimes included purse-snatch, strong-arm robbery, and armed robbery. Prior to conducting an in-depth crime analysis, it was anticipated that one of the recommendations would be to improve street lighting, based upon the assumption that high percentages of street crimes were committed during the hours of darkness. Fortunately, no action was taken before surveys, data collections, and analyses were conducted. It was then found that peak victimization hours were between 10 a.m. and 4 p.m., with very low rates at night.

The state of Florida, with a high percentage of older residents, understandably has built-in concerns for its elderly population. A state-wide rape-specific program was instituted, targeted toward older women. Fortunately, the director of the program consulted information based upon a crime analysis of rape patterns and found the most frequent victims to be women under 30 years old. The emphasis of the program was soon shifted to the primary audiences for a rape prevention program.

There are now so many successful models of effective, low cost crime prevention that it is baffling as to why they are not more widely practiced by communities and law enforcement agencies. For instance, this author has made hundreds of on-site inspections throughout the United States over the past nine years. One example was an inspection made of a garden-type public housing project in Albuquerque, New Mexico. By preference of the elderly tenants, the project was age-segregated. During afternoons, when the elderly tenants were away on social visits and shopping trips, a number of burglaries were being committed. A simple hardware change—from spring latch to deadbolt on exterior doors—completely solved their burglary problem. It appeared that the offenders were very young teenagers, with low skill levels, who were deterred by the increased security afforded by the deadbolt hardware.

Another example is a mobile home retirement complex in Tucson, Arizona. A security check of the premises revealed every conceivable deficiency. No perimeter barriers, poor lighting, profuse shrubbery, no police visible on the premises, located in a moderately high crime area, and adjacent to much through traffic. Yet the project manager stated that there had not been a single case of vandalism or any other crime for a period longer than five years, despite the fact that the occupants had high concentrations of pilferable possessions. In addition, there were many unoccupied dwellings while residents were away during the hot summer months. The answer was a highly effective but unstructured neighborhood watch program. The tenants looked out for each other with great diligence.

By these few brief examples, it should be clear that a local crime analysis is essential to avoid the mistakes so often made in dealing with crime problems. The products of crime analysis are innumerable, and aside from being essential to crime reduction programs, it can produce information to assist in planning, administration, and management. Some of the "intangibles," such as levels of impact and fear, become more tangible through good crime analysis. So often the perceived problem is the basis for action, but many times the perception is at variance with the facts.

Elderly Involvement
In Crime Prevention Programming

Older citizens in the United States constitute a valuable volunteer resource for the crime prevention practitioner. Many older persons are available as volunteers. This is true of most communities in the United States. There are more than 24 million Americans 65 years old or older. That is over 11 percent of the total population—one of every nine persons—a percentage that is increasing year by year. As a general rule, as persons reach 65 and older, they no longer have the time-consuming responsibilities of full-time work or raising a young family. They have time to give and are available as volunteers (National Retired Teachers Association/American Association of Retired Persons 1980).

There are several advantages to using the elderly as volunteers in crime prevention programs. First, the elderly are skilled. At least half of the persons in this "retired" category already have the skills to serve as volunteers, or they can easily be trained to do so.

Second, the elderly bring with them a wide range of experience, knowledge, insights, know-how, and personal contacts—a store of valuable experience accumulated over the years. Fourth, some elderly are a community-relations resource. Many have personal contacts in business, industry, government, and the local community, developed over their living and working in the area. Examples abound of elderly persons forming into groups to support law enforcement in general and crime prevention programs in particular. Fifth, older citizens often possess a sense of local history unknown to and sometimes unappreciated by younger professionals. Hence, they are more sensitive to local attitudes which have been formed among community members as a result of past events. Finally, the elderly are especially mindful of the need for the peace-keeping and law enforcement mission.

What kinds of services can elderly volunteers provide in crime prevention programming? There are many local and national models, even though elderly volunteers in crime prevention is a relatively new concept. In a small Oregon town, for example, four elderly volunteers successfully completed a formal crime prevention training program. They began surveying households of other older residents, making security recommendations regarding locks, windows, doors and lights, and they promoted an Operations Identification program. In an Arizona retirement community, elderly volunteers operated a Neighborhood Watch Program, provided crime prevention education, assumed traffic-control functions at civic and community events, and some have completed comprehensive first aid training. In a large eastern metropolitan area, fourteen elderly volunteers, each working a four-hour shift one-day-a-week, assisted police in monitoring radio dispatches, making follow-up telephone calls, and taking and transmitting messages. There now exists numerous examples like these throughout the nation (National Retired Teachers Association/American Association of Retired Persons, 1980).

A practitioner cannot afford the luxury of dreaming about what might have been nor of awaiting the uncertain future of utopia and unfulfilled ideals of what should work. The practitioner implements and manages what is now or what will be at the most in the next five years. The above examples of opportunity-reduction programs illustrate successful methods for addressing local crime problems.

Summary

Available performance indicators suggest much room for improvement in many current crime reduction approaches. The crime causation approach has yet to provide viable explanations of why people commit crime. Likewise, performance levels, as measured by conviction rates, reflect poorly on the court system. In addition, law enforcement must contend with high caseloads, which reduces their ability to apprehend criminals. The juvenile justice system has been concerned with "stigmatization" of the young offender, often to the sacrifice of administering punishment. Finally, rehabilitative programs in the prisons have failed to significantly reduce recidivism rates. The results are that crime has been an attractive career for many people.

From the viewpoint of the crime prevention practitioner, other alternative approaches must be initiated. The idea of citizen-oriented crime prevention programs represents one such alternative. There are now many local and national models of crime prevention efforts that have proved effective in actual practice. The police will then have more time to devote to the apprehension of the "career" criminal who is not as likely to be thwarted by community preventive measures. If we do not choose to use them, we will have the crimes we deserve.

References

Adams, Virginia, editor. 1976. *Human Behavior: Crime.* New York: Time-Life Books.

Blum, Richard. 1972. *Deceivers and Deceived: Observations on Confidence Men and the Victims, Informants and their Quarry, Political and Industrial Spies and Ordinary Citizens.* Springfield, Illinois: Charles C. Thomas.

Carlson, Norman. 1978. Testimony before Subcommittee of the House Judiciary Committee. April 10.

Clemente, Frank and Michael B. Kleiman. 1976. "Fear of Crime Among the Aged." *The Gerontologist* 16 (3): 207-19.

Conklin, John E. 1975. *The Impact of Crime.* New York: Macmillan Publishing Co., Inc.

Crime Control Digest. 1978. "Nashville Sting." December 11.

Gallup, George. 1968. "George Gallup Poll Reports." February.

Institute for Law and Social Research. 1977. *Expanding the Perspective of Crime Data: Performance Implications for Policymakers.* Washington, D.C.: Institute for Law and Social Research.

Lebowitz, Barry D. 1978. Statement of Barry D. Lebowitz before the Subcommittee on Domestic and International Scientific Planning Analysis, and Cooperation Committee on Science and Technology. U.S. House of Representatives. January 31.

Martinson, Robert. 1977. "What Works?—Comparative Assessment." In Sir Leon Radzinowicz and Martin E. Wolfgang, eds. *Crime and Justice*. New York: Basic Books, Inc., Publishers.

Methvin, Eugene H. 1978. "The Criminal Mind: A Startling New Look." *Reader's Digest*. May: 120-124.

Morris, Norval and Gordon Hawkins. 1970. *The Honest Politician's Guide to Crime Control*. Chicago: University of Chicago Press.

National Retired Teachers Association/American Association of Retired Persons. 1980. *Law Enforcement and Older Persons*. Washington, D.C.: National Retired Teachers Association/American Association of Retired Persons.

Nettler, Gwynn. 1974. *Explaining Crime*. New York: McGraw-Hill.

President's Commission on Law Enforcement and Administration of Justice. 1967. *The Challenge of Crime in a Free Society*. Washington, D.C.: U.S. Government Printing Office.

Rothman, David J. 1978. "Punishment: A Historical Perspective." *Law Enforcement Journal*. June.

Silberman, Charles E. 1979. *Criminal Violence, Criminal Justice*. New York: Random House.

U.S. Department of Health, Education, and Welfare. 1978. *The Elderly Population—Estimates by County, 1976*. U.S. Department of Health, Education, and Welfare, National Clearinghouse on Aging.

U.S. Department of Justice, Federal Bureau of Investigation. 1959-80. *Uniform Crime Reports*. Washington, D.C.: U.S. Government Printing Office.

U.S. Department of Justice, Law Enforcement Assistance Administration, National Criminal Justice Information and Statistics Section. 1979. *Criminal Victimization in the United States, 1977*. Washington, D.C.: U.S. Government Printing Office.

U.S. Department of Justice, National Institute of Law Enforcement and Criminal Justice. 1978. *Criminal Careers of Habitual Felons*. Washington, D.C.: U.S. Government Printing Office.

Wilson, James Q. 1975. *Thinking About Crime*. New York: Basic Books Inc.

12

Crime Prevention Philosophy and Practice

B.M. GRAY

Crime is a commonplace term meaning a variety of things to people. Our interpretation and the images we think of when we hear the term depend greatly upon our personal experiences and education. A senior citizen who has been victimized by a fraud, the youth who has been extorted for lunch money, and the farmer who returns home to find that burglers now possess his gun collection all view crime in relation to their experiences. Even professionals in the criminal justice field tend to think first of those types of crimes and criminal offenders with which they deal most often.

Crime is a broad and pluralist term used to define specific acts and behaviors which our society has legislatively prohibited. The spectrum of prohibited activity ranges from the stealing of property to the harming of another person. From a prevention viewpoint, each crime type requires different strategies.

Myriad surveys, conducted at the local, state and national levels during the past ten years, have shown that crime ranks as one of the top concerns of the American public. Yet, our society's record regarding the reduction and control of criminal activity is not enviable. We have not only failed to prevent the initial occurrence of crime but also have failed to deal effectively with criminal offenders, both juvenile and adult. If our efforts had been effective, we would have witnessed a reduction in the recidivism rates. Instead, we continue to develop more hardened criminals. Our concerns with crime and crime prevention are not new. We are, however, more sophisticated than our forefathers in our ability to articulate, define, and specify our concerns and desires. These abilities are absolutely required if we are to be effective.

History of Crime Prevention

The history of crime prevention is as old as mankind. The earliest of cave dwellers banded together in tribes for mutual protection. The forms of crime prevention and justice administration they practiced were very physical and brutal when compared to today's activities. Might, rather than strong mores, folkways, or law, was the determining factor for right.

It was only with the rise to power of a king, emperor or other central authority figure that duly authorized officials took on the task of dealing with wrongdoers on behalf of society. The state's reaction to crime tended to be punitive, but the punishment inflicted did not necessarily reflect a belief that offender's pain itself had some redeeming value. Instead, the purposes of punishment were thought to be very pragmatic. In some cultures, a criminal was fined, mutilated, or killed. A fine was levied to repay the victim's loss. Mutilation served to show others that the offender was untrustworthy. Execution was used to settle a family feud or remove a "wild beast" offender from society (Sutherland and Cressey 1974: 301).

Codification of laws began with the advent of Hammurabi's Code, in Babylon, about 1800 B.C. This code reflected a variety of philosophies, some of which still influence our way of thinking today. Requirements for punishment and restitution were specifically defined and even the beginning of what we now refer to as crime prevention through environmental design was present. Codification was furthered with the Mosaic Code and is reflected in historic biblical writings.

Roots of the American criminal justice system's crime prevention philosophies are found in England. Our approach to assigning police to enforcement, courts to adjudication, and the correctional system to rehabilitation of criminal offenders is largely based on the English tradition. Though the cloning of the British system was not perfect, our perspective on the role of police closely resembles England's.

Sir Henry Fielding is the well-known molder of the first police force in London in the mid 1700's. He believed that effectiveness was based on a strong police force and the help of the people served, and that efforts to remove the causes of crime had to be undertaken. He published in a newspaper a list of the crimes that had been committed and urged people to report crime to him in order to gain better insight into the scope of the problem(s) with which he was dealing. Fielding's successor, 100 years later, was Sir Robert Peel. Peel stressed that prevention of crime was the primary responsibility of the police. He emphasized that police are sworn, full-time representatives of the public regarding law enforcement, but emphasized as well that all citizens had a responsibility to uphold the law and control criminal activity. The reasoning of Fielding and Peel holds true in our modern democracy and for modern policing.[1]

American policing has developed over the past 200 years as a highly localized service. Thousands of local law enforcement agencies have been formed in the United States. Their efforts are complemented by the existence of a variety of state and federal agencies. During the past 50 years, an unfortunate phenomenon has occurred. Law enforcement chief executives have told the public that they (law enforcement) would take care of crime and that we (the general citizenry) should rely on them. While the primary crime control responsibility may legally be assigned to police, the primary responsibility still rests functionally with the public.

Responsibility of this scope cannot be delegated. The police cannot control crime if the public does not take prudent precautions. Citizens have responsibility to avoid victimization, notify the police when a crime occurs, testify in court when necessary, and support, with funds and volunteer time, the criminal justice system process. The first responsibility noted above, that of avoiding victimization, is of critical importance to the reduction of the occurrence of criminal acts. Actions that potentially can protect the citizen from victimization, that is, practicing crime prevention, are essential if we are to reduce losses of life and property.

Crime Prevention Defined

The term "crime prevention" conjures up as many images and interpretations as does the word "crime." Sociologists, psychologists, policemen, and lay citizens all think of different approaches, techniques or programs when the term is mentioned. This same definitional morass used to exist when "disease" prevention was mentioned. The medical field developed a conceptual framework so that levels of disease prevention were specified. By doing so, practitioners were able to be specific about their meanings. This framework, involving *primary, secondary* and *tertiary* levels of disease prevention has been adapted to provide a framework for crime prevention discussions. According to Brantingham and Faust (1976: 284), the three levels of crime prevention are defined as follows:

> Primary prevention techniques are directed at modification of criminogenic conditions in the physical and social environment at large, such as citizen education programs, household and business precautions, and modification of the physical environment to reduce criminal opportunity. Secondary prevention is directed at early identification and intervention in the lives of individuals or groups in criminogenic circumstances. Secondary crime prevention techniques include patrol peace-keeping actions, diversion, predelinquent screening, educational intervention programs, employee screening and crime location analysis for neighborhood education and modification programs. Tertiary prevention is directed at the prevention of recidivism through post adjudications diversion, reform, rehabilitation, incapacitation, hiring ex-offenders, aftercare services, and other techniques.

Primary prevention efforts are sometimes defined as "direct," while others are defined as "indirect." Still others in the crime prevention field refer to "operative" crime prevention as opposed to "curative." The main point is that there are a variety of activities that people can undertake, individually and collectively, to affect directly their probability of being victimized by certain types of crime. These efforts, which attempt to reduce criminal opportunity, must be based upon analysis of how crimes occur, not in why they may occur.

Opportunity Reduction and Crime Risk Management

Opportunity reduction efforts are a form of primary crime prevention. They are based on the assumption that prudent people can and will take precautions to minimize their chances of being victimized and, if victimized, to reduce their losses. This line of thinking is based on the premise that three factors must be present for a crime to occur: (1) desire; (2) ability; and, (3) opportunity. Of the three, the majority of citizens are most likely to influence the third, that is, opportunity. The capability to prevent crimes runs a continuum from total control by the potential victim to little ability to affect. For example, the potential victim totally controls the crime of fraud (con games). If the victim does not cooperate, the crime cannot occur. On the other hand, the average citizen cannot affect the outcome of random violence, such as that which occurs when a wild gunshot goes off during a bank robbery. Fate largely determines the chance of injury or death. The types of crimes that Americans fear most, that is, burglary, robbery, larceny, and rape, are controllable to some extent.

In rural applications, the premise of risk management regarding crime prevention is evident. Farmers and other rural residents must make a decision whether or not to accept the risk of burglary, by leaving homes and barns unsecured, or to reduce that risk by locking up. Equipment left in fields can be easily stolen, unless the risk is reduced by placing it in an easily observable place, locking it up with a strong chain, removing the rotor on a tractor motor, or by taking some similar incapacitating action.

For most criminal offenses, there are some preventive steps that can be taken. Possible actions must be determined by examining the target, the means of attack, and the probability of the crime occurring. Often pure target hardening will not work, so observation to increase the likelihood of detecting the offender comes into play. Programs such as Neighborhood Watch, where citizens look out for one another, are important to reduce vandalism, burglary, and theft.

These ideas are not only common-sensical but are based on the concept of crime risk management. Rural businesses operate under two forms of risk management. The first is dynamic risk, which is exemplified by there being an opportunity for profit in some endeavor, which might range from operating a store and having to predict (taking a chance) what line of items will sell best, to the planting of crops (always chancy). Although the risk exists, there is a possibility for gain or profit in any dynamic risk situation. The same is not true for a pure risk situation, such as crime risk.

A pure risk, such as crime, is one that does not have a potential benefit, but only liability since no profit or gain can accrue to the victim of a crime. Since the risk exists, it must be managed as much as possible so that the probability of victimization is decreased to an acceptable level and so that the loss, if the victimization occurs, is minimal. The decision process takes into consideration the following possibilities: risk avoidance; risk reduction; risk spreading; risk transfer; and risk acceptance. The decision points are usually the cost effectiveness of each option considered.

Crime risk management decisions should be based upon analysis, not simply on hunches, and should take into consideration such criteria as the probable maximum loss that could be experienced. For example, is the purchase and installation of lights for the barnyard and locking devices for the farm's gas tank desirable or necessary? Would it not be wiser to install these prior to a theft instead of after one, thus automatically amortizing the investment in terms of savings from theft? Is it worth the time to put an identification number on all heavy farm equipment in order to prove a claim if it is recovered, or will insurance pay full replacement costs? These are simply examples of the practical reasoning process that should be followed in determining what risk patterns to follow.

Tools of the Trade

Once crime risks are identified, the vulnerability and criticality of possible targets should be assessed in order to make a cost effective decision. Expensive or time-consuming preventive efforts should not be directed toward non-critical targets or expendable items. The safety of one's home would usually dictate that good locking hardware should be installed in doors and windows. The risk of losing livestock would dictate that frequent checks on the herd and headcounts should be made. Time also becomes an important factor, as exemplified by a soybean farmer losing the use of his tractor to theft during harvest time, thus possibly losing his profits from all the work done to that point.

The tools of the trade in crime prevention are mechanical, electronic, and procedural. The mechanical includes the various locking devices that one might use to secure a home, chain a tractor wheel, or padlock the motor to a gas pump. The electronic security tools are primarily alarm systems designed to alert the potential victim and generate a response. The procedural element involves the prudent use of mechanical and electronic equipment, but also, involves the observation of possible targets. For example, removing the rotor from a tractor left in a field and locking the door to the barn or the garage door in a rural nonfarm setting are all procedural activities. Similarly, the rural business manager who uses a time operated drop box to reduce the amount of cash on hand practices procedural security. The three must be carefully interwoven and used routinely to be effective.

These three types of tools of the trade are to crime prevention what medications and good health care practices are to disease prevention. They are the means, not the end. Having a lock is no good unless it is used, just as getting a prescription is of no value if it is not taken as directed.

The crime prevention tools are meant to *deter* would be criminals from committing the crime, *deny* them success if they attempt it by *delaying* their actions and causing them to be *detected* if the crime occurs. These four "D's" of crime prevention are important as no one, no matter how prudent, is guaranteed that they will not be victimized. Changing the odds to favor the potential victim as much as possible and increasing the likelihood of the offenders being apprehended are the essence of primary crime prevention.

Program Development

Crime prevention programming seems simple at the first blush. If the environment is right, certain types of static and focused program efforts are easy to start. However, if one is concerned with developing activities or a program with staying power, the simplicity begins to wane. From a management perspective, crime prevention programs are designed to educate the public, increase their awareness of a problem, introduce them to recommended solutions, and stimulate their action. This holds true no matter if the activity is a theft reduction program or if the concern involves the educational development of values in school children. To be successful, a management planning process must be followed.

The basic requirements for the development of effective crime prevention programs begin with the identification and analysis of the problem. The nature of the crime(s) that are of concern to the community must be specified and articulated. Just knowing that residential burglary is a problem, for example, is not enough. Information like the nature of the crime, its volume, frequency, method of attack, time, and types of articles stolen, give clues to identifying the type(s) of offenders and what preventive actions might be effective. This type of analysis not only assists the potential victim in taking the necessary precautions but aids police in making apprehensions.

The next step, after problem identification and analysis, is the identification of resources. Who is being affected? Will they form neighborhood watch groups? Will merchants set up a telephone daisy chain to warn each other of bad check rings passing through town? Will the bank print warning flyers or offer a reward for certain types of apprehensions? How much time and how many dollars can the Sheriff allocate to the problem? These are the types of basic resource questions that need to be examined. It should be done in such a manner that those to be affected, directly or indirectly, by the program are offered a chance to participate in the setting of goals and objectives.

Goals and objectives need to be established early-on so that the desired outcomes are known to everyone. If these are not developed carefully, the strategies being developed will not be complete and will fail to address all aspects of the problem.

Obtaining feedback from an evaluation of the effort is the last component of the planning cycle. The important criteria for judging effectiveness must be spelled out. Are the fears of people being reduced? Has the incidence of crime been reduced? Is the educational program for youth doing what was expected? This evaluation gets plugged back into the planning cycle for the continuation of the program.

Whatever the program type, the energies expended and the persons involved should be coordinated and their efforts integrated. If not, turf issues appear or gaps in strategies doom the effort. Just imagine the confusion if nonfarm residents of a subdivision meet and form a neighborhood watch program, receive the guidance of the Sheriff, call when suspicious behavior is spotted, yet no patrol car is dispatched. Or, what if farmers join an Operation Identification program and mark their heavy equipment only to find out that Sheriff's deputies have not been trained to look for the identification numbers? Failure is assured if efforts are not integrated.

The developer of crime prevention programs must be analytic, understand human nature, have some tenacity for following through, and be success-oriented. Without this orientation the collective efforts of business, religious, education, service club leaders, and elected officials will not be directed at the problem over a long enough time period to solve a local crime problem.

Specific Rural Programs

Specific crime prevention steps and programs can be designed for most types of crime. The list of potential activities is very dependent upon the environment and the people involved in designing the response. The ideas presented here are exemplary of what can be done for a few selected crimes. When designing the program, one should keep in mind that the conditions that encourage criminal activity, such as a low potential for observation and a high potential for access, are very present in a rural setting. To get people to accent the types of programs listed below, they must be given the knowledge of the problem, justification to become involved, and an opportunity to participate. Here are some approaches (U.S. Department of Justice, 1980).

PROTECTING LIVESTOCK

Modern technology has made livestock theft one of the easiest and most profitable of crimes. The modern rustler may use a car, light plane, or helicopter to spot a likely target. The offender's prey are usually stock in isolated pastures and unlocked corrals. Once their quarry have been selected, the thieves move in quickly with trucks or vans, trailers or campers, load up 10 to 15 head and drive away, easily putting hundreds of miles between victim and buyer within a matter of a few hours. The whole process can often be completed in ten minutes and can net the rustler $3000 for a night's work. The risk is low. Too often the theft is undetected for several days.

What can be done to safeguard animals from today's sophisticated rustlers? These suggestions are made to farmers.

1. Check your stock frequently. If possible, take a daily count. If you're going to be away, arrange to have a neighbor keep track of your animals. Do the same for your neighbors when they're away.
2. Mark your animals. Be sure to make marks distinct and to identify young stock soon after birth. Your marks and brands should be registered with the Marks and Brands Unit of the Department of Agriculture and Consumer Services. The preferred method of cattle marking is branding with a hot iron, often used in conjunction with lip and ear tattooing or with earmarks or eartags. Brands and tattoos are hard to alter and provide a permanent record. *To be safe, do not rely on earmarks or tags alone.*
3. Let rustlers know your cattle are permanently marked. Thieves are less likely to take property they know can be traced. Ask your county Farm Bureau for warning signs or stickers to post on your barn and on fences and gates. *Do not use the signs or stickers unless you have actually marked your stock.*
4. Check your fences and gates regularly to make sure they are in good repair and locked. Lock corrals and loading chutes. Use case hardened chains at least 3/8'' thick and a good quality padlock with a hardened steel shackle. Be sure to scratch out the serial number on the bottom of the padlock, or a resourceful rustler may copy it and return later to let himself in with a duplicate key.
5. Never leave livestock penned overnight without supervision.
6. Report missing stock immediately. Rustlers move fast, so report the loss even if you aren't sure whether the missing animals are stolen or have strayed. As many as 30 to 40 percent of all livestock thefts are never reported and less than half are reported promptly. Don't wait—delay insures the rustler a safe getaway.

PROTECTING FARM PRODUCTS

Livestock is not the only target of today's rural thieves. Corn, wheat, soybeans, hay, tobacco, and even oats are being stolen by rustlers. They have discovered there is big money in their kind of crime.

Here are some useful tips to farmers to help protect farm products.

1. Keep your property where it can be watched. Store grain and tobacco in protected locations, and stack hay where you or your neighbors can see it from home.
2. Lock your gates and grain elevator at all times.
3. Mark your grain or tobacco with numbered or coded non-toxic confetti. This confetti can be mixed with the grain, hay and tobacco for identification at point of sale. It is easily removed by mills and has substantially reduced theft in areas where it is used.

PROTECTING EQUIPMENT AND SUPPLIES

Farms or ranches contain many items attractive to thieves. Tools, motors, batteries, tractors and other valuable farm machinery, and supplies such as gasoline are all things the rural criminal is eager to steal if he can.

To defend your property, use the following security tips:

1. Light it up. Thieves and vandals don't want to be seen. Make sure your house, yard, corrals and gas supply are well-lighted.
2. Lock it up. Gas pumps, gas tanks, storage bins, and grain elevators should be secured with strong locks. So should your house and barn. Use deadbolt locks or a padlock and hasp; spring latches can be opened by even an amateur thief in a matter of minutes. Boats, snowmobiles, bikes, fertilizers, tools and other small equipment should be stored in a locked garage or shed, or secured to a stationary object with a strong padlock. Also, chain and lock drawn implements and irrigation pumps. Never leave tools or guns in an open pick-up.
3. Bring it in. It is not wise to leave major farm equipment out in the fields overnight. If you can't bring your equipment in at night, keep it where you or a neighbor can keep an eye on it. Power-driven implements should be secured with a case-hardened metal tow chain at least 3/8" thick. It is a good idea to take out your CB and bring it in at night too.
4. Disable it. Don't let a thief drive away in your vehicle or use it to carry other stolen property. Tractors, jeeps, trucks, and trailers should be equipped with hidden ignition-kill switches. Remove the rotor and distributor cap to prevent hot-wiring.
5. Identify it. If any of your property were stolen from your farm or ranch, could you prove it was yours? If not, the thief will have no trouble selling your possessions. The chance of recovery, even if the property is found, is slim.

Operation Identification is a program designed to discourage burglary and theft by making sure your property can be easily traced to you. In those communities where a majority of citizens participate in Operation Identification, crime has been reduced dramatically.

Here is how it works: contact your local police department, farm equipment dealer or Farm Bureau representatives. They can lend you an engraving tool for free. Special heavy duty marking equipment is available to mark farm machinery. Mark all your valuables with a permanent ID number. On farm machinery, it is a good idea to use two markings: one in the primary locations discussed below, the other in a hidden location of your choice. That way, your property can be traced even if thieves find and remove your primary marking.

Here are some samples of where to put markings.

Tractor. Place ID number on the rear of the differential housing. The exact location will vary according to the brand of tractor. If access will not allow the mark to be placed on the center housing, place it on the right axle housing at the top or rear.

4-Wheel Drive Tractor. Place the ID number on the right side from the rail, 12" from the front.

Combine. Place the ID number on the frame, above the pivot point of the axle—not on the axle, but on the frame of the machine. Also, place the ID number on the cord head and grain table on the right rear angle iron on the main frame.

Round Baler. Place the ID number on the right side, on top of the tongue, and 12" behind the hitch pin.

Shredder. Place the ID number on the front of the frame, above the draw bar.

Once your property is marked, make a record and store it in a safe place. Then, let the thief know that your belongings and farm equipment are marked by posting Operation Identification stickers. These are available from your local law enforcement office or Farm Bureau.

PROTECTING NEIGHBORS

The best crime fighting technique does not rely on elaborate equipment or police manpower. Instead, it depends on neighbors.

How do neighbors protect each other? Here are some hints:

1. Keep an eye on each other's property. Ask your neighbor to watch your livestock closures and farm machinery. Do the same for him/her.
2. Going away? Don't let thieves know. Arrange for a neighbor to pick up your mail and newspapers, cut your grass, and give your home a "lived-in" look.
3. Be observant. If you see a suspicious person or vehicle on your neighbor's property, report it at once. Write down the description of the person or the vehicle license number in case you are witnessing a theft.
4. Consider organizing a Neighborhood Watch program in your community. In many farming areas, volunteer teams send out one- or two-person patrols at night. They monitor suspicious activities and keep in touch with a base station and the police on CB radios. In communities that have tried this type of program, crime has been cut. Your local law enforcement agency can supply more information.
5. Be cautious. Buy only from reputable dealers. Don't support the thief by buying stolen property. Remember: if a deal looks too good to be true, it probably is.
6. Report all crimes and do it promptly. The faster you report, the more likely it is that the thief will get caught.

Conclusion

The methods that can be used to reduce crime are myriad. This chapter has demonstrated that crime prevention can be multifaceted and geared to many levels of effort. The programs to be developed depend largely on the scope of the problem and the resources that can be focused on it. The ideas to be tried should be creative and not just traditional. For example, why not have the future Farmers of America help mark farm property for a project?

The long-range solutions to crime lie in building the proper value system in our youth. In the meantime, a wide variety of opportunity reduction programs, properly developed and focused, can significantly reduce the incidence of crime and loss due to criminal acts in rural America.

Further information on this topic is available from Farm Bureaus, local and state law enforcement agencies, and the National Rural Crime Prevention Center at The Ohio State University.

Notes

For a more in-depth discussion of the history of crime prevention, see *Understanding Crime Prevention*. Louisville, Ky., National Crime Prevention Institute Press, 1978.

References

Sutherland, Edwin N. and Donald R. Cressy. 1974. *Criminology*. 9th ed. New York: J. B. Lippincott Co.

Brantingham, Paul J. and Frederic L. Faust. 1976. "A Conceptual Model of Crime Prevention." *Crime and Delinquency* 22 (3): 284-96.

U.S. Department of Justice, Office of Justice Assistance, Research and Statistics. 1980. *How to Prevent Rural Crime*. Washington, D.C.: U.S. Government Printing Office.

13

The Operative Approach to Crime Prevention

EDMUND G. JAMES, JR.
and STEVEN D. GLADMAN

Introduction

Crime is certainly not a new phenomenon. It has been with us throughout history. For as long as crime has existed, man has been theorizing as to the causes of crimes and methods to eliminate criminal activity. Crime is indiscriminate, being prevalent in all societies regardless of social, religious, or governmental preference. History indicates that our efforts at preventing crime have not been altogether successful, as the number of reported crimes continues to rise.

In order for a criminal act to occur, the *desire* to commit the crime and the *opportunity* to complete the criminal action must be present simultaneously. If the opportunity exists, but the desire does not, or if the desire is present, but not the opportunity, a crime cannot occur. In theory, preventing crime is quite simple. Eliminate either or both of the components of crime and crime is prevented.

All crime prevention is based on the premise of eliminating either criminal desire or the opportunity to commit a crime. The approach centering on the elimination of criminal desire is referred to as the *curative approach*. The *operative approach* deals with eliminating criminal opportunity.

Curative Approach

The curative approach is so named because if it is successful, it will cure the problem of crime. Its elements are more strategic in nature and its goal is to provide permanent solutions to crime problems. The curative approach hopes to be able to identify why crime is committed and then to develop appropriate strategies to eliminate what motivates the individual to commit a criminal act.

The curative approach centers on the offender or the potential offender, and attempts to identify those characteristics that contribute to his criminal behavior, and to modify these undesired traits. Until very recently, most efforts in crime prevention have been curative in nature centering on the apprehended offender. The process of changing attitudes or behavior is implemented after an individual has established a criminal history. Thus, this form of crime prevention is reactive, occurring after the commission of a crime with the hope that it will prevent future criminal activity.

It goes without saying that to date the curative approach has not been able to prevent crime, since crime still exists. This does not mean that the curative approach is the wrong direction to take to prevent crime. It means that analyzing and understanding all the elements that contribute to criminal desire is an extremely complex and time consuming process. To allow the curative process more time to unravel the proper behavioral developmental techniques and to give society some immediate relief from the ravages of crime, the operative approach to crime prevention has evolved.

Operative Approach

The operative approach to crime prevention is not concerned with why criminal acts are committed, but instead focuses on eliminating the opportunity for a criminal act to occur. Operative crime prevention, unlike curative crime prevention, does not center on the criminal, but rather the environment in which he operates.

The operative approach must be pro-active to be effective. The environment must be modified *before* the criminal commits an illegal act. In short, the operative approach concerns itself with the elimination of opportunity to commit a crime, even if the desire is present.

Operative crime prevention is not the final answer since criminal technology and prevention technology advance at similar paces. Often improvements in security devices occur only after criminals have proven them to be inadequate. The operative approach places barriers between the criminal and his goal: the more sophisticated the barriers, the more sophisticated the criminal must become to be successful. Operative crime prevention will force the criminal to do one of three things:

1. Stop committing crime. Because he no longer has the expertise to commit the crime, his opportunity has been eliminated; or he will attempt the crime but not have the needed expertise and thus will fail in his intended act.
2. Switch to another type of criminal activity. If the opportunity to commit a certain type of crime is eliminated but the criminal still retains the desire to commit a criminal act, he might enter into another type of criminal activity. This could be either bad or good depending upon the type of crime that is selected as an alternative to the original. If, for example, due to proper "target hardening" a burglar no longer commits his crime of choice and is forced to attempt shoplifting, the overall effect would be positive since the potential for personal injury in shoplifting is much less than in burglary. However, if the scenario is reversed, with the criminal turning from shoplifting to burglary, the end result may be less desirable. However, in both cases the criminal would be dealing with a new area which he may not be as familiar with or as accomplished at, and thus might increase the chance that he would be apprehended.
3. Move his geographic location. Criminals, like everyone else, like to work in familiar surroundings. However, if the needed crime prevention techniques are applied in the area a criminal usually works, he may be forced to relocate rather than quit committing crimes or changing the types of crimes he commits. The displacement effect is obviously more desirable for the community from which the criminal is exiting. However, like forcing a criminal to change the type of crime he commits, forcing him to operate in unfamiliar surroundings increases his chance of apprehension.

If the operative approach is properly utilized, it can alter the criminal's behavior by altering his working environment. From this basic theory, the concept of opportunity reduction has emerged.

Opportunity Reduction

The first opportunity reduction programs emphasized physical improvements to homes or businesses as a method for reducing criminal risk. These types of efforts were called target-hardening. In order to make physical security recommendations, police officers had to become proficient in the technical aspects of lights, locks, alarms, and building construction. After this technical knowledge was acquired, it was applied to crime risk management. The underlying principal of crime risk management is that the reduction of criminal opportunity should be approached in a systematic manner, with effective protection being the basis for all recommendations. An out-growth of crime risk management was the development of the security survey. The security survey is the primary method used by crime prevention practitioners to evaluate criminal opportunity and make corrective recommendations.

In conducting a security survey, the crime prevention practitioner systematically examines the physical facility and surrounding property to determine security needs and identify existing deficiencies. This is accomplished by examining all doors, windows, locks, etc. in conjunction with how the building is utilized. Security needs for banks are obviously different from those of a home. The crime prevention practitioner attempts then to make cost effective recommendations that the owner can implement. It is very important to have the correct level of security for each site studied. Too much security will be cost prohibitive and the owner will not view it as being in his best interest to implement the suggestions. Too little security will not diminish the criminal opportunity enough to reduce the owner's vulnerability.

Opportunity reduction has gradually evolved to encompass personal as well as property crimes. The same philosophical basis is maintained for both types of crimes. The system of identifying the potential risks and recommending appropriate action is applied to personal as well as property crimes. Instead of making recommendations regarding locks or the like for personal crimes, recommendations about possible avoidance strategies or defense techniques are stressed. The importance of proactive planning is stressed for both personal and property crimes. In order for opportunity reduction to work, the positive corrective action must occur prior to the commission of the criminal act.

A vital part of opportunity reduction programs is community involvement. All opportunity reduction programs require community support and cooperation to be successful. Law enforcement is only a part of an opportunity reduction program. Law enforcement's role is that of a facilitator, providing technical assistance and public education where needed. The community is the actual implementor. No one can force a homeowner to carry out security recommendations made by a law enforcement officer or to follow the victim avoidance suggestions. The community must do so voluntarily. Opportunity reduction programs are successful when a large segment of the community becomes involved. Improving one house in a subdevelopment will not remove that community's problem of house burglary. Only an organized and concerted effort by the entire community to improve the physical security of the neighborhood will reduce the opportunity for residential burglary.

Opportunity refocuses the responsibility for crime prevention back upon each individual citizen. The trend in the recent past has been to place responsibility for crime prevention solely with law enforcement. Each individual abdicated his own responsibility, reasoning that law enforcement was paid to prevent crimes. There will never be enough money for law enforcement to employ the number of officers to prevent crime effectively. Law enforcement should not be responsible for locking your door, protecting your cash from pickpockets, or properly securing your car. Law enforcement's role is to educate the public as to proper physical security measures and appropriate actions to avoid personal crimes, and to investigate and apprehend criminals when crime prevention techniques either were not used or were inadequate. In a pro-active sense, law enforcement should be viewed as consultants assisting the community in crime prevention.

ADVANTAGES OF OPPORTUNITY REDUCTION CRIME PREVENTION PROGRAMS

The best thing about opportunity reduction crime prevention programs is that they work; crime is actually prevented. These programs have measurable results, that is, reduction in house burglaries, rapes, etc., and many of these programs have been successful in reducing the number of reported offenses they were designed to prevent.

Besides the impact on the crime rate, opportunity reduction programs enhance police-community relationships. Both sides view the other as part of a team working toward a common goal. Improved police-community relations make law enforcement more effective. Increased communications allow law enforcement to make more complete investigations. The improved rapport between the police and the community expands the number of "eyes and ears" available to the police. Increased information will result in more apprehensions and the solving of more crimes. Additionally, the efficiency of law enforcement will increase if opportunity reduction programs are instituted, because more time will be available to investigate serious criminal incidents. The majority of crimes committed are opportunity crimes. A door is left unlocked while you go to the market, and as consequence, you become the victim of a house burglary. For each such opportunity-theft that is reported to the police, a police incident report is filed. The initial report is usually followed up by an investigation, the length of the investigation depending upon the seriousness of the offense. All of this takes time. It takes time for the street officer to take the initial report, time for the detective to investigate and file his report. Multiply this time by the thousands and thousands of opportunity crimes committed daily, and it becomes easy to see why law enforcement is primarily reactive rather than pro-active in its approach to controlling crime. Law enforcement is struggling to keep up with crimes that have already occurred. Little time is left to prevent crimes.

The statistics clearly indicate that law enforcement's present reactive approach is not winning the war against crime. For example, in the State of Ohio in 1977, fewer than 18 percent of the home burglaries were solved. And this percentage merely represents the reported burglaries. An untold number go unreported because the homeowner feels the police can do nothing to help him. And, in a large sense, the home owner is correct; police do not possess magical powers that allow them to solve crimes. If a burglar enters your home without force, takes property that is not uniquely identifiable, and leaves without anyone seeing him, the police will have no better luck at determining who the burglar was than you would. However, if the door were properly secured so force was required to enter, the burglary may never have occurred. If the burglar did break into your house and had the opportunity to take only items of property engraved with the owner's social security number, he may choose not to steal anything. Even if he did break into your house and stole engraved items, the chances for recovering the stolen property and apprehending the burglar are greatly increased. Opportunity reduction programs enhance the effectiveness of law enforcement and prevent crime. Less crime means fewer victims.

GOALS OF OPPORTUNITY REDUCTION PROGRAMS

The ultimate goal of opportunity reduction programs is to make such programs obsolete by eliminating all crime. However, that is not a likely possibility. Opportunity reduction will be a continual process until criminal desire is eliminated. For as long as someone wants to commit a crime, the need for eliminating opportunity will exist. Opportunity reduction techniques continue to become more and more sophisticated. The advance in sophistication is dictated by the criminal, for almost as quickly as crime prevention practitioners develop ways to deny opportunity through various hardware and avoidance practices, the more sophisticated criminal element finds ways to circumvent them. A never-ending spiral seems to have been created.

What opportunity reduction can provide is immediate relief to a serious problem. Opportunity reduction is a band-aid that can hold things together until we can discover the cure. In some respects, opportunity reduction may be helping to find the cure. The community involvement aspects of these programs stress the need for a greater sense of community, and a greater sense for shared responsibility and personal responsibility. These may very well be the key elements in the curative approach to crime prevention.

14

Community Resources for Crime Prevention in Rural Areas

GWENDOLYN D. HALL

Crimes committed within rural communities are increasing year by year. Rural residents are now being deprived of property, privacy, and personal security—features of rural life once guaranteed because of their physical separation from urban settings. Until recently, rural crime problems and the conduct of research for the development of rural crime prevention programs have been largely ignored, in part because of the more visible urban and suburban crime situations.

Several factors may affect the crime rate of a particular rural community. These factors include:

1. the physical isolation of many rural homes and farms
2. population growth
3. suburbanization of rural areas contiguous to large cities
4. the composition of the rural population relative to age, sex and race
5. the economic status of the rural community and surrounding areas
6. the stability of the population, including commuters or transients
7. educational, recreational, social and religious characteristics of the rural community
8. the policies of local government, the court system, and prosecuting officials

9. the effective strength of the police force, which may include its size of manpower, response time, and quality of leadership
10. police-community relations
11. citizen action for crime prevention and control (including crime reporting, willingness to get involved, and citizen action initiatives, such as neighborhood watch and volunteer service programs.)

In the past, rural citizens could rely upon a supportive social system for the prevention and control of crime. At an earlier time, rural criminal justice system was supported by other components of rural society, namely, the family, the church, the school, and the local community. Today, however, their supportive roles are slowly diminishing.

Understandably, a system can only remain supportive through cooperative efforts. For example, school vandalism has increased drastically over the last decade. This, according to many social scientists, may be due to a number of causes, including a reduction of family communication and interaction and an increasingly mobile population which does not allow youth the opportunity to establish long-lasting peer group relationships. A cooperative effort among the family, the church, the school, and the neighborhood to provide a support system for youth needs to be developed for crime prevention programs to work effectively. In order to achieve this community-wide support, collective citizen involvement is a necessity. Although individual self-protection efforts are encouraged, collective citizen action wields greater impact for the prevention and control of crime.

Recognizing the central role of law enforcement and the criminal justice system, collective citizen action groups can still make a vital contribution to reducing crime in their community.

Collective citizen action for crime prevention in rural areas should encourage a rekindled sense of alliance, a feeling of safety and security, and a sense of community. It should further foster increased citizen awareness and education, increased civic responsibility, and accountability and should improve police-community relations. Citizen involvement in crime prevention in the rural community thereby should rejuvenate collective interest in the total welfare of the community.

Rural Police-Community Relations

A necessary ingredient for effective citizen involvement in rural crime prevention programs is a high degree of cooperation and understanding between law enforcement and citizen/community organizations. Conventionally, law enforcement has viewed community crime prevention programs as ineffective and unnecessary. However, in recent years, many law enforcement officials have reached the conclusion that the strategic involvement of citizens and citizen organizations is essential if crime is to be significantly reduced. Yet, there still exists doubt as to the capabilities of citizens, the extent to which citizens should become involved (without suggesting fear of vigilantism), and the impact that collective citizen involvement may have on the overall reduction and control of crime.

In the recent past, rural citizens generally assumed that the police had the sole responsibility for protection of the citizen and his property. Therefore, citizens perhaps were less likely to become directly involved and, in many instances, even to voluntarily report a crime they had witnessed. Also, because of the sense of security felt by residents in rural areas, individual self-protection crime prevention efforts were not practiced. In addition, collective citizen actions to reduce crime through citizens' organizations were not perceived as necessary.

As law enforcement and citizens alike become aware of their increasing rural crime problem, the prospects for better rural police-community relations will be improved. Crime prevention in the rural community will be recognized as a joint responsibility of the police and the community.

Cooperative citizen/law enforcement action for crime prevention and control provides numerous economic benefits. Most rural law enforcement agencies have experienced budgetary problems that will not allow them to implement a separate crime prevention unit. The citizen/community organization can supplement the critical shortage of law enforcement manpower for carrying out crime prevention activities. Moreover, the citizen, when involved in crime prevention training and public education programs in the rural community, can promote greater community awareness of crime prevention techniques. At the same time, this awareness serves to reduce citizen vulnerability to crime and victimization. Additional economic benefits of crime prevention may include insurance premium discounts to policyholders who implement crime prevention measures. Furthermore, there are the obvious economic benefits of reduction in losses due to property theft for both citizens and businesses.

Police input and cooperation are crucial elements in the planning, development, and implementation of crime prevention programs by rural community organizations. Conducting crime prevention training programs for members of community organizations is one important role the police can perform. Furthermore, the police can provide analysis of crime prevention needs and identify appropriate crime prevention resources. "Operation Identification" and residential security programs are examples of such crime prevention activities.

Conducting a Community Crime Analysis

In order to develop a relevant and effective community crime prevention program that encourages citizen involvement, a community crime analysis should be conducted. The crime analysis would inform law enforcement and citizens alike of the types and percentages of crime occurring and of when and where they are occurring, differentiate between actual and perceived crime rates, and provide information on offender and victim characteristics. Further, the crime analysis would assist law enforcement agencies, crime prevention practitioners, and concerned citizen leaders and citizen groups in prioritizing those major crime problems occurring, and in designing a "Plan of Action" to alleviate those crime problems.

The "Plan of Action" should include a well-developed statement of measurable goals and objectives. Short-range, immediate action goals and objectives, as well as long-range, long-term action goals and objectives should be included. In addition, a workplan (with a specific timetable and task assignments) and a monitoring process should be designed. These steps will help community members to determine what they hope to accomplish, how and when to accomplish it, how reasonable their approach is, and what level of effectiveness can be reached.

Further, after a community organization determines its "Plan of Action," an assessment of the rural community's crime prevention resources should be conducted. The assessment should be based on whether the resources are free or at a cost, whether they are located within the community or outside the community, and, most importantly, the availability of the resources. Volunteer community organizations implementing crime prevention programs without a source of funding would greatly benefit from a realistic resource assessment, in order not to falter after the program is initiated. A major advantage to resource assessment is the development of coalitions. Because of geographic conditions and, in most instances, shortages of law enforcement manpower in rural communities, coalitions provide numerous benefits to the planning, development, and implementation of crime prevention programs in rural communities. Some of the positive aspects of coalitions are that they:

1. stimulate collective action for the coordination of individual/group crime prevention activities/projects
2. establish a network of resources, (both manpower and financial)
3. develop a support system to address new and ongoing rural community needs
4. establish a power base to address a common cause and

5. allow for the development of an organizational structure to encourage a rational decision-making process.

A plan of action, crime prevention resource assessment, and coalition building process will allow the rural community organization to set parameters for the most pressing crime problems; to match resources to needs; to avoid duplication and to improve coordination of crime prevention activities; to enhance individual/group crime prevention projects through an organized support system; to open lines of communication among citizens, law enforcement, and policymakers; and, lastly, to assure follow-through and completion of tasks, which avoids project "burn-out."

For example, vandalism has been reported by researchers (Phillips 1976; Phillips and Bartlett 1976; Smith and Donnermeyer 1979; Donnermeyer 1981) as one of the most pervasive crime problems affecting rural communities today. A rural community organization designing a program to reduce vandalism will be confronted with several problems. Vandalism is usually the result of spontaneous youth group action (i.e. gangs, peer group pressure). Many incidences of vandalism go unreported. As well, vandalism has both direct and indirect costs. Direct costs include damage to property such as schools and mailboxes, and indirect costs include increased cost for insurance coverage, lowered property value, costs to replace damaged property, and loss of privacy and personal enjoyment. The rural community organization must decide, therefore, which aspect of vandalism will be addressed by the crime prevention program. Possibly, a vandalism prevention program providing recreational activities for youth can serve as a deterrent to the crime of vandalism, and can produce both short-range and long-range results.

In summary, it is essential to assess and to establish the crime-related needs of a rural community before developing a crime prevention program. Following the need assessment, a plan of action should be developed. Finally, activities must be initiated to encourage collective citizen action for crime prevention in the community.

Organizing the Rural Community for Crime Prevention Involvement

According to the National Commission on the Causes and Prevention of Violence (1969:278):

Government programs for the control of crime are unlikely to succeed all alone. Informed private citizens, playing a variety of roles, can make a decisive difference in the prevention, detection, and prosecution of crime, the fair administration of justice, and the restoration of offenders to the community.

This theme was later initiated by the National Advisory Commission on Criminal Justice Standards and Goals (1974: 7): "Citizen involvement in crime prevention efforts is not merely desirable, but necessary."

Because of the increasing shortage of law enforcement manpower in rural communities, citizens must assume an increased responsibility for community protection. The essential element in mobilizing community resources for crime prevention involvement is *Organization*.

Citizens derive many benefits from participating in crime prevention activities in a rural community. For example, they learn what crimes are occurring, where, *and* at what rate; what crime prevention programs can work in their area; how to develop and implement rural crime prevention programs; how to match resources to those crime prevention needs (who is best qualified to do what); and how effective each crime prevention activity may be.

To achieve maximum results, in most cases a community crime prevention program or support system must be developed. The purpose of this organized effort is to encourage police/community relations, disseminate crime prevention information and materials, respond to citizen input, and motivate citizens for continuous collective crime prevention action. Additionally, leaders of the community organization need to follow-up on programmatic procedures and evaluate those activities engaged in by rural citizens in terms of performance and impact on crime prevention programs. To identify a community's resources, the following is suggested:

- Develop a potential list of existing resources (civic, business, professional, community, etc.).
- Determine the rural community's power structure.
- Identify those community organizations having positions of authority in the community.
- Assess the leadership capabilities of those citizens engaged in a wide range of civic and voluntary activities.
- Find out who the rural community sees as its leaders. Often the appointed leader is not the acknowledged leader.
- Identify the appointed and acknowledged leaders' track record in participation on issues that affect the rural community.
- Make initial contacts with selected resources; have a systematic plan— whom to involve and why, and be precise on what is expected of those you wish to involve; discuss the benefits to be received from involvement such as the opportunity for voluntary involvement and being informed of the rural community's crime situation, in addition to the benefits you will receive, such as public awareness and education and responsibility of citizens for self-protection.

The next step is to mobilize resources by developing a facilitative relationship with those existing resources in the rural community involved in the process, and then, to design methods for jointly: (1) establishing open lines of communication; (2) setting goals and objectives; (3) problem solving; (4) decision making; (5) assigning tasks and responsibilities according to capabilities; (6) insuring follow-through and completion of tasks; (7) developing collaboration of effort; and (8) insuring an appropriate support system that will let people feel accepted and that their input is beneficial and needed, yet keep issues open for discussion and disagreement.

In order to develop "new" rural community crime prevention resources, the list of all community based organizations suggested above should be examined periodically to see how nonparticipating organizations/individuals might be involved in the program. Meetings should be established with these "new" resources to explain the crime prevention program and why crime prevention is needed in a rural community. The goals and objectives of potentially "new" participants should be discussed and ways of working together decided. Coalitions are more effective for utilization of new and existing groups because a coalition establishes a power base to address common causes and provides strength for new, but less powerful participants.

Summary

Every rural community in America has a multitude of agencies and organizations, many of which are anxious to find ways to help with the task of reducing the growing crime problem. Local law enforcement officials and community leaders are generally aware of those with local programs. The key is to find the common thread and the leadership to link them together in order to seek solutions to their collective crime problem.

References

Donnermeyer, Joseph F. 1981. "Crime Prevention Programming for Rural Environments: A Systematic Approach." Paper presented at the annual meeting of the Academy of Criminal Justice Sciences. Philadelphia. March.

National Advisory Commission on Criminal Justice Standards and Goals. 1974. *Community Crime Prevention*. Washington, D.C.: U.S. Government Printing Office.

National Commission on the Causes and Prevention of Violence. 1969. *Staff Report: Law and Order Reconsidered*. Washington, D.C.: U.S. Government Printing Office.

Phillips, G. Howard. 1976. EB-613. *Rural Crime and Rural Offenders*. Columbus, Ohio: Ohio Cooperative Extension Service, The Ohio State University. EB-613.

————. 1976. *Vandals and Vandalism in Rural Ohio*. Wooster, Ohio: Ohio Agricultural Research and Development Center, Research Circular 222. October.

Smith, Brent, L. and Joseph F. Donnermeyer. 1979. "Criminal Victimization in Rural and Urban Areas." Paper presented at the annual meeting of the Rural Sociological Society, Burlington, Vermont. August.

15

Preventing Youth Involvement: The Role of Family and School

TODD N. WURSCHMIDT
and G. HOWARD PHILLIPS

Introduction

If one were asked how rural communities have for years gone about the business of solving their crime problem, the most typical response would probably center on the operation of three organizational components which comprise the criminal justice system: police and sheriff's departments; courts; and penal institutions. These elements make up the formal system relegated the responsibility for maintaining civil peace and enforcing the laws.

What is often overlooked is the fact that operating in concert with the formal system were informal means of social control which operated effectively and motivated the greatest proportion of people to obey the law. Laying the foundation for this informal social control network fell within the realm of responsibility of such rural institutions and socializing agents as the family, school, and church. Only so long as the vast majority of people were unwilling to steal or destroy their neighbor's property were policing agencies provided sufficient resources and manpower to deal with the few who were willing.

In addition, the low level of the crime problem and the nature of rural living permitted rural people the luxury of going about daily routines without much conscious regard for protection of their selves or their belongings. For example, the absence of concern for security is reflected in the manner in which farmers have for years designed and constructed out-buildings. The barn, the symbol of rurality, was built as a shelter and storage place. Little or no thought was given to securing contents from theft. A hardy roof overlaying ample storage space nicely met the requirements of the farmer.

Traditional criteria, however, underlying barn construction no longer suffice to satisfy contemporary conditions. The farmer is increasingly reminded that disregard for protection of his property increases vulnerability to uninvited intruders. Examples are plentiful. The point is, rural people were not constrained from allocating resources from preferred uses to those which involved security measures.

Unfortunately, times have changed for rural residents, and with them the need to reassess some long-held assumptions concerning approaches to resolving the rural crime problem.

The purpose of this chapter is to argue for the importance of an educational approach to crime prevention. In the opinion of the authors, the educational approach appears to offer the greatest potential for reducing the growing crime problem as it is occurring throughout rural America today. This assessment is based on some level of understanding of: (1) the nature of the present rural crime problem (i.e., the types of crimes being committed and a profile of offenders); and (2) the increase in opportunities to commit crimes. These will be explored in this chapter, followed by an examination of two educational approaches to resolving a large proportion of the present rural crime problem.

The Victimization Paradigm

Traditionally, perceptions of crime were heavily focused on the offender. This emphasis on the criminal as the sole factor involved in the criminal incident dominated our philosophy and resulted in an historical inertia. Legislators, criminologists, and the criminal justice system fell into the habit of thinking that resolution of the crime problem rested on society's capacity both to disseminate more sophisticated investigative hardware and to increase police staffs to a sufficient level that would better permit attempts to apprehend and subsequently incarcerate criminals (Adams 1976). Emerging concomitantly was an increasing understanding that the offender's motivation for deviancy was an outcome of that individual's social biography, the consequence of which was to shift the burden of responsibility off the shoulders of the offender onto society. Amelioration efforts became heavily oriented toward intervention and rehabilitation.

Today, the move is under-way to couch the criminal incident in a broader scenario. The core of this orientation is to acknowledge that the offender is but one necessary element for the occurrence of a crime. In addition to the offender, a crime occurs only when two additional elements are present: a target; and an opportunity. It is the convergence of these three elements in space and time (Cohen and Felson 1979) which results in a crime.

This new paradigm introduces a challenge to society's approach to ameliorating crime. No longer are approaches solely confined to improving apprehension techniques and attempts at secondary prevention (e.g., delinquency intervention programs) and tertiary prevention (e.g., rehabilitation programs) (Brantingham and Faust 1976). Rather, what is increasingly being expressed is concern for the "identification of those conditions of the physical and social environment that provide opportunities for or precipitate criminal behavior and the alteration of those conditions so that no crimes occur" (Brantingham and Faust 1976:292). The success of these primary prevention programs are predicated on the active involvement of the noncriminal justice components of rural communities, that is, for example, families and schools. It is hoped that the importance of the role of this informal network of social control will become more apparent as we move to examine that portion of the rural crime problem for which an educational approach shows potential merit. Although the dramatic growth in the number of available targets (i.e., consumer goods by which the needs of legal consumers are served, but which improve the range of suitable targets for criminals) has contributed to the crime problem, the following discussion centers on the changing face of the rural offender and the rise in opportunities for these offenders.

The Nature of Rural Crime

Rural areas have never been crime free, but the extent of crime tended to be manageable, sporadic, and specific in nature. In little more than two decades, crime in the rural United States has changed from a problem of low concern to one that today affects farms, homes, businesses, parks, and recreational areas. According to the only source of longitudinal data available, the FBI's *Uniform Crime Reports,* crime in rural areas began to show an increase during the late 1950s and early 1960s. Since that time, there has been a steady growth in the level of the problem. Over the twenty year period, 1959-79, rural crime increased 445 percent (U.S. Department of Justice). To better understand the nature of the problem, it is necessary to examine the types of crimes being committed in rural areas.

Crimes are classified by the FBI into two major categories: crimes against persons and crimes against property. If these two categories are examined separately for the same 20 year period, what readily becomes apparent is property crimes have markedly increased and accounted for the largest proportion of the total crime problem. Property crimes increased 459 percent, while personal crimes increased 154 percent.

To further support this contention is the observation that for every ten crimes which occur in rural areas today, over nine of these will involve property crimes. Less than one out of every ten crimes involves injury to persons. The growth in the number of property crimes is responsible for the present state of concern, is "clogging up" the rural criminal justice system, and should command the attention of crime prevention practitioners.

In addition, a closer examination of property offenses reveals that vandalism and forms of thievery are the two leading crimes being committed in rural areas. Phillips (1975) noted that of all crimes reported by Ohio rural residents in a statewide victimization study, 38 percent were vandalism. The second leading crime was thievery (19 percent). Smith and Donnermeyer (1979) reported similar findings in a countywide victimization study conducted in Indiana. Vandalism and theft, by definition, involve the illegal destruction and acquisition of public and private property. The rural crime problem, then, has largely become a property crime problem involving the destruction and theft of property.

Rural Offenders

Crimes in rural areas are disproportionately committed by young people. Youth are largely responsible for the sizeable growth in property offenses. Of those persons arrested by rural law enforcement agencies, approximately 75 percent will be under 30 years of age (U.S. Dept. of Justice 1979). This same age cohort, however, represents only 53 percent of the total rural population (U.S. Bureau of Census 1970). And, a further breakdown of these data reveals that teenagers constitute the most often arrested age group. In an Ohio Sheriff's Offenders Study,

Figure 15.1: Percent of offenders apprehended by Ohio sheriffs in rural
areas compared to the rural population by age categories

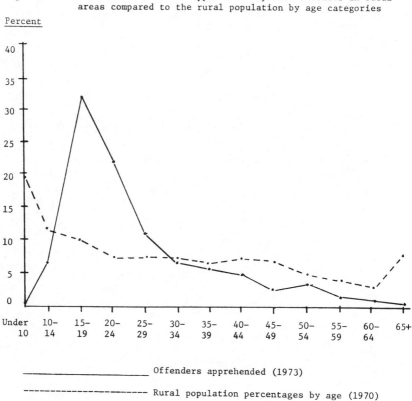

Percent

Offenders apprehended (1973)

Rural population percentages by age (1970)

Phillips (1975) reported that of all persons arrested, one third were teenagers from 15 to 19 years of age. This same age group constituted only 10 percent of the total rural Ohio population (U.S. Bureau of Census 1970) (Figure 15-1).

Although the percentage of teenage apprehensions in Ohio in 1975 tended to be slightly higher than for rural sectors in the United States (27 percent for rural U.S.) (U.S. Dept. of Justice 1975), the implication is clear. Teenagers are the most often arrested age group in rural areas.

The often heard expression, "It is the professional or highly skilled criminal who is responsible for our crime problem," is challenged when data on the residental location of the offender are examined. Of those persons arrested in rural counties in Ohio, 70 percent lived within the same county in which they were arrested (Phillips 1976). Another 18 percent resided in a county adjacent to the one in which they were apprehended. Only 12 percent of the rural offenders travelled across two or more county lines in order to perpetrate their crime. Less than a third of these persons had a previous record.

The facts revealed by these data do not repudiate the notion that skilled criminals or "hardcore" juvenile delinquents ply their trade against rural citizens. They do, however, demonstrate that a vast majority of the rural crime problem is a result of young people committing one-time illegal acts (or at least getting caught for the first time) on locations which are in and around their own communities.

A myth often expressed is that the rural offender is a sophisticated professional who with purposive intent travels from urban dwellings to ply his/her trade in isolated areas of rural America. Corrective action to resolve crime, then, is seen as falling within the duties assigned to law enforcement agencies. The citizens' attitude reflects a belief that little can be done at the level of the private citizen to impair the professional's motivation to intrude into rural areas. On the contrary, the largest percentage of crimes which are committed in rural areas are committed by amateurs and by young people, and nearly all live within local areas.

Peer Acceptance:
The Motivation for Youth Involvement

The most recent research studies on the rural crime problem have consistently supported the contention that the leading crime problem in rural areas is vandalism. This fact, combined with the fact that the teenage population is largely responsible for the rural crime problem, leads one to ask the questions, "Why do young people get involved in crime and under what circumstances do they get involved?"

Insight into these questions was provided by the results of two self-report vandalism studies conducted in Ohio (Phillips and Bartlett 1976) and Indiana (Donnermeyer 1980). The sample in the Ohio study consisted of sophomore high school students (i.e., 15- and 16-year olds). The Indiana sample consisted of junior high school students (i.e., 16- and 17-year olds).

Several important findings surfaced from these studies. The first point to be made is that in both studies a majority of students admitted they had committed one or more acts of vandalism. In fact, students were more likely to have committed three or more acts than to have only committed one or two acts. This leads to the conclusion that vandalism is a crime which is not perpetrated by a select few, but has become acceptable behavior among rural youth.

Second, over 70 percent of these young people did not commit their act in an effort to get back at the property owner (vindictive motivation); nor were they interested in owning the item being vandalized (acquistive vandalism); nor were they destroying property for hedonistic purposes (malicious vandalism) (Ward 1973). The prevading motivation for these young people, that is, their predominant reason for committing vandalism, was peer competition, challenge, fun, contest, etc.

This point is further highlighted by the fact that in over 90 percent of the cases, the individual admitting to vandalistic behavior was with peers at the time the vandalism was done. The notion that vandalism is extensively a "peer acceptance" crime was again supported by the fact that over 70 percent of the youth who were involved believed their acts did not constitute a "crime."

A similar finding was reported in a recent national Gallup poll, conducted among teenagers from 13 to 18 years of age, asking about their involvement in shoplifting (Columbus Dispatch 1980). One-fourth of the teenagers admitted they had shoplifted at least once. There were variations according to sub-regions of the country and as broken down by age group (13-15 vs. 16-18 year olds) and sex. Males from 16-18 years of age were more likely to have shoplifted (37 percent) than young females from 13 to 15 years of age (14 percent). However, the interesting finding is that 72 percent of those admitting involvement said they had done it for "kicks." In other words, teenage involvement in this crime of thievery was very similar to motivations reported in the vandalism studies.

In the words of Glaser (1978:172):

> Extremely relevant to an understanding of adolescent crime is the observation that much of life with others is what Gothman calls a "character game." This is exemplified by challenging, teasing, flirting, showing off, debating, kidding, bluffing, and other interaction in which the response solicited in front of others is meant to suggest a character or ability of the actor. For persons insecure in status—as are most adolescents when their claims to adulthood are placed in doubt by peers who challenge them to do something risky—these 'games' can be extremely decisive. They cannot back out without being humiliated either as "chicken" (timid), as being less sophisticated in adult behavior than they had pretended, or as being dependent on or as being subservient to parents or teachers.

The quest for peer acceptance, the eagerness to search out competitive challenges, and the young person's need for fun have escalated the level of "prankism" beyond tolerable limits.

These pieces of evidence, when combined, present an expanded view of the current crime problem plaguing rural areas and give insight into the changing face of the rural offender. The contention is that rural communities must increasingly recognize that responsibility for prevent-ing a large proportion of rural crimes cannot be delegated to police. "The unspecialized adolescent offender is the criminal type of most concern to American society" (Glaser 1978:161). Preventing involvement by young people, providing alternatives for peer interaction, and devel-oping a strong character of responsibility in youth are tasks for which families, schools, churches, and youth organizations must accept primary obligation.

Opportunities for Young Offenders

Current evidence supports the contention that the peer group is gaining a greater influence on teenagers' lives. Several researchers have reported on the positive correlation between youth who engage in deviant behavior and the fact that this behavior is often initiated and reinforced as a result of associating with peers who are engaging in similar behaviors (Natalino 1979; Akers et al. 1979; Krohn 1974; Jessor et al. 1973). The reason for this increased influence stems in part from the fact that the opportunity to interact with adults has diminished for the young person. Glenn (1980) reported that the "average" parent in a two-parent family today spends approximately 14.5 minutes in a typical 24-hour period in direct com-munication with each of their children. Of this time, 12.5 minutes are spent correcting things that have gone wrong. In other words, approxi-mately two minutes each day are devoted to open-ended conversation between child and parent.

Although seemingly unplausible at first glance, verification of these facts is supported when one realizes that in a 24-hour day, approximately eight hours are spent sleeping, while eight to ten hours separate family members as a result of being away at school and work. Only six hours for potential direct contact remain. But, as Glenn points out, the "av-erage" American family in 1980 spent close to five hours watching television. The residual, that is, one hour, is quickly divided up as a consequence of accomplishing routine matters (e.g., grocery shopping, visiting friends, doing homework, etc.). It quickly becomes apparent that, for those young people whose parents are not available for routine interaction, the next most likely available group will be those young persons' friends. The peer group, although ill-prepared to deal with the development of a strong value and attitudinal base, gains increasing importance, principally as a consequence of their being accessible.

In addition, economic necessity, coupled with a changing image of both the role of women and the division of labor for marriage partners, has found an increasing number of rural households vacated during normal working hours. For example, in 1950, 29 percent of farm women worked at off-the-farm jobs (U.S. Bureau of Census 1961:19). In 1977, 41 percent of farm women worked away from home (U.S. Bureau of Census 198:9). For rural nonfarm wives, the percentage is even higher. For those families with children, the need for both parents to work, and the increasing numbers of one parent families, has created a situation whereby school-aged youngsters find themselves arriving home, alone and unsupervised, for some period of time. Although limited in documentation, it seems likely that the daily requirement for young people to assume responsibility for themselves may produce predicaments which might otherwise never occur. Data from the vandalism study, for example, revealed that over one-third of the vandalism acts occurred during the hours immediately following school (Phillips and Bartlett 1976:21). The situation falls squarely into the realm of long-standing discussion concerning young people's need for supervised and structured activity.

In addition, with the growth in construction of county, state, and federal highways and the dramatic increase in availability of automobiles, would-be offenders have an opportunity for travelling, for example, 50 miles in any direction in the course of one hour. In years gone by, a similar distance would have required preparation for a two-day excursion.

In addition, the remoteness and isolation of rural communities in the past created a situation wherein confinement bred familiarity and contributed to the visibility of strangers once they intruded into the community space. With increased mobility, who belongs is no longer always apparent. The consequence of being recognized served, in the past, as a strong deterrent to young people. Messages in a close-knit, homogeneous community were likely to fall on the ears of the young person's parents. Today, with the rising number of families owning two cars, the young person, in the company of his/her peers, accomplishes easy escape into unfamiliar neighborhoods. Achieving anonymity is easy, undercutting the effective operation of one more component of the informal system for maintaining social control.

As well, technological changes have dramatically affected today's family lifestyles by: (1) preempting many of the opportunities for young people to share experiences in meaningful ways with members of their immediate and extended families; (2) replacing convenience at the expense of having the need to make plans in order to meet basic requirements for food and shelter; and (3) negating the traditional process whereby young people learned responsibility as a byproduct of learning the consequences or penalties a family endured if each member did not carry out assigned tasks and chores (Glenn 1980).

For example, 50 years ago, this country was characterized as a traditional, agrarian society with approximately 54 million people living in rural areas of the United States. Although the total number of people residing in rural places has not substantially changed (U.S. Bureau of Census 1930-70), the proportions of farm to nonfarm families have dramatically shifted. In 1930, a vast majority of rural families made their living farming. Today, less than one in twenty families' major occupation is farming (U.S. Department of Agriculture 1978). And, for these farm families, accomplishing the task has become heavily skewed toward mechanization. The point of this discussion is to note that the children growing up in the agrarian tradition became involved early-on in contributing to the operation of the family enterprise. Ten to twelve hours each day were spent interacting with family members. The outcome of this interaction was learning responsibility. The consequence of not bringing in the firewood, for example, and stoking the fire before bedtime was the family was cold upon rising in the morning. If plans were not properly made prior to the weekly trip to town and each member did not follow through once in town, the family went without for the week. In the process of carrying out these daily routines, the young person learned the nature of being responsible. The consequence of not being responsible was going without some needed or desired item or being cold in the morning.

Today, the thermostat replaces the need to make preparation for heating. A turn of the wrist brings warmth quickly. The automobile and proliferation of easy accessibility to consumer goods replaces the need to make careful preparation for food and supply needs. If something is forgotten, a quick trip to the convenience store quells potential inconvenience.

This discussion has not been presented as a challenge to return to the old ways of doing things. The potential for meaningful opportunities for our youth has never been better. Yet it requires that parents, educators, youth workers, etc. realize that young people are today growing up in a world much different than that of a few decades ago. Learning to become a responsible and functional adult is not an ability people are born with, but a capability that is learned through "practice and experience" (Glenn 1978). Learning how to operate successfully in one's social environment is largely based on having the opportunity to interact with others who are operating successfully. Today, many of the opportunities for young people to learn how to become successful adults have been replaced, leaving them greater opportunity to get involved in peer-centered activities. The results of these activities have increasingly been the committing of crimes which are motivated by challenge and contest.

These crimes are not premeditated, vindictive, or malicious. The outcomes are most often not planned. Rather, they reflect poor judgment or a failure to examine the consequences of their actions. For example, driving through the crop fields of a farmer, destroying mailboxes and street signs, or stealing clothes from a department store can undoubtedly be fun to the young person, but doing it competitively increases the level of excitement. The youth becomes stimulated as his/her higher skills are called into play. Add a certain level of risk to the mix, and a dull act becomes exciting. In the excitement, judgment is impaired, especially as to examining rationally the consequences to the victims of a hastily conceived act.

A Search for Strategies

It is the contention herein, then, that much of the dramatic rise in crime rates in rural areas has been due to the increase in opportunities for young people to get involved with their peers in illegal acts. The types of crimes for which these youth are responsible are virtually impossible to control by target-hardening approaches (i.e., improving home and business security through the installation of quality locks, lights and alarms) or by catching a significant number of vandals or young thieves in the act. The only appropriate strategy is one that causes potential perpetrators not to commit the act willfully. This seemingly idealistic statement was actually the predominating behavior in rural areas not more than two decades ago. It still prevails in selected areas. Responsibility for instilling the motivation or teaching skills that will enable teenagers to avoid participation in illegal acts belongs in the home and classroom. Although the family and school are not often thought of as institutions of public safety, these are the two social institutions the criminal justice system relies upon most heavily to provide the foundation in which the majority of people learn to become responsible and capable adults.

THE EDUCATIONAL APPROACH

All approaches to crime prevention have some element of education associated with them. Although particular crime prevention programs have diverse objectives to be achieved, the process of accomplishing these objectives entails education of the actors for whom the program is targeted. Education is the means to an end. Each prevention effort requires that those involved communicate useful information in ways that will heighten the awareness and motivation level of potential audiences.

For purposes of this discussion, the "educational approach" means deliberate strategies employed to help youth become responsible and capable people. These are directed primarily at the potential offender.

CRIME PREVENTION IN SCHOOLS

The educational approach to crime prevention for schools centers on assisting young people to understand the consequences of committing a criminal act, to examine their attitudes relative to various deviant acts, and to provide skilled training in peer group behavior. Consequences are formally examined in terms of legal, economic, social, and psychological costs to both offenders and victims.

The criminal penalties associated with some crimes may be sufficient to deter some individuals from committing a crime. In others, this risk may only add excitement. Many youth, however, are simply not aware of the legal consequences of particular acts. The two most often arrested age groups in the Ohio Sheriff's Offenders Study (Phillips 1975) were 19- and 16-year olds. The vandalism studies conducted among 15 to 17 year olds (Phillips and Bartlett 1976; Donnermeyer 1980) demonstrated that a majority of these students had previously committed vandalism. For these teenagers, their experiences may not have been of the nature that would cause them to be aware of the consequences of their involvement. And so, the question is asked, "Who will be the source of their experience or skill training?"

For example, one of the suggested methods of developing skills that will help a teenager better cope with those occasions when peer challenge creates an uncomfortable situation, is classroom presentation of "contrived experiences." Real-life situations that create potential troublesome predicaments for youth are read to the class or acted out in skits. Excluded, however, is a conclusion to the story. Once the dilemma is introduced, the class is asked to consider the many ways the actors might seek resolution to the predicament. The premise is that the young person may not always want to be involved in the proposed vandalism or shoplifting act, but peer pressure and the lack of skills to remove him/herself from the dilemma may override their perception that the behavior is wrong. The purpose of the classroom exercise is to enhance the probability that youth have gained at least a little experience in thinking about the consequences of involvement and ways to avoid or excuse themselves from participating.

Although this type of exercise may appear on the surface to be simplistic, the reader might consider the intensity of the argument it would take from one of your peers to convince you to commit a vandalistic act, rob a bank, shoplift, etc. Most readers would have acquired the skills to reject the notion easily, let alone the offer.

There are many teacher's guides in crime prevention available, ranging from kindergarten to twelfth grade (Hamrick 1978; Wurschmidt and Phillips 1977; Miller Productions, Inc. 1976; Commercial Union Assurance Co.'s 1978). They have been tested and shown to have an affect on young people's attitudes, behaviors, and knowledge levels (Thomas 1978; Hamrick 1980; Wurschmidt 1977). Perhaps the rural classroom will continue to be reorganized as a primary force in preventing crime.

THE FAMILY'S ROLE IN CRIME PREVENTION

The family is generally the most influential unit in a young person's life. As such, it obviously has a major role in building positive skills and attitudes in children.

As discussed earlier, significant social and cultural changes have impinged on the nature of parent-child relationships (Glenn 1980). These relationships in the past had built-in mechanisms that assured the development of needed attitudes and skills in young people. The nature of these relationships can no longer be taken for granted.

As Glenn (1980) points out:

> A family in the past could assume that if they brought a child into the world, fed and clothed it, they could reasonably expect that the child would grow up to be a responsible adult. This assumption was based on the fact that the old world was filled with activities that provided the child with practice and experience to become capable. Cultural change has preempted many of those opportunities.

The family today must realize that the result of these changes requires that they provide by "intent and design" opportunities now suppressed by contemporary lifestyles. The diversity of rural families makes it impossible to offer a precise prescription concerning the kinds of experiences young people need. But the following general guidelines serve as a basis for potentially reducing the vulnerability of young people. These guidelines are derived from a series of videotape programs titled "Developing Capable People" in which Dr. Stephen Glenn outlines positive action approaches for the family, as well as for youth program workers, school teachers, and law enforcement personnel.[1]

First, families need to find ways to increase the amount of time shared with their children. Shared time does not mean watching television, where the only conversation centers on the selection of a program. Rather, it means time in which parents give their undivided attention to a young person thus providing them opportunities to learn the skills of living successfully with others. For example, this might be accomplished by turning off the television in order to discuss what each person has viewed.

A second guideline involves learning the consequences of one's behavior. Maturity is the ability to be able to examine the consequences of behavior and paying the consequences when poor judgments are made or reaping the benefits of good judgments. Parents have to give their children the chance to test ideas and occasionally fail if they are to learn how to make sound judgments.

Perhaps the third guideline could best be defined as on-the-job-training for adulthood. That is, if a young person at 18 is expected to assume adult roles, then they must be provided with opportunities to have experiences which help them learn the skills of adult living. How can one be expected to live within one's means when he/she has never had to pay a bill, settle a debt, or balance a checkbook? How can one expect to choose a career wisely when he/she has never experienced meaningful work? Today, young persons have plentiful opportunities for these experiences, but no one is taking the time to discuss the implications of these experiences with them. Experiences which are left uninterpreted may have little effect in developing skills for adult living.

Stability in adulthood appears to be related to stability in one's childhood. A fourth guideline involves family rituals and traditions. It does not seem to matter so much what the rituals are. What is important is that the family engages in regular, systematic activities such as family discussions, birthday celebrations, Thanksgiving dinners, family prayers, and family outings on the weekend. Rituals, if regularly carried out, are important to teaching order and regularity to young people.

A final guideline important for families to consider in preparing the young person to accept adult roles involves technology. What the wise family today must recognize is that the widespread adoption of technology in each of our lives has preempted many of the opportunities for families to interact. For example, dishwashers have replaced the need for family members to work together in a setting that would cause them to discuss their daily activities (i.e., washing and drying dishes as a routinized activity after the evening meal).

Technology has certainly taken the drudgery from many necessary tasks. However, at the same time, it has eroded the nature of family life.

The above examples function as crime prevention because they influence the quality of socialization provided by families, which in turn is intimately associated with the behavior patterns of adolescents. In spite of the fact that these are indirect and long-term approaches to resolving the crime problem, the family approach may hold more promise for resolving the growing crime issue than any other solution. However, other shorter-term programs (i.e., targethardening) need to be addressed in concert with the longer-run solutions. Nevertheless, the ultimate solution in returning to a relatively crime-free rural environment must by necessity involve the family and the community of which it is a part.

Summary

What we have tried to demonstrate in this chapter is that a large proportion of the present rural crime problem is perpetrated by young people. Their involvement is largely based on the fact that there has been dramatic changes in rural areas over the last few decades, one outcome of which has been to increase young people's opportunities to interact with peers. This increase in peer-centered activities has been at the expense of diminished time spent with their families.

The concerned family today is increasingly adjusting to a new set of conditions by consciously providing innovative ways for young people to gain the experiences necessary for becoming a successful adult in a constantly changing society.

In an educational-conscious society, school consumes much of the young person's life outside of the family. This rural institution is a significant force in the formation of a youth's attitudes and behaviors. The school serves as a source of knowledge, a forum for the testing of new ideas, and an environment for new experiences. Rural schools have a definite responsibility and opportunity to teach youth the consequences of illegal behavior and the skills to remove themselves from potentially troublesome predicaments.

Crime prevention professionals must recognize the potential contribution of these rural institutions. Often parents and teachers simply do not know how to deal with the issue of crime prevention. Crime prevention professionals will find acceptance among many concerned citizens who likewise realize the impact of the family and school on the behavior of young people and, therefore, on the rate of crime in the community. With the support of the local community, the crime prevention practitioner has the opportunity to initiate successfully these long-term prevention programs.

Notes

1. The videotapes were produced by the National Rural Crime Prevention Center. Dr. Stephen Glenn is Director, Family Development Institute, Washington, D.C.

References

Akers, R.L. 1973. *Deviant Behavior: A Social Learning Approach.* Belmont, California: Wadsworth Publishing Co., Inc.

Brantingham, Paul J., and Frederic L. Faust. 1976. "A Conceptual Model of Crime Prevention." *Crime and Delinquency* 22 (3): 284-96.

Cohen, L.E. and Marcus Felson. 1979. "Social Change and Crime Rate Trends: A Routine Activity Approach." *American Sociological Review* 44 (August): 588-608.

Columbus Dispatch. 1980. "Teen Thievery is Major Trend." February 6.

Commercial Union Assurance Company. 1978. *Play a Part in Prevention.* Boston, Massachusetts: Ziff-Davis Publishing Co.

Donnermeyer, Joseph F. and G. Howard Phillips. 1980. "The Nature of Vandalism Among Rural Youth." Paper presented at the Annual Meeting of the Rural Sociological Society, Ithaca, New York. August.

Glaser, Daniel. 1978. *Crime in Our Changing Society.* N.Y.: Holt, Rinehart, and Winston.

Glenn, Stephen H. 1978. "Education for Alternative Behavior." Keynote Address, Proceedings of the 1st Annual Southeast Drug Conference, Georgia State University, Atlanta.

————. 1980. "Developing Capable People." Video-tape series. NCRPC 102. Columbus, Ohio: National Rural Crime Prevention Center, The Ohio State University.

Hamrick, Scott. 1979. *The Charlottesville/Albermarle Crime Resistance Program.* Charlottesville, Virginia: Charlottesville/Albermarle Public Schools.

Jessor, Richard. 1976. "Predicting Time of Onset of Marijuana Use: A Developmental Study of High School Youth." *Journal of Consulting and Clinical Psychology* 44: 125-34.

Krohn, Marvin D. 1974. "An Investigation of the Effect of Parental and Peer Associations on Marijuana Use: An Empirical Test of Differential Association Theory." In Marc Reidel and Terrence P. Thornberry, eds. *Crime and Delinquency: Dimensions of Deviance.* New York: Praeger.

Miller Productions Incorporated. 1976. *The Child's Keys to Crime Prevention.* Wichita Falls, Texas: Education Support Services.

Natalino, Kathleen W. 1979. "A Rural-Urban Comparison of Delinquency, Home Factors, and Peer Group Involvement." Paper presented at the Annual Meeting of the North Central Sociological Association, Akron, Ohio. April.

Phillips, G. Howard. 1975. *Crime in Rural Ohio.* ESO 363. Columbus, Ohio: Department of Agricultural Economics and Rural Sociology, The Ohio State University.

————. 1976. Rural Crimes and Rural Offenders. EB-613. Columbus, Ohio: Department of Agricultural Economics and Rural Sociology, The Ohio State University.

Phillips, G. Howard and Kaye Bartlett. 1976. *Vandals and Vandalism in Rural Ohio.* Research Circular 222. Wooster, Ohio: Ohio Agricultural Research and Development Center.

Smith, Brent L., and Joseph F. Donnermeyer. 1979. "Criminal Victimization among Rural Residents: A Case Study of Benton County, Indiana." Paper presented at the Annual Meeting of the Rural Sociological Society, Burlington, Vermont. August.

Thomas, Donald W. and Douglas C. Bachtel. 1978. *The Rural Turnaround in Southern Ohio: A Five County Study.* ESO 514. Columbus, Ohio: Department of Agricultural Economics and Rural Sociology, The Ohio State University and the Ohio Agricultural Research and Development Center.

U.S. Department of Agriculture. 1978. *Farm Population Estimates.* Series P-27. Washington, D.C.: U.S. Government Printing Office.

U.S. Bureau of Census. 1930-1970. *Current Population Studies.* Washington, D.C.: U.S. Government Printing Office.

U.S. Department of Justice, Federal Bureau of Investigation. 1959-1979. *Uniform Crime Reports.* Washington, D.C.: U.S. Government Printing Office.

Ward, Colin, ed. 1973. *Vandalism.* New York: Van Nostrand Reinhold Company.

Wurschmidt, Todd N. 1978. *Final Report: Ohio Rural Crime Fighter's Project.* Columbus, Ohio: Ohio Farm Bureau Federation.

Wurschmidt, Todd N. and G. Howard Phillips. 1977. *Teacher's Guide: Rural Crime Prevention Guide for Young People.* ESO-486. Columbus, Ohio: Department of Agricultural Economics and Rural Sociology, Ohio Cooperative Extension Service, and The Ohio State University.

16

Rural Law Enforcement and Crime Prevention: A Role in Transition

GARY R. WILSON

Crime is rapidly becoming an especially ominous, new kind of blight for both citizens and police in rural areas. The incidence of rural crime in 1980 has now actually surpassed the mid-1960 level of crime in America's urban areas. That level of urban crime in 1968 precipitated massive federal aid programs through the passage of the National Safe Streets Act and the creation of the Law Enforcement Assistance Administration. One researcher has found strong indications of as much as a fourfold increase in rural crime since 1960 and by almost 300 percent during the last decade alone in one area (Phillips 1975). In other words, instead of just an overall rise in the number of incidents, there has been an alarming upward trend in the actual rate of increase in criminal occurrences.

Crime in the countryside would seem to be getting worse faster than ever. Concern about the problem has put it on practically everyone's agenda. Some have been impelled to action, albeit too often only by an unthinking castigation of an inadequate, anachronistic rural police service. Given the complexities of crime causation and control, this makes as much sense as the patient blaming the treating physician for having contracted the plague. However, a case can be made against such a "professional" who is willing to settle for treating only symptoms or consequences, rather than advising others of their vulnerability and the available countermeasures or joining with them in programs designed to reduce threat.

The purpose of this chapter is to argue that rising crime rates in rural areas are causing rural law enforcement agencies to rethink traditional approaches to solving crime. In the process of rethinking, what is emerging is increasing attention to the concept of crime prevention. Discussed are the roles and limitations of both reactive and pro-active approaches to accomplishing law enforcement and several organizational implications rural police agencies must consider if they are to adopt an effective prevention strategy.

Reactive Responses: An Essential But Limited Approach

Rural policing finds itself in a predicament regarding crime in the country. This predicament may not be too unlike that dilemma of medical practice in the past, that is, before someone thought to inoculate against disease, promote hygiene, or drain swamps. A crossroad is presented where the choice of direction may not only be critical to the future of police service in rural areas, but vital to the very quality of rural life. Most who have looked seriously at the problem would agree that we are farther behind in the fight against rural crime.

Sheriffs and other rural police administrators have certainly felt the pressure of public expectation to do something about crime, and many are doing something. They must share a sense of professional frustration over an apparently diminishing resource in proportion to the crime problem. Indeed, it must seem that during the recent past, rural law enforcement agencies have been kept in an almost constant state of flux. Many progressive officials have worked at making important and necessary changes in rural police programs. Considerable attention is being given to efficiency factors in this era of declining public enthusiasm for tax increases in support of more police resources. These range from replacing sworn personnel with "civilians" in office and support functions, so that more officers are freed for field duty, to shedding or splitting off organizationally such extraneous functions as jailer, court guard, prisoner escort, and server of court orders.

Perhaps as important to productivity are continuing efforts to upgrade qualifications and performance standards, civil service status, and general as well as specialized training. There are innovations in patrol, like task grouping, directed patrol, and helicopter patrol, to enhance response time and patrol coverage (little crime occurs in roads other than traffic offenses and consequently few are encountered by random car patrol). Given the multiplicity of jurisdictions in rural areas, mutual aid agreements as well as plans for the consolidation of shared support services, or of separate organizations, could conceivably yield more and better police resources and more police presence.

Seen one way, these efforts at change (which are by no means universal) are commendable as attempts to catch up or keep up with the demands of the task. On the other hand, they may also be seen as too short-sighted, promising at best only to delay the inevitable or slow down the rate of falling behind. In this view, there are to be heard echoes of the time-honored displacements of responsibility for failure—"Just give us more men, more public support . . . more money . . . fewer court system obstacles. . ." In all probability, these changes could at best make possible the continuance of the status quo, doing more and more of the same things. There is no assurance that increasing the density of or concentrating patrol forces materially affects the crime rate anyway. In fact, there are strong indications to the contrary (Kelling et al. 1974). The primary triggering mechanism for police involvement in a criminal enterprise, the report of crime, is not even materially influenced by police. An overwhelming majority of crime reports appear to result from citizen-initiated contact, rather than fortuitous police encounter.

Continued overreliance on response as the major countercrime strategy seems even less feasible in rural areas than in the city. Taking into consideration the hundreds or even thousands of square miles of area to cover, response time will likely continue to be too long under the best of circumstances to assure timely intervention in crimes in progress or to even match the response times in town. Working mainly from "cold" reports inevitably frustrates officers and investigators alike, lowers clearance rates, and extends the time required for successful follow-up investigation. The resultant selection among cases and prioritization will probably continue the mere formality of report-taking which citizens perceive with futility, further reducing inclinations to report crimes. An overly reactive stance inevitably limits the impact of officers to the range of one individual's personal perceptions and reaction to problems.

Given the public's growing reluctance to pay more (or the same) level of taxes and rural government's lack of willingness to fund more improvements of the sort described earlier, it seems that many may not be fully realizeable anyway (at least not quickly enough). If crime rates continue to rise essentially unchecked, other more harmful effects may be felt. Spontaneous, unaffiliated self-help programs (e.g., vigilantism) may be foreseen which would acknowledge and further erode public confidence in rural police or add to the problem directly. Resentments may develop, and police become increasingly unwelcome in rural areas. Vigilante activities could cause even more lawlessness. Fear and suspicion could fractionate communities and recreate fortified neighborhoods. Something else is needed other than a reactive police response to crime which offers both to offset more effectively the threat of escalating crime and to restore a reasonable prospect for a relatively crime-free rural environment without being repressive.

Pro-active Responses: A More Balanced Approach

Although what is needed may be a significant departure from modern police over-reliance on methods effectively furthering only their law enforcement/order maintenance role, it should be seen more as a return to fundamental, traditional conceptions of the police role in crime control. Crime prevention may have been a revolutionary concept when Henry Fielding first proposed it in the mid-1800s or as part of the Peelian reforms. Anglo-Saxon police function and purpose were to have centered on responsibility for the prevention of crime. Brown's (1979: 1050) citing of Sir Richard Mayne's first principle, "the primary object of an efficient police is the prevention of crime," serves as a basic statement of purpose for police in a free society. He argues the need for the modern police service "to restore primacy to its generalist, preventive functions, and to bring these functions into more balanced relationship with specialist, reactive functions" (Brown 1979:1053). Both British and American police have increasingly departed from this common heritage of role prescription. Meadows (1979) gives authoritative support to an expansion of U.S. police practice into the broader role of crime prevention. In a later similar article, he quotes American police pioneer August Vollmer (Berkeley, Calif. Ornia Chief of Police 1905-32) who said:

> I have spent my life enforcing the law. It is a stupid procedure, and has not, nor will it ever, solve the problem (of crime) unless it is supplemented by preventive measures. (Robert J. Meadows, 1980)

For whatever reasons, police seem recently to have drifted away from this essential role commitment, so much so that to one writer, most rural agencies "are structured to enforce laws. Few seriously attempt to serve the crime prevention function" (Donnermeyer 1979). A redirection of the police enterprise into more pro-active channels is called for, even more urgently for the rural agency which has the most limited prospects for success in reactivity alone. A basic change in role for rural police agencies from a mostly reactive force to a pro-active, prevention orientation is not only traditionally consistent, but necessary and feasible, as well.

In addition, the potential for prevention acceptability in the country may be enlarged given the more fundamental characteristics of rural folk. Brown (1979:1050) points out that "the primary police force in any society is the ability for that society to regulate itself." Rural folk are sometimes described as being more independent and self-reliant. From the farmer who does not have close neighbors to the urban visitor who leaves his customary world at home, self-help is a way of life in the country. Rural self-policing has been more the rule than the exception. Chronically undermanned agencies have historically even had to call on the community to help enforce the law (i.e., the posse). Beyond that, rural law enforcement has always been closer to the people than in urban areas. Whether this is due to lower population density or country origins is immaterial. The point is that people in the country are more accustomed to a close working relationship with their police authority, and a tactic which is essentially familiar and preferred seems to offer a lot of promise.

Curative vs Operative Crime Prevention

Insight into the full potential of prevention as a countercrime strategy is hampered by confusion between types of crime prevention, as well as inadequate translation into concrete terms. The concept is most readily distinguishable in two major categories: (1) direct; and (2) indirect.

INDIRECT OR "CURATIVE" CRIME PREVENTION

Indirect or "Curative" Crime Prevention addresses crime causation, motivation, and the dynamics of criminal behavior—the social, economic, or psychological genesis of crime. It has been essentially the province of sociologists, social workers, and criminologists, although social planners, government, and community service agencies are increasingly involved out of desperation in broad general programs of this sort.

One is concerned in curative prevention with influencing or removing root causes of crime/criminality and the restoration or preservation of the social health of individuals and communities. Major research and implementation of programs of long duration can be identified here, such as juvenile delinquency control, corrections, drug abuse control, and family counseling. Indeed, the argument can be made that, indirectly, crime prevention must begin with education and extend to enlightened rule-making, even assured incomes. However, unless it can be assumed that crime would have been a lot worse without such programs until now, it can be said that curative efforts have not yet stemmed the tide of crime.

Curative programs and theories of crime causation and deviance have been around for hundreds of years, and still exist imperfectly today. This has probably not been due to error as much as to incrementalism and excessive zeal (reflecting the depths of concern and commitment which have prevailed). Being heavily theory-based, each new factor discovered or claimed as a prime factor in crime is consumed fadistically and rejected, or different explanations or philosophies have competed with each other and been jealously guarded, diluting the effects of each. It seems that crime and criminals tend to be extremely complex, while cures have been either too simplistic or too exclusive. A total or comprehensive program of so-called cures may even be inconsistent with the idea of a free society with decentralized authority, lacking the compulsion that would be necessary to define every deviant or criminal as ill in order to "commit" them to the cure. Many answers or explanations for criminality have been found, but no single theory with a derived master plan has yet been accepted as providing all or most of the answers. Each person is still free to make his own decision about whether to commit a criminal act or explore a criminal career. We seem to be limited to juvenile diversion, voluntary family counseling, and crowded jails, unless we want to contemplate brainwashing at an early age.

DIRECT OR "OPERANT" CRIME PREVENTION

Direct, or "operant," crime prevention is more pragmatic, more immediate than the curative variety. It is concerned with the target of crimes and the circumstances of a criminal occurrence, specifically with reduction of the opportunity for crime through target hardening. Consideration is given to mechanical, instrumental, or behavioral victim avoidance processes depending on the victim's assumption of responsibility and participation. Operant prevention capitalizes on vested interest as well as on the strength of self-help motives of the potential victim. Obviously, the potential victim is most critically concerned about his vulnerability and the availability of counter-measures within his own capability to implement. It is comparatively easy to show a person the practicality in doing something for himself, as long as potential effectiveness can be demonstrated and costs do not exceed the potential loss. People tend to identify more readily for the purposes of collaboration with family, friends, neighbors, or members of an organization to which they belong.

Community programs tied to such identities are feasible. The "territorial imperative" cited by Davis (1972:96) as motivating neighborhood involvement in the city should be even more compelling in the country. Many rural people are assumed to have a great affinity for the land or at least for their own turf. Rural demographics are changing, but there is still more continuity for people and patterns in the country than in the city.

Curative and operant crime prevention have similar objectives, namely sparing people the experience of being either crime victim or criminal, and alleviating the societal as well as community costs of crime. However, police are probably not as qualified academically or officially for curative crime prevention as are other professionals. With their constraints closely defined legally, budgetarily, and socially, police agencies cannot show too great an affinity for nonspecific, nebulous objectives. Snibbe (1972:29-30) says that even though "human behavioral descriptions and classifications of crime will provide more useful information to the police than legal definitions . . . many factors leading to crime are beyond the control of police, (and) preventive policing must be based on those which the police can predict and influence."

Organizations work best with limited objectives and immediate goals, tending for the sake of their continued existence to put priority on properly limited, operationally consistent objectives. This is not to say that concerned professionals including police should not be as involved in curative programs as anyone else. Given an assumed interest in shared objectives and the service ethic they subscribe to, it is not surprising that many police officers contribute their own time to such efforts. For instance, the durable Police Athletic League (PAL) programs have been among the most effective juvenile diversion programs.

The problem is organizational, not personal, but police operations still have a certain built-in compatability with curative programs extending even to actual criminal justice system modifications. These include the special juvenile justice system and concomitant police procedures, laws prescribing referrals, treatment, etc. for even adult criminals, and legal provisions such as mitigations and defenses to criminal culpability.

Considerations for Adopting a Prevention Strategy

Seen in terms of untapped potential effect, the time has never been better for the adoption of pro-active, preventive policing. A harried, frustrated rural police resource looking for something truly new can find in prevention an effective countercrime mechanism, while there is still time for it to achieve its full potential. An alarmed public can be helped to avoid crime with workable answers that reduce feelings of futility. Perhaps best of all, in our society a repressive reaction is made less likely. To move itself in this direction developmentally, the rural police agency must address some organizational implications of a prevention strategy in three basic areas: (1) organizational considerations; (2) community considerations; and (3) specific programs.

ORGANIZATIONAL CONSIDERATIONS

Rural law enforcement agencies cannot simply stop responding to calls for service and work at prevention. They will continue to represent the source of urgently needed intervention for citizens in trouble. They will still be the ready access into the criminal justice system, as well as a source for referral to other community services. Officers must continue to go out and take "cold" reports (for insurance or other purposes) which have little prospect for clearance but consume valuable time, until someone develops a better way (mail-in or phone reports, citizen reports in person at the agency, etc.) and educates the public into acceptance.

Rural police administrators are not very likely to appreciate the potential of any alternative as an add-on either, with tighter and tighter budgets making it hard even to continue present operations, much less add a "new" function. Rural police officers, locked into habitual concepts of what their work is, will not readily accept prevention as a bona fide activity ("that's not my job." . . . "let social workers do social work").

Given these reactions, it is perhaps understandable that even where recognition of crime prevention as a popular concept with wide current appeal and support has lead an agency to accept it, it has sometimes only been as a token to validate the claim or to alleviate public pressure. Seeing it perhaps as an intrusive extra, prevention is sometimes relegated under these circumstances to a single officer, typically one with a number of other "ancillary" functions already. Needless to say, prevention effectiveness is ill-served thereby. It does not work, thereby justifying the preconception. Even the dedicated crime prevention officer becomes disillusioned as awareness grows that the task and the potential are beyond him. Perhaps an even worse response to the perceived need for prevention activity is to merely relabel prevailing patrol practices as "preventive patrol."

Operationalizing Prevention. An initial step should be to formalize the commitment of the organization to prevention at least on a par with interception and follow-up investigation. Members of the organization as well as clients and other coordinate agencies must have it made explicit to them that prevention is as much a part of policing as other repressive efforts against crime. Kenny (1972:35) asserts that police involvement in prevention has been traditionally acknowledged as important, but left unclear. The need is to "operationalize" prevention. Some sort of statement of purpose would be appropriate, establishing a high priority for prevention. Such a statement would provide a departure point for internal changes and inform the public. From it, specific operational objectives should be derived (such as to reduce residential burglary), roles developed for all personnel, and support services reoriented as necessary. Derivation of general objectives and specific goals could provide a useful opportunity for participative management, in which the input and commitment of those most directly affected would be assured.

Crime analysis. A capacity for crime analysis must be available, so that the community's crime experience can be known, as well as anticipated, by rate and by character. From this, predictions can be made, targets identified, and priorities established (Snibbe 1972:29). Campaigns to encourage a more dependable reporting of crime by citizens will be needed, but administrators should be especially prepared for one result of this. Crime will initially appear to have gone up markedly, just at a time when great expectations are being made of reductions in crime, since previously unreported offenses will now be counted. Criminal methods, or the specific means by which crimes are committed, must be highlighted so that derived prevention programs more accurately address real factors. For example, sexual assaults may involve physical force, duress or trickery. They may be perpetrated by strangers, acquaintances or relatives, and there can be further differentiation into time and location. Obviously, no single program response can be particularly effective against a general offense category, whether it be rape, theft, or robbery.

Target types, victims, perpetrators, and circumstances all vary and must be made apparent for prevention to be properly designed. Program development must also be able to take into consideration factors other than crime characteristics, such as degree or frequency of threat, public receptivity, and organizational feasibility. However, the effort should be to substitute precise, factual information about crimes for the old intuitive sense based mostly on the accumulated experience of individual officers. A final assessment of the preventive potential in a situation may bring about a whole new constellation of "needs to know"—for instance, what circumstances of the setting of a crime center itself seem to be most conducive to the crime (is it lighting, behavior patterns, even traffic patterns?).

Follow-up investigators have an excellent orientation and opportunity for an in-depth look at contributing factors in criminal events, a most important aspect of the crime analysis function. Already concentrating on the re-creation of crimes, examining dynamics and interaction between victim and perpetrator, they are becoming inevitably the most knowledgeable about criminal methods. The good investigator should not find it too difficult to take the extra step and pass on these insights to program developers and to the public.

Communications. A supportive communications resource must be available to the organization, both internally and externally. Internally, the simplest and most effective means may be through a reporting system where forms read by all officers require information from the reporting officer about how and why a crime occurred, incorporating the very factors which can be used to describe it back to officers. The experience of writing reports differently must be augmented by the circulation of derived summaries or crime breakdowns, pictorially if possible, but shared in any case (such as during briefings of personnel coming on duty). Patrol can be "preventive" to the extent it is thus caused to be focused or directed with current, useful information shared by all. Actually, reporting in terms of criminal methods, crime objective and contributing circumstances (door unlocked, etc.) can cause officers not only to describe a criminal incident in a way more conducive to ultimate prevention, but to investigate it that way from the start. Persons reporting crimes, their friends or family, and even neighbors are at least subtley caused to reflect on factors of crime vulnerability, if officer inquiry is made accordingly.

Organizational legitimation. A department intent on making crime prevention work for it must attend early to certain organizational realities. Support and reinforcement for the idea of prevention's legitimacy and validity as a police talk must be assured if it is to be accepted. Administrative guidance and reinforcement in the form of policies is needed. Job descriptions need to be revised to include prevention responsibilities. The purpose statement mentioned earlier could usefully be elaborated into operational goals and performance objectives, commensurate with all types of assignment—patrol, staff, or investigative. Even performance evaluations should reflect expectations in the area of prevention activities. A breakdown of complementary tasks by assignment can be made.

Staff personnel assigned to crime prevention should be a resource to others who will deliver the product, as much as possible, rather than being an exclusive, specialized function. Just as an overly centralized investigative function can produce preliminary report-takers (street officers) with no stake in the investigative product, prevention activities restricted to the few may cause a continuation or worsening of past levels of internal acceptance. The person who develops programs, resource materials, contacts, etc., must work through others as a primary tactic to assure that the final prevention product will be the very best available. This same person can nonetheless still be a specialist by preparation and inclination, since a higher degree of training for a few is more feasible.

Budgetary support. Given a department's commitment to prevention as both strategy and tactic, budgetary support should be no harder a decision than for any other function. Prevention becomes just one more of the things done to accomplish basic objectives in crime control for the community. Coincidently, community receptivity and support for police agencies seems to go up where a true interest in helping is perceived—not just waiting to pick up the pieces after calamity has struck. Idealistic young officers can avoid the familiar sense of futility in police work with has so often lead to cynicism and defensiveness late in a career. Prevention necessarily involves positive personal contacts with people who show their appreciation. Credibility is enhanced on both sides when perceived remoteness and association of police only with distress are no longer factors.

Training. A major task of the rural police agency getting fully involved in prevention is to train its personnel. Training for prevention skills is just as valid for officers as is preparation for investigation and interception, but unfortunately lacks recent tradition. Internal acceptance, as well as performance/preparation of officers should be enhanced by basic training in prevention at the entry level, including a foundation in theory. In-service training should concentrate on technical aspects such as locks, lights, and alarms; criminal methods by crime type; countercrime strategies and resources; and presentation skills. Supervisors should be among the first trained, instead of, as too often is the case, last or not at all. Officers will find it difficult to perform prevention tasks in spite of an unknowing, unappreciative supervisor. Of course, one or more specialists should be trained as that resource to others, to the degree of expertness this function requires. All need to be made aware of and taught to rise above certain common pitfalls. For instance, the fact that someone could have done something to lessen vulnerability (and did not) does not mean they were asking for it. Blame has no part in prevention. Other important concepts include individual responsibility, collaborative concepts, and how to be a prevention catalyst.

For instance, patrol functions could include detection and response to perceived vulnerabilities, such as getting an open window closed, recommending lighting improvements, and giving situational advice to people. Officers on patrol are best suited routinely for other functions depending on personal contacts—distributing literature, doing security surveys, meeting with neighborhood groups, or delivering brief talks on a wide variety of preventive topics. The patrol officer is the most well-known in the community, and these tasks are consistent with the ready, resourceful presence necessary to interception tasks. Officers doing security surveys will assure an intimate knowledge of the community, while simultaneously defending the community by helping harden specific crime targets both ways—by police presence and residual effects of counseling and advice.

Training in a function or skill will often make it more likely to happen, as will job definition and stated intentions. The department should, however, go the final step and assure that one can succeed as an officer by stressing prevention. Other sanctions besides performance expectations should also be used—commendations, premiums toward promotion or expanded responsibilities, even negative sanctions for nonperformance. There are enough tasks in preventive functions which are compatible with public law enforcement to give everyone a chance. Even the most reticent officer can do a premises survey. Generally, treating accomplishments in prevention activities as commensurate with expertness in policing (the least to be expected of knowledgeable, committed officers) is the way to go. Prevention responsibilities for police can be described as more of a return to traditional values, anyway, if one takes the long view of history.

COMMUNITY CONSIDERATIONS

The capacity for communication externally is also important to the ultimate impact of prevention efforts. Knowledge about how to prevent a crime must be passed on to the primary beneficiary, the victim. Police agencies should be able to prepare and disseminate prevention information to best encourage awareness, impact and retention, whether it be pamphlets, posters, bumper stickers, or visual aids in support of presentations to groups. Potentially a very expensive aspect of prevention programming, significant economies can be achieved at the same time through a community involvement approach, another basic requirement referred to by Kenny (1972:35).

Goal sharing. Potential victim groups to whom prevention is addressed are also served by other organizations which are often willing to make common cause with a police agency in prevention programs for members, or for the whole community, if their objectives are coincidently served (e.g., Chamber of Commerce involvement for antishoplifting campaigns). It is not only feasible to share the cost of printing or obtaining prevention materials, but through this means, the commitment is likewise shared. Support and participation are enhanced to the degree that citizens and other organizations perceive their stake in the outcome.

The media. By working closely with broadcast and print media serving the larger community, as well as proprietary organs such as company or organization newsletters, another extremely important device can be brought into the prevention picture. Access to the media for general prevention messages is available as "public-service spots," a function required of the electronic media. However, these usually tend to be concentrated heavily right before breakfast, after the late movie, or on Sunday morning—not exactly prime viewing periods. By working with media representatives, a better system can be developed involving flash reports of current crime concerns, usually described as a crime alert. Descriptions of trends or specific, episodic series of crimes, such as a roofing scam being perpetrated within or near the jurisdiction, are news and will have a commensurately greater claim on media time as well as public attention. Not surprisingly and particularly with frauds, criminal incidents reporting will increase radically following crime alert broadcasts, since sheepish victims feel better knowing they were not the only ones.

Getting the word out. To be even marginally effective, the police agency must be committed to spreading prevention and crime awareness any way it can, including pamphlet racks in public places. The best way remains a person-to-person (or group) presentation with discussion, so that specific questions and local variations can be dealt with. There should be as great a commitment to this mode as possible. Instead of relying on a single polished presenter of crime prevention programs, the agency should share presentation tasks widely within the organization, particularly for repetitive programs, and support volunteers and outside experts presenting or working in the same programs. Mutuality of concern and involvement are strong impetuses to meetings of the mind as to content and approach, and they are also wonderful extenders of resources.

A facilitator's role. A particularly useful strategy regarding community involvement begins with a concentration on start-up efforts, followed by intermittent but regular program involvement from police. This allows a very necessary transition to achieve the resource extension previously described, as participants make the program their own and continue it. Officers need to enhance the role of others in prevention. Acknowledging the superior expertise and credibility of those like the farm extension agent for program development and implementation in rural areas is necessary to the concept of being a resource rather than all things to all people.

Specific programs. Crime prevention for police in nonurban areas could most readily begin with basic programs which should be common to all agencies, such as targethardening/opportunity reduction campaigns and citizen involvement, and extend to applications and problems uniquely rural. These areas include farm, rural nonfarm, business, recreation, small town, schools, and public utilities.

Specific prevention targets will necessarily vary between or within jurisdictions, and over time, generally. However, there are few strategies which are nearly sure winners. Many programs already demonstrated as successful elsewhere, even in cities, can be readily adapted to the rural circumstance. Conversely, many programs developed in rural areas will probably be found to extend usefully to urban areas, such as programs for parks and recreation centers, school programs, and collaborative concepts like the National Sheriff's Association Neighborhood Watch. Operation Identification programs involving the personalizing of commonly stolen items and advertising that fact have been shown to work, whether it be in apartment houses or strip homes on a country road. The important thing here is that specific program selections as well as the characteristics of a given program should arise from mutual involvement of police and citizenry, and no just its implementation (Webster 1980:10). Prevention activities are a natural for involvement programs like the law enforcement Explorer Scouts with which many rural police are already involved.

Neighborhood Watch is already established as a convenient and effective vehicle for organizing cooperative responses to the threat of crime in the country. New methods of branding cattle (lip tattooing, freeze branding) make disposal of stolen livestock more difficult and a countrified Operation ID metal-stamps farm equipment. Good ideas are being worked out across the country, even internationally, to hamper the criminal further. Trucking operations are working on terminal and transport security. Information repositories such as the National Rural Crime Prevention Center at The Ohio State University not only provide access to what is being done elsewhere, but conduct research and develop innovative approaches as well. The problem and some answers are becoming known. New ideas being considered which offer much promise include a crime prevention curriculum for the full 12 years of school (which acknowledges that the child is more often victim than perpetrator), versions of which are being implemented in Ohio and Virginia. Perhaps someone will go on to develop camperships, farmerships, and other experiential programs to restore an affinity for the land to the young, and a mutuality of regard between various types of rural presence. Preventive design programs for space and facilities offer much promise. But, the major problem now is implementation on a scale which will assure the effectiveness of prevention before it is too late to work.

Summary

The challenge for the rural law enforcement agency and administrator is to have the foresight and determination to overcome the recent tradition of reactivity in policing and to capitalize on the enthusiasm of others to get back to basics for preventing crime. Farm Bureau, local cooperatives, USDA, and other organizations centering on the rural environment, as well as land-grant universities with farm extension programs, constitute real resources to police in this effort. Our response should be to be good at what we are, crime experts, and become better at what we can be— generalists in the best sense. Combine this commitment with a community development approach, capitalizing on the expertise of other professions like teachers, organizational representatives, public officials, and citizen leaders, and the sky's the limit. Rural police will then be change agents, facilitators of the efforts of others, and catalysts in community crime prevention. We need to get back to prevention, and get on with it. One has to agree with Nepote (1972:62-63) that "Police should be known and recognized by the public as an institution for crime prevention . . . by revealing to the public its organization, structure and aims" and by opening up to crime prevention.

References

Brown, John. 1979. "Community Policing." *Police Review* (June): 1050-53.

Davis, Ed. 1972. "Basic Radio Car Plan." In Dan G. Pursuit, John D. Gerletli, Robert M. Brown, and Stephen M. Ward, eds. *Police Programs for Preventing Crime and Delinquency*. Springfield, Illinois: Charles C. Thomas, Publisher.

Donnermeyer, Joseph F. 1979. "Community Development and Crime Prevention for Rural Areas." Paper presented at the Annual Meeting of the Community Development Society, Kansas City, Missouri. August.

Kelling, Pate, et al. 1974. *The Kansas City Preventive Patrol Experiment*. Police Foundation.

Kenny, John P. 1972. "The Police and Crime Prevention." In Dan G. Pursuit, John D. Gerletli, Robert M. Brown and Stephen M. Ward, eds. *Police Programs for Preventing Crime and Delinquency*. Springfield, Illinois: Charles C. Thomas, Publisher.

Meadows, Robert J. 1979. "Perspectives for Change: Expanding the Police Role in Crime Prevention." *The Police Chief* (April): 58-63.

———. 1980. "Crime Prevention and the Police: Moving from a Traditional to a Contemporary Role." *The Police Chief* (June): 62-67.

Nepote, J. 1972. "The Role and Future of the Police in the Field of Crime Prevention." In Dan G. Pursuit, John D. Gerletli, Robert M. Brown, and Stephen M. Ward, eds. *Police Programs for Preventing Crime and Delinquency*. Springfield, Illinois: Charles C. Thomas, Publisher.

Phillips, G. Howard. 1975. *Crime in Rural Ohio*. ESO 363. Columbus, Ohio: Department of Agricultural Economics and Rural Sociology, The Ohio State University.

Snibbe, Richard H. 1972. "A Concept for Police in Crime Prevention." In Dan G. Pursuit, John D. Gerletli, Robert M. Brown and Stephen M. Ward, eds. *Police Programs for Preventing Crime and Delinquency*. Springfield, Illinois: Charles C. Thomas, Publisher.

Webster, William H. 1980. "Ahead in the 80's: New Challenges." *The National Sheriff*. (Feb.-March): 10-11.

Index

Authors

Timothy J. Carter, Associate Professor, Department of Sociology, Anthropology, and Social Work, James Madison University. Ph.D., University of Tennessee. Major Field: Sociology, Specialty Areas: Criminology and Urban Community.

G. Howard Phillips, Full Professor, Department of Agricultural Economics and Rural Sociology, and founder and former Director, National Rural Crime Prevention Center, The Ohio State University. Ph.D., The Ohio State University. Major Field: Rural Sociology, Specialty Area: Rural Crime Prevention.

Joseph F. Donnermeyer, Assistant Professor, Department of Agricultural Economics and Rural Sociology, and Director, National Rural Crime Prevention Center, The Ohio State University. Ph.D., University of Kentucky. Major Field: Rural Sociology, Specialty Areas: Rural Crime Prevention and Community Development.

Todd N. Wurschmidt, Executive Director, Ohio Crime Prevention Association, Columbus, Ohio. M.S., The Ohio State University. Major Field: Rural Sociology, Specialty Area: Rural Crime Prevention.

Ed Sagarin, Full Professor, Department of Sociology, City College of New York and City University of New York. Distinguished Visiting Professor, The Ohio State University (1981). Ph.D., New York University. Major Field: Sociology, Specialty Areas: Crime and Deviance.

Kathleen Weinberger Natalino, Assistant Professor, Department of Urban Studies, Cleveland State University. Ph.D., Bowling Green State University. Major Field: Sociology/Delinquency.

Martin G. Miller, Associate Professor, Department of Sociology, Iowa State University. Ph.D., Michigan State University. Major Field: Criminology/Juvenile Delinquency.

Eric O. Hoiberg, Assistant Professor, Department of Sociology, Iowa State University. Ph.D., University of Nebraska. Major Field: Rural Sociology, Specialty Areas: Agricultural Sociology, Human Ecology.

Rodney F. Ganey, Assistant Director, Social Science Training and Research Laboratory, University of Notre Dame. Ph.D., Iowa State University. Major Field: Rural Sociology, Specialty Areas: Statistics and Methodology, Organizations.

Ted L. Napier, Professor, Department of Agricultural Economics and Rural Sociology, The Ohio State University. Ph.D., The Ohio State University. Major Field: Rural Sociology, Specialty Areas: Rural Development, Leisure and Sports Recreation

Mary Christine Pratt, Director, Brown County Ursuline Center, St. Martin, Ohio. M.S., The Ohio State University. Major Field: Rural Sociology.

Robert O'Block, Associate Professor, Department of Political Science/ Criminal Justice, Appalachian State University, Boone, North Carolina. Ph.D., CPP, Kansas State University. Major Field: Crime Prevention and Private Security.

R. Paul McCauley, Chairman, Department of Criminology, Indiana University of Pennsylvania, Ph.D., Sam Houston University. Major Field: Criminal Justice Administration, Specialty Area: Management Research.

George Sunderland, Senior Coordinator, Criminal Justice Services, American Association of Retired Persons, Washington, D.C.

B.M. Gray, II, Director of Crime Prevention, National Council on Crime and Delinquency, Hackensack, New Jersey. M.S., Eastern Kentucky University. Major Field: Criminal Justice Education.

Edmund G. James, Jr., Director, Ohio Division of Crime Prevention, Department of Economic and Community Development, State of Ohio. Ph.D., The Ohio State University. Major Field: American History. J.D., Capital University Law School, Columbus, Ohio.

Steven D. Gladman, Program Administrator, Home Energy Assistance Program, Department of Economic and Community Development, State of Ohio, and Former Executive Director, Ohio Crime Prevention Association, Columbus, Ohio. B.A., The Ohio State University. Major Field: Political Science.

Gwendolyn D. Hall, Educational Program Manager, National Council on Crime and Delinquency, Hackensack, New Jersey. M.S.W., Florida State University. Major Field: Social Welfare Administration.

Gary R. Wilson, Deputy Chief of Police, University Police Department, The Ohio State University. B.A., Southern Illinois University. Major Field: Psychology.